Mantra Yoga and Primal Sound

Secrets of Seed (Bija) Mantras

By

Dr. David Frawley
(Pandit Vamadeva Shastri)

Disclaimer

This book is not intended to treat, diagnose or prescribe. The information contained herein is in no way to be considered as a substitute for a consultation with a duly licensed health care professional.

Author: Dr. David Frawley

Illustrations: Cover and drawings/ pictures - Hinduism Today, additional line drawings of Goddesses - Kanika Tripathi

First Edition 2010
Printed in the United States of America
ISBN: 978-0-9102-6194-4
Library of Congress Catalog Number:2010921035

LOTUS PRESS

Published by:
Lotus Press, P.O. Box 325, Twin Lakes, WI 53181 USA
web: www.lotuspress.com
Email: lotuspress@lotuspress.com
800.824.6396

Table of Contents

Foreword

Dr. David Frawley, Pandit Vamadeva Shastri, is a modern Renaissance man for Eastern mystical studies.

If one is interested in Vedic Astrology, he has insightful books filled with information and wisdom about this ancient science.

If one is drawn to the ancient science of healing called Ayurveda, again David Frawley has books that will illumine the subject for you and guide you to further reading and studies.

If your interests lie in the area of classical tantric practices – and I don't mean of the sexual variety, but of the true mystical approaches – then you again will do well to consult the books expertly rendered by David Frawley.

But his reach is yet greater. In India he is recognized as an historian of modern importance. He coauthored Hidden Horizons – Unearthing 10,000 Years of Indian Culture, which has been publicly lauded by many Jagadgurus and spiritual leaders in India.[1]

So it is with appreciation for his stellar contributions to Hindu mystical practice, history and thought that I approach this Foreword to yet another great contribution from him: The topic of Sanskrit Mantra.

Classical descriptions of mantra are grounded in the idea that this entire creation at both the manifest and subtle levels is nearly endless combinations of the finite vibrations that scholars and mystics alike call the Matrika – The Mother: The Sanskrit alphabet. Whether it is Satya Loka, the realm of pure Truth at the top of the realms of light, or Patala Loka, the lowest of the seven nether realms, the composition of these lokas and the beings of form that inhabit them are composed of various permutations and combinations of the Matrika: The Sanskrit Alphabet. In various mystical texts the Matrika is commonly referred to as "She who binds and She who sets free."

If we are unaware of the existence, power and operation of the Matrika, we are inexorably bound to the wheel of death and rebirth – Samsara. We are in the thrall of She who binds. But if we understand, even if only a little, and practice ancient spiritual formulas called mantras, we enter the realm of "She who sets us free." Mantra is often referred to as "The Divine Name," called "Nama" in Sanskrit. If one goes to any Hindu Temple and approaches one of the priests and says questioningly, "Nama Eva, Nama Eva . . . " there will invariably come the response, "Kevalam, Kevalam." This exchange roughly translates as, "The Name alone, the Name alone . . . sets one free, sets one free." The understanding between the questioner and responder is that the practice of Sanskrit mantra is the single most efficacious spiritual practice for the current period of Spiritual Winter, called Kali Yuga.

In the last fifty years, Masters such as my own gurus, Sadguru Sant Keshavadas and his wife Sadguru Rama Mata, have both taught extensively and encouraged others like me to spread this knowledge of mantra and make it available to everyone. With his works such as *Inner Tantric Yoga* and this book, David Frawley lends his

1 *Published by the Swaminarayan order (BAPS), famous for its beautifully designed modern Hindu temples in both India and the West.*

authoritative voice to the authentic and reliable resources available to help all of us escape our karmic predicaments.

Dr. Frawley goes into considerable helpful exposition on the subject of mantra. As a preamble to his discussion, here is some beginning explanation of the subject of mantra from my book, *The Ancient Power of Sanskrit Mantra and Ceremony, Volume I.* The word mantra has entered colloquial speech much the same way 'guru' has. Advertising slogans become mantras for products or services. Political campaigns develop popular 'mantras' for convincing voters about platform policies or candidates for office. Yet the true genesis and meaning of the term has become swallowed by popular usage along with a commonly agreed upon definition which does not come close to the original meaning for the word.

For some words, a distinction between what a word truly means and what is generally accepted as the meaning has little importance. But for a word like mantra, the true meaning is important. This is because a mantra is a word or term of power. And the power of every mantra is specific and exact. Therefore, popularly accepted definitions of what mantra is may have no relevance whatsoever to the actual use and effect of the power of a specific Sanskrit mantra.

With this understanding of mantra as an expression of tangible and usable power, we have the first useful item in the application of the science of mantra. Mantras are tools of power and tools for power. They are formidable. They are ancient. They work.

The word mantra is derived from two Sanskrit words. The first is "manas" or "mind," which provides the "man" syllable. The second syllable is drawn from the Sanskrit word "trai" meaning to "protect" or to "free from." Therefore, the word mantra in its most literal sense means "to free from the mind" (the cognitive, creative mind). Mantra is, at its core, a tool used by the mind that eventually frees one from the vagaries of the mind. But the journey from mantra to freedom is a wondrous one. The mind expands, deepens and widens and eventually dips into the essence of cosmic existence. On its journey, the mind comes to understand much about the essence of the vibration of things. And knowledge, as we all know, is power. In the case of mantra, this power is tangible and wieldable.

Historical Background

The historical derivation of the science and study of mantras corresponds with the intricacies of the Sanskrit language. Sanskrit has been called a variety of names: Deva Lingua (language of the gods), the "mother of tongues", or simply a divine language. Why should this be?

Linguists commonly ascribe these descriptions to Sanskrit, because it provides a root tongue for so many languages, but the real reason is more esoteric. The Sanskrit alphabet has the same number of petals or spokes as there are on the flowers or wheels of the total of the first six chakras or esoteric energy centers, located along the spine. This is no accident.

The Sanskrit language is a tool for working with the subtle energy potential represented by each of the many chakras in the etheric body. However, the six major chakras contain the map of sounds written on each of the combined petals on those six chakras.

A saying from the Vedas claims that, "Speech is the essence of humanity." All of what humanity thinks and ultimately becomes is determined by the expression of ideas and actions through speech and its derivative, writing.

Everything comes into being through speech. Ideas remain unactualized until they are created through the power of speech. *The New Testament*, Book of John, starts: "In the beginning was The Word. And the Word was with God and the Word was God . . ."

The parallel for us is that if we wish to attain higher states of being, there are only two ways: Our own effort or Divine Grace. Some spiritual leaders have suggested that the first leads to the second.

In mainstream Vedic practices, most Buddhist techniques and classical Hinduism, mantra is viewed as a necessity for spiritual advancement and high attainment. In *The Kalachakra Tantra*, by the Dalai Lama and Jeffrey Hopkins, the Dalai Lama states, 'Therefore, without depending upon mantra . . . Buddhahood cannot be attained.' Clearly, there is a reason why such widely divergent sources of religious wisdom as the *New Testament* and the Dalai Lama speak in common ideas.

Your Mantra Practice

As the topic of mantra is developed here by David Frawley in specific and expert fashion, you will hopefully be inspired to begin a mantra discipline. But before you do, please begin the important decision-making process of plumbing into the heart of your own spiritual nature. There you will find your spiritual ideal. Having found it, dedicate all of your spiritual practices and disciplines toward the achievement of your ideal nature and its fulfillment. This does not mean that you must give up intermediate goals such as wealth, happy marriage, good job, good health or other things. It merely means that you have framed an ultimate destination that is based in your own nature. From there you proceed with the understanding that the road and the destination are really one.

David Frawley, Vamadeva Shastri, has presented here for our use invaluable information and tools for spiritual advancement that are very hard to find. I urge you to take advantage of this rare opportunity through this masterful work and engage in a mantra discipline with dedication, discipline and intensity. The returns will be more than you ever thought possible. We are all benefited by the learned efforts of Vamadeva contained in this treasured volume, but it is up to us to put it into practice.

Thomas Ashley-Farrand (Namadeva Acharya)
September, 2009
www.sanskritmantra.com

Introductory Note by Swami Veda Bharati

Those who know (vidvaamsah) will confirm that the works of Shri Vamadeva Shastri are distinguished by their authenticity. This is so because they are based on (1) his personal quest and experience (2) deep dwelling into the texts and (3) oral learning received from many authentic teachers who are experts in their areas of knowledge.

Shri Vamadeva Shastri has done this great service to many that he has offered access into knowledge that was often hitherto inaccessible to an average western seeker. He has done so not merely as a scholar of 'words, lexicons and translations', sometimes dubbed in the traditional circles of India as modern 'index aachaaryas'. They provided profound research tools with their untiring efforts. It is a matter of profound delight that we can use their work as well as the first hand of knowledge of the keepers of the Traditions. Those who wish to dive deep into the spiritual treasure beyond words are now more and more highly recognized even in academic circles.

Shri Vamadeva Shastri is of the generation that now respects the Traditions and articulates the ancient knowledge of those who would otherwise remain inarticulate because they do not always speak the languages of our contemporary world power structures. The present work on Mantra-yoga by Shri Vamadeva Shastri is a delight to read as it leaves out no corner of multigonic truths unexplored with regard to the complex science of mantras.

Attached to the mantras is always a pra-yoga-shastra, the science of their application. Shri Shastri has given glimpses of these applications. The true details are to be learnt not by a student but by a disciple who submits to traditional disciplines under an accomplished guide.

An example of such pra-yoga-shastra is Rg-vidhana of the Rishi Shaunaka. This very ancient text gives the applications of only a select number of hymns and mantras of Rg-veda, out of the 10,000 mantras of Rg-veda. For the hymns selected, the sage Shaunaka not only states the power of each hymn, the end-result of using the mantra, but also, most important, how the mantra is to be used, for example with what kind of wood the fire offerings with that mantra are to be performed, how many times, with what herbal oblations, and so forth. It may even prescribe the posture in which one should sit for such endeavour.

In the age of instant fixes, those who know the disciplines are often disinclined to give out the knowledge to those whose very long term dedication to a discipline is not yet proven. For instance, in writing the above paragraph on the work of Shaunaka, I am not revealing, for example, which hymn may be mentally recited, with what fire offerings, if one wishes to remember one's past life or if one wishes that the knowledge of this life may be remembered in the next life. Who will follow the discipline of correct daily schedule, the attitude of devotion-- not mechanical recitation – and sit in the prescribed posture at the prescribed hours of the day ?

Can I become a doctor by reading one book on medical science? Can I start prescribing, even to oneself, ayurvedic medicines after reading one book? Can one choose a mantra for oneself so as 'one's spouse would begin to listen to him/her!'

What we write in modern languages is often an appetiser; for an invitation to the full feast, may each reader become an adhikarin. Shri Vamadeva Shastri's work guides one on the path to becoming a qualified disciple. Congratulations to those who would truly pursue the Path of nih-shreyasa (summum bonum), the Supreme Good.

Swami Veda Bharati
Swami Rama Sadhaka Gram, Rishikesh, India

Introductory Note by Sampadananda Mishra

A Mantra, as Sri Aurobindo puts it, "is a word of power and light that comes from the overmind inspiration or from a very high plane of intuition." (*The Future Poetry*, SABCL, vol 9, p. 369) A Mantra is thus an inspired and intuitive and rhythmic utterance, a revealed seeing. It comes out of the "realisation of some inmost truth of God and self and man and Nature and cosmos and life and thing and thought and experience and deed." (*The Future Poetry*, SABCL, Vol. 9,P. 199)

Every Mantra contains in its vibrations a certain power. The very etymology of the word Mantra reveals that it serves as an instrument to elevate the Mind, an instrument which helps the mind to contemplate and plunge into the oceanic depth of silence. The word Mantra is derived from the root sound 'man' which means to think, to contemplate or meditate on, to perceive, to understand or comprehend. The sound tra at the end of the word Mantra is a suffix added in the sense of instrumentality. So, Mantra, as per its etymology, is an instrument of or a means for contemplation, meditation, comprehension, perception and of thought. Mantra, in fact, unites the mind with the pure sound. And this union of the mind with the pure sound is considered by the Vedic and Tantric tradition as the highest kind of Yoga. It is in this state that mind becomes free from all its activities and gets absorbed in the silence (the unmanifest speech) which is the source of all sounds.

The book, *Mantra Yoga and the Primal Sound* by Dr. David Frawley is not simply a collection of Mantras or an expression of their moral significance; it is an interpretation of the philosophy and the reality of the mantric approach to intelligence and knowledge held within the sound code or vibratory pattern behind the universe itself.

It is believed that all the answers we search for, all the vital responses we seek after, and all the information we need are stored on an energy matrix called the non-local intelligence and that is available to all of us at any time. It is the function of the higher selves and can be accessed through the mantras. But one has to learn the impeccable procedures meant for it. The perfection in approach should result from a dedication of intelligence and mental activity to a projected plane and world of consciousness. The perfect mantric approach and knowledge aligns the energy of the body and mind with the fundamental frequency of the universe and with a consciousness linked energetically to the subtler universal fabric.

The book aims at a perfect explanation of the mantras and a revelation of their perpetual relevance and significance. Now, mantra in the traditional sense no longer exists. There is mantra causing the innovation and invention of modern knowledge and wisdom. A mantric approach to science, technology, information, marketing, media and streams of knowledge is being constantly emphasized.

Sri Aurobindo has presented his longest epic poem, savitri as a mantra for the transformation of the world. Mantra can only cause transformation as it is the essence of the cosmic response and the invocation of the eternity. Dr. Frawley in his book explores the use of mantras for improving our karmas and actions in life. He also goes on to unravel the profounder mystery besetting the conceptual philosophy of the mantras. His sole aim is to arouse an insight and awareness into the practicalities of mantras.

The author has taken care of explaining the bijamantras, starting with the letters of the Sanskrit alphabet, and leading up to the mantra purusha or body of sound which is considered an important practice in mantra yoga. Gradually he explores the main methods of the mantra yoga starting with mantra and pranayama, mantra and traditional kundalini yoga and the use of divine names and bhakti yoga. The application of the mantra therapy in the Vedic sciences of Ayurvedic medicines, Vedic astrology and vastu sciences, too, form important part of the book.

Here it is mentioned that the mantras alongside pranayama bring greater awareness and energy into both mind and body. Such Pranayama-mantra vibrations can lift the mind into Samadhi or higher states of oneness, which it would otherwise not have access to. The power of mantra can unfold the movement of mind and its habitual pattern and their constant transmutation.

The fundamental significance of the mantra, as indicated by the book, lies solely in exploring deep into the deeper recesses of reality. All existence - as the mind and sense know existence - is manifestation of an eternal and infinite which is to the mind and sense unknowable but not unknowable to its own self awareness. The unmanifest supreme is beyond all definition and description. Whatever the manifestation may be it has behind it something that is beyond itself. Mantra through its positive and constructive vibrations integrates the mind into growing to the vastness of truth and inspiration.

Mantra carries with it the essences of yoga and the yogic consciousness. As man is a mental being, he naturally imagines that mind is the one great leader and an indispensable agent in the universe. But mind is not the greatest possible power of consciousness and not the instrument of truth and knowledge. It is only their ignorant seeker. To rise to the higher levels of consciousness, mind has to be silent, thought- free and immobile. Sri Aurobindo has said that when the mind is still, then truth gets her chance to be heard in the purity of silence. Truth cannot be attained by the mind's thought but only by identity and silent vision. Mantra plays a great role in creating a blessed quietude and silence in mind, felt by an elevating vibration, to rise to the highest level of yogic consciousness.

The book ultimately reflects that mantra causes a holistic transformation for a perfect realization of truth. It takes the awareness beyond the mental man and its limits. The book teaches us that there is an eternal closeness between the yogic mind and the ever living cosmic vibrations of the universe. The mantras act like a bridge, internally solid but externally unmanifest, from the outer layer of the consciousness to the inner, from within to without and from the surface to the absolute and the supramental. The book stresses the very fact that Mantras are instrumental for the great yogic teaching as well as its primary practices. The mantra gains its own life and consciousness in the very ground of our being.

-Dr. Sampadananda Mishra, Sri Aurobindo Society, Pondicherry

Author's Preface

Mantra is the key to Yoga in the deeper sense and to awakening a higher intelligence within us. Yet mantra remains a subject filled with mystery, illusion and misapplication that would benefit from a clear, systematic and in-depth explication, such as other aspects of Yoga have already received. I have aimed at such a presentation here, not just an introductory book on the subject.

Over the past few decades, I have written several books on different aspects of Yogic knowledge, Ayurvedic healing and Vedic astrology, in which I have alluded to various mantras and their application. At the same time, I was conducting research for a book devoted entirely to the subject of mantra, which has now come to fruition. I have tried to distill what is most essential and easiest to apply from that greater study and placed it in the present volume.

The book focuses on bija or 'seed mantras' – single syllable mantras that reflect the primal sounds of the universe. The Mantra Purusha, the person of sound or 'sound body' is the main subject of these correlations. This examination emphasizes the letters of the Sanskrit alphabet, which are the building blocks of all mantras, as well as the primary Shakti mantras that are the most powerful of bija mantras. Yet the book is not meant simply as a list of mantras. It contains an examination of the profound philosophy behind mantra and the important rules of attitude and application necessary to follow in order to allow mantras to work in the best possible manner.

Mantra has been the most intriguing and fascinating aspect of yogic studies for me and the one I have devoted the greatest amount of time to exploring. Mantra perhaps uniquely represents both the teaching and its practice at the same time. It holds the key to the greater Yoga tradition and its continual adaptation. It links the human mind with the cosmic mind. Yet mantra is also something very accessible that we can begin with at any stage of our inner quest.

My study of mantra and sacred sound began with the poetic and literary explorations of my youth. I was attracted to French symbolists like Rimbaud, English Romantics like Wordsworth and German symbolists like Rilke. I found additional inspiration through the novels of Herman Hesse and the alchemical studies of the noted psychologist C.G. Jung. There seemed to be a deeper universal language of sound and image hidden behind such different depictions of symbolic languages.

My study moved further into the mystical sphere, to the East and to the ancient world. This included looking into the symbolism of the *Chinese I Ching* or *Book of Changes* and the *Egyptian Book of the Dead*. I found that images like the Sun, Moon, dawn, night, fire, wind and lightning possessed a great evocative power for understanding the mysteries of the psyche and the universe as a whole. I discovered astrology as a cosmic symbolism that reflected a higher language of light.

However, it was in the yogic traditions of India that I discovered the deepest connections to symbolic language and primal sound, which appeared inherent to the great Sanskrit language, the language of mantra. I became fascinated not just by the philosophy but by the symbolism of Hindu scriptures in the *Upanishads* and *Bhagavad Gita*. The great diversity of Hindu deities and their rich symbolic portrayals of multiple arms, gestures, ornaments, weapons and colors reflected to me a deeper understanding of the universal meaning of light, color, form, symbol and movement.

I was similarly drawn both to Yoga philosophy and to yogic imagery, particularly in the Tantra and its inner alchemy of the Sun and the Moon, fire and water, Shiva and Shakti, the mountain God and the mountain Goddess.

The great modern Yogi, poet and philosopher Sri Aurobindo proved to be the central inspiration in this early endeavor. He composed profound poetic works like the monumental epic *Savitri* – the longest epic poem in the English language – which features a symbolic journey through all the worlds and planes of consciousness from the Earth to the Absolute beyond all manifestation.[1] He also wrote on the philosophy of poetry and its deeper connection to mantra.[2] Most importantly, his study of ancient Vedic texts opened up the yogic symbolism hidden behind the ancient Vedic mantras. Through his influence I began to understand them at a deeper level than what the academic mind considered them to be.[3]

In my meditations, I learned to enter into the Vedic world of primal sound that preceded the rational age of philosophies and breathed with the spirit of the Gods. I spent several years in my twenties reading the *Rigveda*, the Vedic book of mantra, in the original Sanskrit and repeating its rhythmical hymns, noting how the power of certain alliterations and root meanings granted multiple levels and dimensions of meaning to its teaching. I gradually examined the entire field of Vedic mantras, deities and symbolisms in all ten books or mandalas of the *Rigveda* and over time translated many of them[4].

Over time, I expanded my Sanskrit studies to classical *Stotras*, poetic hymns to Hindu deities composed in special intricate meters and melodies. Most notable were the beautiful Saundarya Lahiri (The Wave of Beauty) and Ananda Lahiri (The Wave of Bliss) by the great Advaitic sage Shankara, which were dedicated to the Goddess as Tripura Sundari, the 'Beauty of the Three Worlds' and unfolded all the secret meanings of Shakti and the chakras. I discovered the power of *Stotras* as an invocation of the Divine presence, a sacred connection to the entire universe and its indwelling Being.

Besides such symbolic explorations, Vedantic philosophy provided another great source of inspiration, including the philosophy of mantra and cosmic sound that are commonly found in these teachings. I meditated upon the great mantric phrases of non-dualistic Vedanta like 'Everything is Brahman' (the supreme Godhead)[5], learning to ride the waves of cosmic sound and meaning beyond the mind and senses.I contemplated the Sanskrit verses of great classics of the Yoga of knowledge like the Yoga Vasishta, which are mantric verses in their own right, combining the highest yogic knowledge with profound poetic utterances. Most importantly, I explored bija mantras (seed syllables) and primal sounds in Tantric Yoga, including Shakti mantras and sounds of the chakras and nadis, whether from the traditions of Kashmiri Shaivism, Bengali Tantra, Advaitic Tantra or the Shakta or Goddess tradition as a whole in which mantra is the prime method, the Goddess herself equated with the Divine Word.[6]

I learned to use mantras along with the practice of pranayama for bringing greater awareness and energy into both mind and body. Such pranayama-mantra vibrations can lift the mind into samadhi or higher states of oneness, which it would otherwise not have access to. I recall falling into such states of higher consciousness, not even knowing what they were, evoked through prana and mantra in a simple and direct manner. Through the power of mantra I could witness the mind and its habitual patterns becoming unraveled back to the Void, the pure space of cosmic sound and the higher electrical forces beyond all creaturely limitations.

During my many trips to India, I received special mantras from several great gurus and teachers, both known and unknown. Sometimes these mantras were complex, other times very simple. These included special Vedic mantras, particularly to Indra, Agni and Soma, and Tantric bija mantras, used both in outer ritual and inner meditations. It included mantric verses to Shiva, the Goddess, Krishna, Rama, Ganesha, Hanuman and the whole range of Hindu deities. I was taught how to use these mantras along with the forces of nature like fire and water, as well as with the inner senses, inner sound and light vibrations.

I discovered such great modern Sanskrit teachers and Mantra Yoga experts as Ganapati Muni, the chief disciple of the great sage, Ramana Maharshi. Ganapati's main living disciple K. Natesan passed on the entire corpus of Ganapati's Sanskrit works to me to study, preserve and share. I learned the important role of mantra in Hindu life overall and in the great festivals of India, as well as the mantras that resound at the great temples of the land from Tamil Nadu in the south to the snow covered Himalayas in the north.

Besides the role of mantra in higher Yoga practices, I explored the place of mantra therapy in Ayurvedic medicine as a tool for psychological and physical healing, particularly how mantras can remove deep seated negative emotional patterns and karmic blockages from the mind and heart. I learned the use of mantras as potent remedial measures in Vedic astrology to balance out difficult karmic influences transmitted by the planets, particularly malefic Saturn and Rahu that cause many obstacles and limitations in life.

The language of mantra provides a foundation for integrating all the Vedic and yogic disciplines and sciences into a single great teaching. Such key yogic concepts as the five elements, the seven chakras, and three gunas are part of a mantric tapestry, linking us back to the cosmic mind and our true Self beyond name and form. Mantra is the essence of the great yogic teaching as well as its primary practice. It turns teaching into practice and allows our practice to directly teach us, as the mantra gains its own life and consciousness in the very ground of our being.

I would like to thank Yogi Baba Prem, Nicolai Bachman, Pavan Kanwar and Don Diggs for going over the manuscript and Hinduism Today for providing its wonderful illustrations for this as in several of my previous books. If I succeed in encouraging the reader to a deeper study and practice, my goal of writing will be fulfilled.

In closing, I would like to dedicate the book to K. Natesan, who recently passed away at the age of ninety-six in Tiruvannamalai, India. Natesan was a source of great inspiration for my Sanskrit studies through his gurus Bhagavan Ramana Maharshi and Kavyakantha Ganapati Muni; he was close to both since his childhood. Ganapati Muni's Sanskrit works were particularly helpful as the Muni explains the secrets of Vedic and Tantric mantras with both precision and grace that I have not seen elsewhere. May such great Yogis and Rishis continue to guide us!

David Frawley (Pandit Vamadeva Shastri)
Santa Fe, New Mexico
Nov. 2009

Note on Spelling and Pronunciation of Mantras

The book uses the 'transliterated Sanskrit alphabet' to indicate the proper pronunciation of the mantras. Please note that the transliterated alphabet has its own phonetics that are not always equivalent to how these letters are pronounced in English. Sanskrit letters do not always correspond with English letters or even with English phonetics. This transliterated alphabet, though perhaps a little cumbersome to use at first, allows us to pronounce Sanskrit correctly.

However, for Sanskrit terms that are not approached as mantras in the book and may already be part of the English language, like Purusha or Shakti, I have not used the transliterated alphabet.

Please take the time to learn the basic sounds of the Sanskrit alphabet in order to pronounce the mantras correctly. Note the description of the transliterated alphabet at the end of the book. Be willing to take as much time with Sanskrit as you would any other language that has a different pronunciation. The rewards of such diligence will be unlimited in Mantra Yoga!

Orientation of the Book

1) The first section of the book explores the background of Mantra Yoga, the use of mantra for improving our karmas or actions in life, and the profound philosophy that mantra is based upon. This is to enable the reader to approach the practicalities of mantras with awareness, insight and discrimination.

2) The second section explains the main bija mantras, starting with the letters of the Sanskrit alphabet, leading up to the Mantra Purusha or body of sound, which is a very important practice in Mantra Yoga that has not been afforded much examination in the existing literature. Shakti bija mantras are also explored in detail, along with their application with the Mantra Purusha. This can help the reader understand the energies and indications of the bija mantras that they are using and how to adapt them for greater efficacy.

3) The third section explores the main methods of Mantra Yoga starting with mantra and pranayama, mantra and traditional Kundalini Yoga, and the use of Divine names and Bhakti Yoga. It is followed by the application of Mantra therapy in the Vedic sciences of Ayurvedic medicine, Vedic astrology, Vastu (directional science), and the Vedic usage of mantras overall.

4) The appendix contains advanced technical material as well as background resources, including reference to a series of mantra CDs of Yogini Shambhavi Chopra that can help with the pronunciation of the mantras in the book.

Part I

Mantra Yoga And
Mantra as a Karmic Tool

Ganesha, the Lord of Speech

Chapter 1:

Mantra and Primal Sound

The Universal Tradition of Sacred Sound

All over the world we find traditions of special words of power, magical phrases or secret codes that can unlock the great mysteries of life otherwise unapproachable to the human mind. Such traditions occur in religion, occult sciences, mysticism, shamanism, and almost every known spiritual path. Poetry, literature and philosophy worldwide similarly recognize the power of the word, sound or prime concept to influence and move us at a very deep level. While accessing the cosmic powers may not be as simple as repeating a phrase like 'open sesame', there are key sounds and words that can dramatically reveal new vistas of insight and energy within us.

While the Yoga practitioners of India have developed sacred sound into an extensive science of mantra as discussed in detail in the following chapters, it is important to note that the tradition of the transformative power of 'the Word' is universal. What makes the yogic approach so important and compelling is that it looks at the power of sound and the Word in an experiential manner as part of a sacred approach to the whole of life and consciousness.

The Judeo-Christian tradition starts with God creating the universe through the Word: "Let there be light," and there was light. The *New Testament* ponders, "In the beginning was the Word." The monastic history of Christianity includes prayer, chant and formalized words of meditation. Church services frequently include responsive chants of 'Amen'. The Jewish *Kabala* has mystic syllables and explains the Hebrew alphabet in a similar way relative to cosmology as the Yoga tradition does the Sanskrit alphabet. Sufism relies on the power of oft repeated prayers and Divine names to bring life into harmony with the Spirit.

Taoism has an important tradition of healing sounds for body and mind that are used in Taoist Yoga and traditional Chinese medicine. Buddhism has its own rich tradition of mantras, particularly in the Buddhist Tantras and in Tibetan Buddhism. These are largely Sanskrit mantras and include many of the same mantras as in the Hindu Yoga tradition mentioned in this book. Shamanic healing from all over the world invokes healing powers through chant and prayer, with diseases expelled in its rituals through the use of an emphatic phrase or mantra. We find traditions of sacred sound in all ancient cultures from Egypt and Babylonia to India, China and the Americas, as the ancient world lived more closely to the magic of the Divine Word.

Many traditions teach that if you know the Name of something you can gain mastery over it. This is an expression of the occult, mystical sense of being able to create the vibration or resonance of the object to fully identify with it. It is not the outer name, such as we find in a dictionary, which grants this power but the inner Name that is a mantric vibration. There is a sound code or vibratory pattern behind the universe itself, embedded in the fabric of existence that holds the intelligence, information and energy forms through which all processes of life operate. Connecting to this universal vibration is the basis for the yogic pursuit of mantra.

Yet apart from the mysticism of mantra, there is a practical side to mantra that is also gaining wide recognition today. Mantra as a term has entered into languages worldwide. Mantra is now commonly used to indicate a key word or phrase employed by various groups or individuals to summarize their views or relate their prime focus. This practical idea of mantra fits in well with the computer age, in which complex information is passed on in concentrated data bits that connect us to wider fields of knowledge and energy. It is what we could call 'the mantric approach of information technology'. A mantric like condensation of knowledge has become essential to modern communication and higher education. It is the ancient basis of the 'power point' presentation among many other such concentrated teaching devices.

The power of the Word is easily seen in our everyday lives as the words help create the environment within which we live, for good or ill. Road rage is frequently accompanied by expletives and the pent up energy behind them frequently breaks out in fights, tension and traffic accidents. Political rallies and sports competitions use key phrases and chants to create a mass energy to stimulate action and bring about victory, to get the crowd involved as it were, which can have positive or negative effects on a large scale.

The mass media world relies on key words, slogans and advertising phrases. Such short statements become the news stories in brief and can impact public opinion and sentiment globally, affecting us at subconscious and conscious levels. These concentrated sound messages are all mantras or power words of sorts. Through the science of Mantra Yoga, we can navigate our way through the influences of the dominant words reverberating around us to a higher truth, discerning the sounds that weigh down our consciousness from those that elevate it.

The reality behind these sacred or mundane uses of words of power is that words carry energy, creating and embodying the inner essence and forms of manifestations in the world. Each outer object has its own characteristic sound vibration that sustains it. Our own bodies, minds and hearts have their own characteristic sound patterns, which in turn are affected by the spectrum of sounds around us.

Mantra Yoga, Yoga as Sound

Mantra Yoga provides us a means to understand sacred sound from the perspective of a tradition that has taken it beyond mysticism into an organized and codified spiritual science. Mantra Yoga includes a study of the qualities inherent in sound itself, through which words and meanings are either properly shaped or deformed. It shows how sounds impact the nervous system, mind and heart, and how we can modify them to improve our lives. Regardless of which background or tradition you may personally follow, the insights provided in Mantra Yoga can be of enormous value to enable you to manifest your destiny creatively, effectively and completely through understanding the power of the Word.

The 'energetics of sound' discussed from the standpoint of Mantra Yoga can help you understand the sounds that you are setting in motion in your own life, and what their likely impact is going to be. The methods of Mantra Yoga can help you apply mantra and sacred sound in a practical manner, just as you can use Yoga asanas or pranayama to improve your health and awareness. While most of what is taught here is placed in the context of the Yoga tradition, Ayurvedic medicine and Vedic science, these teachings have a relevance to the whole of life. Mantra Yoga can take your Yoga or meditation practice to a higher level, but it is also helpful in terms of any healing arts for body or mind, and for any literary or philosophical pursuits.

Mantra is a tool for connecting us with the spiritual wisdom and the energy of consciousness hidden in the universe as a whole. Mantra is a doorway to an awareness that exists beyond all limited bits of information or technical knowledge. Mantra summarizes an inner view of reality as a play of consciousness that can instantly comprehend the whole, grasping the totality in a single point focus of direct perception and immediate experience. The universe itself is ultimately an expression of a single mantra or vibratory sound energy.

Mantra in the yogic sense relates to the prime energies, ideas, principles or archetypes of the cosmic intelligence that directs the forces of nature and the movements of our own minds and hearts. Mantra is part of a universal language rooted in sound, image, number and symbol, reflecting a 'cosmic thinking' beyond the preconceptions and biases of human thought. Mantra functions according to the inner mathematics of cosmic law. It serves to link our individual intelligence with the greater intelligence that pervades all space, extending our awareness into the Infinite and Eternal. To chant a mantra at a deeper yogic level is to think with the entire universe and to access the wisdom and experience of all beings.

There are mantric sounds that can awaken the higher potentials of the brain and change the flow of energy in the nervous system. Each one of us has a unique sound pattern that sustains all that we do, and allows our energies to move and grow or stagnate and decline. Unless we learn to harmonize our inner sound vibrations, our lives will likely remain in disharmony and suffering. Mantra is the most important tool for attuning our bodies and minds to their proper resonance, which is not with the outer world, but with the Divine presence that constitutes our own deepest Self.

Mantra and Modern Yoga

Today the interest in Yoga, which has largely been focused on asana or posture, is expanding beyond the physical back to Yoga's core concern with consciousness. In this process a new popular usage of mantras is arising. In yogic circles, mantras may be recommended as part of inner spiritual practices or for outer personal gains and achievements. Some groups emphasize special mantras to improve prosperity, health or well-being. They claim that those who chant these will gain wealth, status or whatever they really want in life. Other groups emphasize special spiritual mantras to help induce higher states of consciousness. They maintain that those who chant their mantras will more quickly reach levels of awareness not otherwise easily accessible. Many Yoga students chant mantras, using a personal mantra given by their guru or sanctified by their lineage, or add mantras to their Yoga classes, passing them on to their students.

However, in spite of this new interest in mantra, the full science of mantra is not well understood or even appreciated. There is often a secrecy maintained around mantras in order to preserve their power, which must be respected. In addition, few people know the complete science of mantra, as this requires a practice and study of mantras on many levels, not merely repeating a few common mantras for one's personal benefit. We find many people today chanting mantras that they don't know or teaching mantras that they have not practiced or brought to life on an inner level. The situation is ripe for a deeper approach to mantra, so that serious students can learn how to apply mantras with discrimination, insight and a higher aspiration.

Modern Yoga emphasizes Yoga asanas which place the body into special poses through which a transformative stillness can arise. Perhaps the easiest way for us to understand mantra is as a kind of asana for the mind. Mantras provide focus, strength, plasticity and adaptability to the mind, just as asanas do for the body. Mantras exercise our mental energy and give it poise and stability, just as asanas improve our physical condition. Most importantly, mantras harmonize the mental field, drawing our consciousness into a state of stillness that is inspirational.

Just as each asana puts the body into a certain energetic posture in which higher forces can be released, so too each mantra puts the mind into a certain pose in which it can become a conduit for a higher flow of energy and grace. Each mantra like each asana has its intention, form, and means of adaptation. Much like each asana, each mantra has its signature energy that brings about a specific effect upon the mind and can be understood according to its sound, meaning and application. Unless we learn to use mantra in our Yoga practice, we may succeed in putting our body into wonderful asanas, but our mind may remain rigid, agitated or distracted. As asana is the key to the flexibility of the body, the right use of mantra is the key to the flexibility of the mind!

In the world of Yoga today, chanting or kirtan is another important practice that is rapidly growing in popularity. Kirtan is based upon the repetition of mantric sounds, names and phrases; though not all who perform kirtan may be aware of the meanings involved. Kirtan, we could say, is mantric music and song. It sets in motion the power of mantra within us, not just as a mental pattern but as a current of deeper energy and feeling.[7] If we want to know the spiritual essence of Kirtan, we need to look more deeply into the subject of mantra.

Many modern Yoga groups give importance to mantra and primal sound. The mantra *Oṁ* has become the main word and sound of Yoga. The chanting of Shanti or peace mantras is another important part of modern Yoga gatherings. The TM or Transcendental Meditation movement has for decades promoted mantra meditation and primal sound as its main technique. The Krishna movement has promoted the *Hare Kṛṣṇa* mantra as its primary means of developing devotion and higher awareness. Even the Yogic greeting, Namaste, 'I bow to the Divine within you', is a kind of mantra.

The great Shiva mantra – *Oṁ Namaḥ Śivāya*! – is used by many Yoga groups, particularly those rooted in the Sivananda and Siddha Yoga traditions. Pranic mantras like *So'ham* and *Hamsa* (Hong Sau) are emphasized by groups like Self-realization Fellowship (SRF) or Siddha Yoga. Many Yoga Gurus initiate their students with mantras or combine mantra with the pranayama, asana or meditation approaches that they teach.

Mantras are one of the easiest of Yoga practices to perform, unlike complicated Yoga postures or strong pranayamas that many people are unable to do. There are simple mantras that any sincere student can be taught and gain much benefit from. However, mantra is also a very deep subject that can require more study and focus than outer Yoga practices working on the body and breath. Mantra connects us to the profoundest Yoga philosophies and the most powerful forms of meditation. Such a deeper use of mantras requires special training and adaptation at an individual level with a teacher trained in the tradition. As Yoga spreads and develops, the role of Mantra Yoga is bound to become more important, crucial and transformative both for the new student and for the advanced teacher.

Traditions of Mantra Yoga

In the following chapters, we will examine the yogic science of mantra, its philosophy, energetics and rules of application, so that we can employ mantras with clarity, comprehension and greater efficacy. We will also address the issue of how to keep mantras sacred so that they can raise our consciousness in life, rather than just become another tool for our transient desires.

For this exploration, we will rely upon the great mantric traditions of India - the Vedic and the Tantric – in which the subject of mantra and sacred sound is most fully addressed. There is a profound art and science of mantra, described in a number of traditional texts, which is seldom studied today. The fact that few of these texts are available in translation, or that existing translations are often defective, contributes to this condition.

The great *Upanishads*, the prime source books of spiritual knowledge for the Hindu tradition, contain sections on mantra and primal sound, connecting back to older Vedic teachings given in cryptic mantras. The Tantric tradition explores the different mantras and the Sanskrit alphabet in great detail as divine powers. The Shabda Brahman or 'Sound Yoga' tradition shows how mantra and sound can lead us to the highest reality. It states, "Two forms of knowledge are to be known, the Sound Brahman (Shabda Brahman) and the Supreme Brahman. Becoming immersed in the Sound Brahman, one reaches the Supreme Brahman."[8]

In addition, our study will bring in the work of modern mantra masters starting with the great Sanskrit poet and Raja yogi, Ganapati Muni, the chief disciple of the great sage Ramana Maharshi. We will use the insights of Ganapati's disciple Brahmarshi Daivarata, who was an important inspiration to Maharishi Mahesh Yogi of the TM movement and his promotion of Vedic knowledge. We will note the views of Sri Aurobindo, perhaps modern India's greatest philosopher and poet, who wrote in an English idiom but with a full understanding of older Sanskrit traditions.

However, our study of mantra will be practical as well, showing how we can use mantra to improve our lives on all levels. Mantra is a means of both enhancing awareness and of improving all our actions. The reader should be able to add mantra to their practices of asana, pranayama and meditation in a way that is rational, respectful and in harmony with the deeper teachings of the great Yogis, using mantras for physical, psychological and spiritual well-being. We need an intelligent, discerning and sacred approach to mantra, so that more people can benefit from this great tool of Yoga, without compromising its essence, power or purity.

Mantra is part of a great yogic technology for unfolding the higher powers both of our own core awareness and of the vast universe of consciousness. Through mantra we can gain access to and mastery over the forces of Nature, like the five great elements, and the very well-springs of creation itself. We can understand our own inner being through mantra and go beyond the ego and its limitations. Through mantra we can communicate with subtler regions beyond this dense physical realm and learn to ascend the ladder of the worlds to the Absolute beyond all manifestation.

Back to Primal Sound

To approach the essence of mantra, we will focus on the foundation of mantra in 'primal sound' and bija mantras, the shorter single-syllable 'seed mantras' that are among the most powerful mantras and the easiest to pronounce. We will emphasize two types of bija mantras. The first is the letters of the Sanskrit alphabet, which are the basis of all mantras and hold the key to cosmic sound. The letters of the Sanskrit alphabet reflect the prime powers of creation through which everything in the universe is structured, down to the physical body itself.

Second, we will examine the key Shakti mantras, which are more complex sounds, like the commonly used *Oṁ* and *Hrīṁ*. Shakti mantras reflect the prime forces of the universe and can be used to direct higher energies in specific ways, including awakening the Kundalini Shakti, the inner power of higher consciousness.

We will explore the meaning and usage of both types of bija mantras relative to Yoga, Ayurveda (Vedic medicine), Jyotish (Vedic astrology), and Vastu (Vedic architecture), where they are crucial. Mantra therapy is probably the main therapy used in all Vedic sciences for promoting our greater well-being, inwardly and outwardly.

Along with bija mantras, the book will examine important 'Name mantras' to different deities. We will also mention longer mantras, verses and Sanskrit hymns like Vedic Sukta and Sanskrit *Stotras*, which develop the power of mantra into the realm of prayer, deep devotion and meditation.

Chapter 2:

Mantra and Classical Yoga

Classical Yoga is one of the world's most important approaches to Self-realization, to understanding our true nature beyond time and space, birth and death, suffering and limitation. Mantra in Sanskrit means the tool 'tra' of the mind 'manas'. It is the primary tool of Yoga for calming the mind, which is necessary to allow us access to the higher Self. While classical Yoga through the *Yoga Sutras* of Patanjali does not make mantra specifically into one of Yoga's eight limbs, it does regard mantra as a key practice relative to all aspects of Yoga.[9]

- Mantra creates the orientation of mind necessary for the yamas and niyamas, the prime yogic observances, attitudes and life-style measures, to work. Such yogic observances as non-violence (ahimsa) and truthfulness (satya) are mantras themselves as it were, prime principles to repeat in our minds and hearts in order to guide our lives.
- Asanas performed while repeating the appropriate mantras bring a greater energy and awareness into the bones, muscles, joints and nerves, and help us transcend body consciousness.
- Pranayama practiced along with special 'prana mantras' can connect us to the cosmic prana and draw it into our deeper mind and heart for greater vitality and awareness.
- Mantra, by its ability to internalize the mind, is a prime tool of pratyahara, the yogic internalization of the senses necessary to bring our awareness to our deeper mind and heart. There are special 'pratyahara mantras' for this purpose.
- Concentration on a mantra is an important method for developing the power of attention that is the basis of dharana or concentration practices. There are special 'dharana mantras', which are connected to holding the gaze at various outer or inner locations like the chakras.
- Meditating on the sound or meaning of a mantra is one of the best and simplest meditations to perform, and one of the main approaches to dhyana. There are special 'dhyana mantras' for this purpose.
- The use of sacred sound and music is one of the best means to bring the mind into the state of samadhi or yogic oneness, absorption and bliss.

There are many mantras that can go along with asana practice. Many Yoga students chant the names of the Sun while doing the Sun salutation, for example. Most importantly, certain bija mantras can be used to direct or alter the power of the asana and make it more effective. However, we must remember that mantra is a sacred practice, not just an adjunct to a physical exercise, and treat it with respect. To do this requires making our asanas into mantras, prayers or rituals, not simply adding mantras as ornaments to physical movements.

Repeating special mantras along with the breath increases the energy of prana, helping to revitalize not only the body but also the mind. Mantra adds a sacred dimension and higher vibration to the practice and can transform pranayama into meditation.

Mantra is an important method of pratyahara or internalization of our energy. The mind and senses can follow the mantra to turn within, leaving all distractions aside. For this to occur, we must be able to energize the mantra, not only with prana, but with the power of the senses. We must learn to sense the mantra as resonance behind all of our senses.

Focusing on a particular mantra – particularly holding to a bija mantra – is one of the main methods of dharana or yogic concentration. Continuously directing the mantra to a particular location like the tip of the nose or to a particular chakra turns it into a dharana practice. Very helpful in this regard is 'Mantra Drishti' or the gaze of the mantra, in which one concentrates one's gaze along with the mantra, particularly on sites in the body like the heart, the third eye, the navel or the base of the spine.

As asana controls the body and pranayama controls the breath, so mantra controls the mind, not artificially but through a natural development of energy and attention. Mantra maintains the strength and integrity of our mental field, so that the mind no longer wanders off or loses its composure. Mantra sustains the proper circulation of energies in the sphere of the mind, so that we are no longer vulnerable to external conditioning which, after all, is based largely on reactive patterns of words and names.

Just as asanas place the body in a calm and relaxed state, so mantras puts the mind into a steady and relaxed state for meditation. For example, repeating the mantra *Oṁ* has the same calming and uplifting affect upon the mind and heart that the lotus pose does for the body.

Mantra Meditation

Mantra is not only an important preparation for meditation, 'Mantra Meditation' is one of the main types of meditation, with many variations. After all, our main mental fixation is with words. Mantra allows us to turn this negative attachment into a positive inspiration, as we replace our ordinary words and phrases with mantras.

Mantra practice gradually calms and integrates the mind. The mind becomes silent, concentrated and reflective, allowing our awareness to vibrate with the mantra. This naturally leads to deeper meditation, in which the mantra may fall away. Formless meditation is hard to achieve directly but becomes easily accessible once one builds the power of mantra in the mind. When we repeat a mantra, or do various forms of chanting, a more refined vibration develops and begins to assume the background pattern of our minds, down to a subconscious level. If we continually return to the mantra each time our mind becomes agitated, then the mantra's power to calm the mind will increase.

It should be beneath our dignity as a Divine soul to allow our minds to dwell on negative thoughts and emotions, fears, desires, jealousy and hatred, or to be controlled and distracted by external influences. With the mantra, we have a tool for redirecting the energy of the mind within so that we can reclaim our inner composure. Mantra can help us break up deep-seated mental and emotional patterns, conditioning and traumas even from childhood.

Traditional Yoga practice consists of two primary stages:

1) To develop sattva guna or 'purity of body and mind'.

2) To still the mind and go beyond it to the higher Self or Purusha.

The first stage of Yoga requires promoting sattva guna to create the proper balance in the mind, removing toxins and doshas from the body, and neutralizing the residual energies of rajas and tamas or agitation and inertia from the subconscious. The second stage consists of going beyond the mind-body complex and all of its conditioning, even that of sattva guna, to pure awareness.

Generally, we cannot succeed at the second step, if we have not first accomplished the first, which is its prerequisite. Many problems in Yoga practice arise from attempting the second step when the first has not been accomplished (in some cases it may not have even been attempted!). People may try to meditate in stillness, or enter into the oneness, while their minds remain outwardly oriented and caught in the disturbances of the body and senses. The proper practice of mantra helps neutralize such difficulties, developing sattva or harmony in the deeper mental field.

If our minds are noisy, disturbed, hypersensitive, reactive, opinionated, critical, or just constantly busy, we cannot silence them. If we are addicted to sensory sources of stimulation and entertainment, we are not even in control of our minds and so cannot focus them in any consistent manner for meditation. First, we must set in motion forces to take the mind from its disturbed (rajasic) or dull (tamasic) state to its natural clear quality (sattva). Mantra is the main practice for changing the nature of the mind from tamas and rajas to sattva. At the same time, it provides us the focus and energy for going beyond the mind.

Mantra and the Main Branches of Yoga

Mantra is probably the main practice that characterizes Yoga as a whole and its many different branches. All yogic paths use mantras and have special mantras of their own. Special mantras and chants pervade the primary Yogas of knowledge (Jnana), devotion (Bhakti) and service (Karma) in which asana does not have an important role. Yet even in Hatha Yoga, where asana can be very important, mantra remains significant and is the main method employed to prepare the mind for deeper Yoga practices.

The Yoga Sutras and its tradition of Raja Yoga emphasizes the role of the Pranava,[10] which literally refers to 'primal sound', and specifically to the mantra *Oṁ*, as the main means of connecting with the Divine or Cosmic Lord, Ishvara, the primordial guru of gurus in the Yoga tradition.[11] Just like the *Upanishads*, the *Yoga Sutras* stresses the importance of chanting and meditating upon *Oṁ*, which is the essence of all the mantras. This means that mantra is the guiding power of Yoga, not just one of its many practices!

Bhakti Yoga, the Yoga of devotion, centers on chanting, singing and the internal repetition of Divine names like *Namaḥ Śivāya* or the *Hare Kṛṣṇa* mantra are the best means of developing deep devotion and Divine love. In fact, the word of the heart is always mantra!

Jnana Yoga, the Yoga of knowledge, focuses on prime Atmic or Self-revealing mantras like *So'haṁ*, 'He am I" or the great sayings (Mahavakyas) of Vedantic philosophy. *Oṁ* is also important as the sound of the Self.[12] Such mantras are the foundation for the meditation and Self-inquiry practices that characterize Jnana Yoga practice.

Karma Yoga involves an extensive performance of rituals, like pujas and yajnas, all of which have their accompanying mantras to empower and sanctify them. It includes various forms of service (seva) to others, which are best performed while repeating a mantra. Unless the mind is engaged inwardly in mantra, one may not be effectively practicing Karma Yoga even when performing service.

Hatha Yoga and Tantric Yoga use pranic mantras like *Hūṁ* to arouse the Kundalini and open the chakras. The fifty main Sanskrit letters form the petals of the chakras and serve to energize them. The Kundalini Shakti or inner power of Yoga is said to be composed of the letters or sounds of the Sanskrit alphabet and is primarily a higher mantric force.[13] Kundalini is an electrical energy of speech at a deeper level of consciousness.

The practice of Yoga usually begins with the chanting of mantras, which may be mantras to the guru, to the aspect of the Divine one worships, or to the higher Self in order to create the proper atmosphere for teaching, or mantras to sanctify the ground on which one sits. Mantra grants sanctity and concentration to Yoga, which otherwise easily descends into another form of physical exercise or a seeking of personal empowerment.

Mantra Yoga, Nada and the Yoga of Sound

Mantra Yoga reflects an entire 'Yoga of Sound' (Shabda Yoga). The Yoga of Sound formulates the supreme reality as Shabda Brahman or transcendent sound. This tradition goes back to the Vedas, where the entire universe is said to rest in a single imperishable sound. Aspects of this teaching continue in all the different branches of Yoga.[14]

The main insight behind the Yoga of Sound is that reality consists of vibration, which in essence is sound. Even the formless silent Absolute has its own vibration or Shabda but remains contained in itself, a kind of breathing without the breath as it were. This sound of consciousness is called the 'non-elemental sound'[15] as distinguished from the elemental sound that arises through the ether element. By going back to the reality of primal sound, we can return to the very heart of creation and reach the Absolute beyond time and space from which all creation arises. We can reach the state of silence or pure stillness that is total communication and complete unity.

The profound study of scriptures, which are manifestations of Divine sound, is included in the Yoga of Sound. True scripture is not the literal word of God in human language, but rather the expression of primal sound as mantra. The Sanskrit word for scripture or Veda is Shruti, which means what has been heard at the level of the spiritual heart. The true revelation is not mere words that one can read in a book. It is the mantra revealed in the state of awakened listening, which reveals the essence of truth.

The state of awakened listening serves to open the head or crown chakra, whose organ of reception is the ears. True mantra is not just about speaking but about listening. Unless one can listen to the spirit of the mantra, the mantra cannot reveal its secrets to us. To truly study the Divine Word is to dwell in the state of revelation, in which each object in the universe proclaims the highest reality. This is to be receptive to the aspect of the Divine Word that each thing symbolizes and expresses in its vibration.

A related yogic science in the Yoga of Sound is called Laya Yoga, the 'Yoga of mergence'. This involves meditation on the inner sound current called nada, which arises when the mind becomes pure and clear. We can hear this vibratory sound if we close our ears and listen deeply with attentive awareness. Several types of nada exist. These are said to be like the sounds of a bell, a drum, a flute, the ocean or other sounds. Nada is the celestial music within us. We hear these sounds with our inner ear, the subtle counterpart of our gross organ of hearing. They reflect the sound of the cosmic intelligence inherent in space, which is the source of all knowledge.

Nada is the inner power behind the mantra. The outer mantra works to awaken the inner nada. Then the nada repeats the mantra, which is held in our inner sound current. The nada itself can assume the form of the mantra. This indicates that the mantra is resonating with our inner being. Several Tantric texts indicate that the real

One method of Yoga is to concentrate on the sound current and allow it to take us into the Divine, as this is its natural movement, drawing our energy up the spine and out through the top of the head. Other systems of Yoga use a meditation on the sound current but reinforce it through the use of mantras, pranayama, asanas, devotional or knowledge oriented meditations. The sound current is emphasized in traditional Hatha Yoga, where it is an important means to enter into samadhi or the yogic experience of bliss.

To meditate upon the nada is not just to listen to or to repeat a sound. It is also to inquire into the origin of sound, to follow the sound current back to its origin. This is to inquire into the origin of our own consciousness, which itself is a manifestation of sound. It is to contact our inner Self in the spiritual heart from which the sound current arises.

All forms of spiritual music come under the Yoga of Sound if we follow their vibrations back to the Divine Word within us. This includes vocal and instrumental music in all their beauty and diversity. Music in turn may be allied with poetry, drama and dance. Poetry is a kind of verbal music. Drama is the enactment of poetry. Dance is its expression. The internal usage of music can energize the various chakras that reflect the music of our soul. Music therapy and now poetry therapy have entered into alternative medicine in the West. The Yoga of Sound shows how they can be integrated as a sadhana or spiritual practice bringing us to the state of Self-realization.

Vedic Mantra Yoga

Yoga historically likely began with Mantra Yoga as its original form. The oldest yogic text and spiritual teaching coming out of India, the *Rigveda*, is primarily a teaching of Mantra Yoga. The *Rigveda* is composed of sacred chants like the Gayatri mantra to the Sun God designed to invoke the cosmic powers within us for their blessings and guidance. The Vedic ritual is based upon Agni or the 'sacred fire', which is regarded first of all as a power of Divine speech and mantra. This sacred fire, which is inwardly the power of speech, serves to invoke and manifest all the deeper powers of the psyche and the greater cosmos.

This Vedic Mantra Yoga is still accessible to us through learning Vedic chanting. Yet we should learn to use Vedic mantras along with the breath and meditate upon their profound meanings, if we want the deeper aspects of the Vedic Yoga to become clear to us.

Tantric Mantra Yoga

Mantra is the prime practice of Tantric Yoga, particularly the use of bija mantras or single syllables like *Oṁ*, *Hrīṁ* or *Śrīṁ*. As Tantra consists of devotional worship of various Gods and Goddesses, particularly Shiva and the Devi, the name mantras and bijas of these deities have an important role within it. In Tantra, the mantra is the sound form of the deity that reveals its inner truths. Tantric texts contain many teachings on mantra and reveal many powerful mantras for all aspects of life.

Mantra is the Shakti, the Yogini or inner power of Tantric Yoga. Indeed Tantra is largely synonymous with mantra. Mantra is the teaching of Tantra, which is the inner technology of mantra. Most of the teaching in this book will be based upon Tantric Mantra Yoga approaches.

Chapter 3:

Managing Your Karma with Mantra

Though mantra is central to all the branches of Yoga, the importance of mantra is not limited to Yoga and spiritual practices. There are special mantras to improve all human activities and our connections with the whole of life. In fact, mantra can help us do whatever we are doing better, with more awareness, more in tune with the greater universe of consciousness.

Mantra is relevant for everyone for creating the greater harmony and well-being that we are all seeking. There are many different types of mantras and different ways to apply them depending upon our aims and intentions. There are mantras that each person can benefit from in his or her own way at any stage or circumstance of life.

Mantra is perhaps the main tool we have for optimizing our karma in life. Through the right use of mantra, we can call upon the benefic powers of the universe to bring us the higher karmas that we are seeking and to remove the lower karmas that afflict us. Through the right use of mantra, we can restructure our samskaras or 'karmic patterns', changing the types of karmas we set in motion, so that our lives move in the direction that we would really like them to go. Through mantric sound vibrations, we can align ourselves with higher karmic energy currents that can lift us beyond our personal and collective limitations and open up our deeper potentials, which in the case of every human being are unlimited.

Mantra is probably our best tool available for psychological well-being. It allows us to detach ourselves from the outer world and its disturbances, including the conditioning power of the mass media that prevents us from moving within. It is a way to turn our minds, which are often our worst enemy, into a friend of our higher Self. It allows us to remove bad habits, addictions and inertia from our emotions and replace them with a peaceful and content mantric flow.

Mantra is probably the most important practice that we can do in life, whether to achieve our goals, to better communicate with others, or to develop a higher awareness. A conscious life – a life of grace, beauty, sanctity and peace – is best rooted in mantra. Each person should have his or her own prime mantras that they repeat daily for this purpose. In this way, our mantras are among our best friends and an important refuge for us in the face of life's complex challenges.

Mantra and the Main Goals of Life

Mantras are traditionally used for all the main goals of human life, which are defined in four categories according to Vedic thought.

- Dharma, one's primary purpose, vocation, work or career in life.
- Artha, achievement of necessary goals and objects, including wealth and property, to facilitate one's dharma.
- Kama, achievement of happiness and fulfillment of desires including relationship, family, and children that support, express and expand one's dharma.
- Moksha, liberation of the spirit, Self-realization, which is the highest

goal, achieved mainly through the practice of Yoga and meditation, and the fulfillment of our inner dharma as an immortal soul.

There is a fifth foundational goal of arogya or physical and psychological health and well-being. Without proper health and well-being, we are restricted in pursuing any of the goals of life. Vedic thought teaches that each human being has the right to achieve all these goals of life according to their temperament, inclination and karmas.

There are mantras to help with all these goals. Generally speaking, dharma, artha and kama are preliminary or outer goals of life, while moksha is the final or supreme goal. Yoga in the broader sense is the pursuit of moksha or liberation. Yoga is another term for moksha, and the Yoga Dharma in the classical sense is also moksha dharma. The use of mantras for Yoga and meditation comes under moksha dharma.

Mantras and the Prime Goals of Life	
Dharma mantras	Develop our life purpose and vocation, along with the necessary skills, power and knowledge
Artha mantras	Develop prosperity, abundance and resources that allow us to achieve our goals
Kama mantras	Help us fulfill our desires and wishes and gain happiness and contentment
Moksha mantras	Help us achieve liberation, unity with the Divine or higher Self and release from all sorrow
Arogya mantras	Counter disease for body and mind; promote positive well-being, health and longevity.

You may choose to focus on one goal or have some concern for all. Yet one should start with understanding one's dharma – one's real role and purpose in life – or what one seeks may not be harmonious to one's inner being. Then one should make sure to have the proper physical and psychological health in order to go forward.

Often the same mantra can be used for different goals. For example, the bija or seed mantra *Śrīṁ*, which relates to the Goddess Lakshmi, the aspect of the Divine Mother who grants the fulfillment of our desires, can be used for dharma, artha, kama, or moksha depending upon which goal we focus upon in our practice. The mantra can also bestow health and peace of mind, if we know how to awaken its healing powers.

Many of us begin our mantra practice with kama mantras to fulfill our outer desires for personal or family happiness. There is nothing wrong with kama mantras as a first step of mantra practice, but we must go deeper if we wish to discover the real secrets of mantra. One may needlessly increase one's desires, if one carelessly uses mantras to achieve one's desires without considering any higher goals. First of all, consider whether what you are asking for is a real desire of your soul or just a casual wish of the ego.

Many people repeat mantras to achieve artha as wealth and prosperity. This too has its value as long as the wealth is used for dharmic purposes, not for self-indulgence or wasteful consumption. In this regard, there are mantras that can aid us in business practices and facilitate material gains.

Relative to dharma, mantra can be used to reinforce our vocation in life, unfolding the deeper purpose of our existence. For example, there are mantras that help promote artistic skills, such as mantras like *Aiṁ* to the Goddess Sarasvati, the patron of the fine arts. Every vocation has its patron deities, mantras and sacred sounds.

We should consider carefully the nature of what we are seeking in our mantra practice because the mantra will not only grant us our wishes but also connect us to the corresponding karmas. We will be bound to the karma of the goals that we seek through our use of mantras. If these goals are unspiritual, then we will increase the unspiritual energies in our lives.

Right Attitude and Intention in the Use of Mantra

Some of us find a book on mantras and choose the mantra that seems to quickly offer us what we most want in life, like a mantra to attract the right partner or mate. We may repeat the mantra haphazardly for a few days and then wonder why our life hasn't changed in a radical manner. We may not even pronounce the mantra correctly.

Mantras are not simply random sounds that we can pick up by casual reading and expect wonders from. The sound form of the mantra only has value if applied in the right manner, just as a tool will only work if used by one trained in how to handle it. As mantras directly impact our psyche, we should be discriminating in how we use them and try to learn something of the science of mantra as well.

The application of mantra rests on the intention, samkalpa in Sanskrit, according to which the mantra is approached. These intentions are defined according to the three gunas or qualities of Nature that are widely considered in yogic thought: sattva (harmony), rajas (aggression) and tamas (inertia).

In Yoga philosophy, all the forces of nature and human life are made up of the interaction of these three gunas. To gain real happiness and well-being, we need to promote sattva guna – the clear quality necessary for the mind to be aware and the heart to be at peace – for which the right use of mantra is perhaps the most important method.

Mantras and the Three Gunas	
Sattvic Mantras	For liberation (moksha), the well-being of all, the fulfillment of deeper soul wishes, and gaining our real needs in life, like our legitimate needs of security, home and family.
Rajasic Mantras	For the achievement of outer goals in life like wealth, career, power or relationship, as if these were the highest aims, to gain power and prestige for the ego.
Tamasic Mantras	To control, harm or hypnotize others or otherwise employing mantras in an ignorant or destructive manner.

Mantras can work at rajasic and tamasic levels as well as at sattvic levels. There is no doubt about it. You can use mantras to get anything that you want in life, even if these desires may not be what you really need. However, there is an important qualification to these usages. At the same time, we are creating sattva, rajas or tamas as energies in our own minds according to how we employ these mantras.

If we use mantras in a rajasic way, to further our ego expectations, the mantras will work. They can help us get a better job, a good partner, more money, a better career, more power and so on. But if these desires are beyond our real needs, the mantras will increase the quality of rajas in our minds, making us more aggressive and worldly, restless and unhappy, even if we get what we want.

Similarly, it is fine to use mantras to protect ourselves from negative influences such as abound in human life with all of its gossip, jealousy and enmity. But when we use mantras to project negative energy on to others, that energy can rebound back upon us. If we use 'tamasic mantras' to control or harm others, for example, we will create more tamas in ourselves, bringing deception, ignorance and suffering into our lives and darkening our emotions and thought processes.

For this reason, it is best not do any mantras for rajasic or tamasic goals. You will likely increase your own negative karmas if you do. Tantrics who perform or prescribe such rajasic and tamasic mantras usually end up with suffering and create negative karmic forces that eventually overwhelm them. Unfortunately, many books on mantra and Tantra, particularly out of India, contain such rajasic and tamasic mantras. These mantras, like magic spells and potions, are dramatic, exciting and appealing to our ego nature. But the same books may not adequately warn us of the negative karmic consequences of such mantras, which can be considerable.

The first principle of mantra practice is to make sure that you have a good intention or 'sattvic samkalpa'. The mantra should be used to increase the force of good in ourselves and in the world and not to harm anyone.

In addition, one should perform mantras according to a sattvic life style. A great aid for this is to follow a sattvic or vegetarian diet at least while doing the mantra practice. A pure diet helps keep the mind pure in order to hold the higher vibration of the mantra.[16] Traditional approaches to mantra require a ritualistic purification of the body, mind, senses and prana that can be quite engaging.[17] While we may not be able to do all such purification practices, we should at least strive to keep our bodies, minds and hearts in a pure condition while we are seeking the blessings of a mantra.

Perhaps the simplest way to make sure that our mantras are based upon right intentions is to treat mantras as prayers and to make a prayer to the deity or guru along with the mantra. One can dedicate the mantra to the deity and to the fulfillment of the Divine Will. Holding an attitude of ahimsa, not wishing harm to any living being, is another important aid.

Finally, we should note that mantras have inner power only to the extent that we are truthful in life. If our minds and speech is truthful, if we say what we mean and mean what we say, if we follow out our words in action, then a mantra will likely work for us. Mantra reflects our own power of speech, however we have cultivated it.

Mantra Therapy

Mantra therapy can be used to direct a higher prana or healing energy to wherever it is needed within us. Special healing mantras exist for both physical and psychological afflictions that can literally work wonders, if they are applied in the proper manner.

Mantra therapy can be found in Yoga and in all the Vedic sciences, which have their own special mantras, particularly Ayurvedic medicine, Vedic astrology (Jyotish) and Vastu (Vedic architecture). Vedic astrology is also used for choosing mantras and for the timing of mantra practice, making it the most important adjunct Vedic science for Mantra Yoga.

Energetics of Mantras

We can compare the use of mantras with that of herbs. It is very different to just pick an herb out of an herb book that appeals to us than it is to go to a qualified herbalist and get a good herbal formula that really addresses our condition as a whole.

Mantras, like foods and herbs in Ayurvedic medicine, have particular energetic effects. They can be expanding or contracting, heating or cooling, light or heavy, soft or harsh in their effects. Just as any herbal therapy rests upon the right understanding of herbal energetics, the application of mantras rests upon a right understanding of the energetics of the mantra. The overall energetics of mantra depends upon three primary factors:

- Sound Factor: First, the effect of a mantra relates to the energy inherent in the nature of its sound, in the different qualities of vowels and consonants and the particularities of pronunciation. Each sound has a certain quality that reflects the potential meanings that it can serve as a vehicle for. The sound factor is like the 'body' of the mantra.
- Pranic Factor: Second, the effect of a mantra depends upon how its sound is made. The same sound can be made with more or less force, intensity, velocity or prana, which naturally will alter its energy, meaning and impact. Different tones come into play here and how the mantra is aligned with the breath. This is like the 'life-force' of the mantra.
- Mental Factor: Third, the effect of a mantra depends upon how we energize it with thought, meaning, intention and emotion. This is like the 'mind and heart' of the mantra.

There are energetics relative to the sound quality of a mantra and its application. Some sounds like 'sh' or 'm' tend to be soft sounds, while 'p' or 't' tend to be hard. In addition, sounds are connected to prana and reflect the conditions of our own prana or vital energy. If our prana is disturbed, our speech and mantra will be disturbed. If our prana is calm, then our speech and mantra will be calm. Relative to intentionality, the meaning of a word is more important than its sound, but a word will have a stronger effect if the sound supports its meaning. That is the difference between poetry and ordinary speech. An effective mantra requires the appropriate sound, intonation and deep sense of meaning.

The energetics of mantras are subtle and can be modified significantly by the way in which they are applied. For example, the mantra *Laṁ* indicates the earth element with its density, inertia, calm and delight, but also has some watery and nourishing qualities. Applied with harshness (tamas) and force (rajas), the mantra can literally be used to crush things into the ground with the power of stone. Applied with softness (sattva), grace and beauty, it can be used to dance lightly, slowly and rhythmically on the ground, releasing the joy inherent in all creation!

Root sounds, like those of the Sanskrit alphabet, have spectrums of potential meaning. They are not ordinary nouns, like a 'house' or a 'tree', that have a specific meaning only. Some sounds reflect a range of opposites in Sanskrit. For example, the root 'Yu' means both to unite and to separate, and consequently to coordinate and classify. In addition, the sound quality of the mantra, much like poetry, requires a subtle and sattvic mind to appreciate. This entails deconditioning the mind from its habitual sound associations. For example, the English word 'bum' connotes a worthless person, which meaning we automatically attach to the sound. Yet the seed mantra *Baṁ* (which is pronounced the same way as bum in English), is used to project light. Unless we disconnect a sound from its conventional meaning, we may not be able to connect to its underlying mantric seed power.

Bija mantras and primal sounds help us release negative experiences and painful memories that we may be holding in the sound patterns of different words. Mantra prepares the mind for meditation by clearing out conditioned sounds and the emotional reactions they allow to continue unconsciously within us. Yet mantras can also help us improve our actions in the outer world, by providing us with the insight and creativity to respond to the challenges of the moment, no longer burdened by our previous psychological baggage.

Chapter 4:

Energizing Mantras with Power and with Grace

Mantras require the proper energization for them to work in the best possible manner. How to awaken and empower the mantra is one of the most important considerations in the usage of any mantra. In the following chapter, we will explore the main methods and approaches for doing this. One must bring life to the mantra, which is to make the mantra not only part of your personal life but of the universal life around you. Energization of mantra in turn requires some guidance and connection with the greater tradition of Mantra Yoga.

The term mantra traditionally suggests a mantra guru. A guru or spiritual guide is often defined as one who gives us a mantra and makes it work. The special word or instruction of the guru can itself be called mantra and can function as a mantra for us. The guru is usually part of a yogic tradition that has its own mantras, through which the tradition is sustained, linking us back to previous gurus and a line of teachers and teachings.

An important factor to consider before taking up any mantra is the source the mantra has come from. Who is giving you the mantra and according to what authority or sanction? What kind of teacher or therapist is necessary to provide a mantra that really works for your particular issues in life? What constitutes a real mantra guru and what types of mantra teachers can be helpful to consult?

We have already discussed the importance of first knowing what we are seeking from a mantra and how we are applying it. A mantra by itself is a mere sound. Unless we have some means to bring it to life, the mantra may not become effective, even if we have a good mantra to begin with.

If we are looking to choose our own mantras, there is the danger that we may not have enough inner knowledge to determine the best mantra in the first place. It is better to consult a mantra guru or mantra teacher before taking up a mantra, even if we have carefully considered different mantras and how to use them. Just as in any other Yoga practice, like asana, pranayama or meditation, a teacher is an important aid and in many instances indispensable.

Generally, for a mantra to grant moksha or liberation,' it requires the energization of a Self-realized guru or a tradition going back to Self-realized gurus. Mantras for the outer goals of life are not as stringent in their rules of choice or application.

Some spiritual groups hold that only mantras given by a great guru will work. While this reflects the concerns of moksha or liberation mantras, it is not true of all mantras, though any mantra given by a great master will naturally have a greater efficacy. In India, there are mantras for everything, and mantras are passed on by a variety of sources. Parents teach mantras to their children from family traditions relative to family gurus and family deities. School teachers teach mantras to aid students in the learning process, like chants to Sarasvati and Ganesha, the main deities who govern the learning process. India's traditional music contains mantras and sacred chants as part of common songs. *Clearly one doesn't have to go to an enlightened guru for any mantra, but for the higher mantras we need if not an outer connection with a great guru, at least a profound inner connection with a guru, deity or tradition.*

Traditional mantras connect us with the energy and aspiration of the many people that have used the mantras over time, putting us in touch with special currents and rivers of spiritual energy so generated. Of course, we should make sure to choose a mantra from a tradition that we resonate with, and that directs us to the goal that we are really seeking. A traditional guru can empower the mantra for us or instruct us how to do so. There are also traditional rules of receiving mantras, times for taking up mantras, and rituals for using mantras that make them more effective.

Rules of Mantric Applications

Each application of mantra has particular rules of usage. If you are using a mantra for healing purposes, the mantra should be correctly prescribed and applied just like herbs, diet or any other healing therapy. A good Ayurvedic practitioner – particularly one trained in traditional Yoga and Ayurveda – should be able to recommend suitable healing mantras for you. If you are seeking a mantra for astrological purposes, for removing negative planetary energies and their resultant karmas, you need to consult a good astrologer trained in the astrological application of mantra. If you want to use mantras for Vastu or purposes of protecting your dwelling, you need someone who knows the rules of Vastu and the mantras that go along with these.

However, such mantra teachers or therapists need to practice the mantras in order to be really able to pass them on to others, preferably having the siddhi or power of the mantra that arises from deep and long term practice. For example, if an astrologer recommends a traditional mantra for an afflicted Saturn in your chart, the mantra can help. But if the astrologer has practiced these Saturn mantras for years and has gained the grace of Saturn as a cosmic power, then the same mantras will be much more effective.

If you are looking for a mantra for ritualistic purposes – such as to aid in achieving the outer goals of home, family or career – a Hindu priest can help you and recommend both mantras and rituals that will aid in your actions. The work of Hindu priests and pandits largely consists of performing mantras and rituals for the benefit of others, and they are carefully trained how to do this.

Besides mantras that require special prescriptions, there are 'universal mantras' that can be recommended for everyone. Certain spiritual mantras like *Oṁ* or peace chants (Shanti mantras) are general in their application and are often widely prescribed. Many traditions pass on certain mantras to their followers like the Gayatri mantra by the Arya Samaj or Gayatri Pariwar.[18]

There are certain 'personal mantras' that we can choose for ourselves. Each person can develop his or her own personal mantra favorites according to the form of the Divine they worship (their Ishta Devata mantra), their own inclination, or what simply resonates best with them. You don't have to get an approval to chant a mantra to the Divine as you best relate to it, though certainly the mantra will have more power if given by a teacher in the tradition.[19]

However, if one wants a powerful moksha or liberation mantra, it is best to seek a Self-realized guru, or a teacher in the tradition of Self-realized masters, to initiate you. Yet even here one has to exercise a great deal of discrimination. Of the many who may claim to be Self-realized teachers, only a few may be so, particularly those who stand outside of any formal tradition.

Mantra and Shakti

For a mantra to be really effective, it must be electrified as it were. There must be prana in it, along with a power of deeper feeling and a concentration of mind and heart. Repeating such an energized mantra can be compared with the effect of saying the name of one's beloved as opposed to saying the name of a person that one does not know.

There is an inner *Mantra Shakti* that must be brought into function for a mantra to become really effective. This empowerment of the mantra can come through the guru, through tradition, through intense practice, deep devotion, or even by grace – or may require all of these. When the Mantra Shakti is awakened, the mantra will resonate with dynamic energy and repeat itself by its own power. It will connect you to the deity in a form or relationship that communicates to you. It will follow an internal light and sound vibration, stimulating a higher form of contemplation and meditation within you. Its inner meaning and broader associations will become clear as the mantra begins to speak to you and teach you. You will see the mantra vibrating in the world around you and resonating through your entire being.

Once the Mantra Shakti is awakened with a single mantra, any number of mantras can be energized by transferring its power to them. One can compare this Mantra Shakti to poetic inspiration, through which the power and beauty of any number of words can be developed. We must learn how to bring life to the mantra, which requires making our own lives and thoughts into mantras. Mantra can bring a cosmic energy into all the sounds that we hear, whether it is the beating of our hearts, the howling of the wind, or even the barking of a dog.

Awakening the mantra Shakti is the foundation of effective mantra practice. Mantras cannot be made to work mechanically or merely according to our personal wishes. To enliven a mantra requires a sense of the sacred, particularly an honoring of the Goddess, who holds the power of sacred sound. However, there is no outer formula according to which this inner mantric power can be awakened, though a frequent and dedicated repetition of a mantra is helpful. We must remain receptive to the Mantra Shakti, allowing its grace to flow. This entails repeating the mantra as a prayer and a meditation with a receptive mind and heart. Those who have the Mantra Shakti fully developed within themselves become true mantra gurus. They know intuitively the different powers of sounds and intentions and can recommend what an individual may need at any stage of life.

Each mantra has a consciousness of its own that is connected to the universal consciousness. Unless we link to that mantra consciousness (Mantra Chaitanya) and work with it, then the mantra is likely to remain without vitality or direction. Once we have awakened the Mantra Shakti, it will then bring to life the Mantra Chaitanya. The mantra will become a repository of wisdom, perception and insight.

Mantra and the Deity

Mantras relate to the Divine in various names, forms and functions, from the outer forces of nature to the Absolute transcending all time and space. These forms and aspects of the Divine, called *Devatas* in Hindu thought, are usually referred to as Gods and Goddesses in the West, though these terms, we should note can be misleading, as they are not separate deities but different Divine qualities and functions.

Such deities provide us with an intimate and personal connection with the Divine and our higher Self. Whether for spiritual or mundane purposes, a mantra is usually connected to the propitiation of the appropriate deity or aspect of the Divine for the purpose involved, like Lakshmi for wealth, Sarasvati for learning, Kali for strength, or Shiva for peace.

Mantras are usually addressed to the deity in order to bring a Divine power and grace into our lives. The Devatas have their own special mantras through which we can call upon them and gain their grace: Lakshmi mantras like *Śrīṁ*, Sarasvati mantras like *Aiṁ* and so on. The mantra is said to be the subtle body of the deity, the mental counterpart to its representational form. The mantra is often a name of the deity we seek to connect with. Divine names are among the most powerful mantras. They represent Divine attributes and powers and can bring these into our lives.

It is best to look at the mantra as a vehicle for communion with the Deity – as a kind prayer – not as a power to manipulate for personal ends. Mantras are usually performed along with devotional practices and dedicated to the deity. This is one of the most important ways for empowering a mantra and awakening its inner energy. The deity can be defined according to one's Ishta Devata or the form of the Divine that one personally worships, or to God in a relationship sense as Divine Father or Divine Mother. Your primary, root or *mula mantra* is usually that of your Ishta Devata or form of the Divine that you worship.

The inner honoring of the deity helps us approach the mantra with the proper respect, so that it can yield the blessings it is endowed with. It is the grace of the deity that grants the fruit of the mantra, not just the mantra as our personal expression. Naturally, if we are calling upon the Divine with mantra, we must do so with the right attitude, intention and action. You don't expect God to answer your prayers and mantras if you approach the deity carelessly or thoughtlessly! Treat any mantra with devotion and it will give you back the rewards of Divine love.

Mantra and Ritual

What is done in a sacramental manner has more power, a greater karmic effect and leaves a stronger *samskara* or residual effect in order to guide our actions for the future. Rituals and sacraments are an important way to make our lives more meaningful by connecting us with the greater universe. Healing also works best if done as a ritual or in a sacred manner, which aids in the flow of healing energies.

Mantras are commonly part of rituals. Mantra, we could say, is 'sacred thought' and ritual is 'sacred action'. Sacred thought naturally embodies and expresses itself in sacred action. Generally, it is best to perform some ritual before or along with reciting a mantra.

One can look at a ritual as a kind of mantric gesture or expression of mantra in action. There is a whole science of ritual in Vedic thought that involves special fire offerings called *yajnas* and ritual worship of images called *pujas*. Yoga is meant to be such an inner ritual, sacrifice or sacred action.

Empowering Mantras with Substances

An important way to energize mantras is through the five elements of nature, particularly through water and fire. Mantras chanted in water gain more power, for example, while bathing or while standing in a river or in the ocean. Mantras can be used to purify or energize water. You can chant mantras over water before drinking it or using it to make herbal beverages or foods. It is good to have such mantrically energized water in your home, in your kitchen and in your meditation room. Water is a vehicle for prana and for emotion. We should make sure to use mantras to create water that can really nourish our souls.

Mantras chanted while meditating in the presence of a sacred fire are also more powerful. The fire magnifies and carries their influence into the greater universe. It is best to use mantras along with specially performed Vedic fire rituals, sanctified by special offerings. You can write mantras down and burn them in a sacred fire to purify and energize them and to convey your intentions to the cosmic powers.

Relative to the force of air, you can use mantras along with prayer flags placed on your house, nearby trees or in a temple environment. Another way to use the air element is to chant mantras along with special forms of incense. Or we can recite a mantra to clear the air of negative energies. Relative to the forces of ether, one can chant mantras around flowers or to define sacred spaces, or around the space that you wish to sanctify or protect. You can use mantras to consecrate your house, healing room or meditation room.

Mantras gain more power if they are recited relative to a statue or form of a deity that you worship regularly and feel a divine presence in. In fact, you can use mantras to empower all the material forces around you. This includes using mantras to energize sacred stones, crystals or other forms of the earth element.Mantras can be used to energize, sanctify or spiritualize whatever we do. Once we have brought energy to the mantra, the mantra can pass that energy wherever we direct it, empowering both the objects and actions around us.

In the practice of Yoga, mantras can be used to sanctify our asana or meditation seat. They can be used to spiritualize our Yoga room or Yoga class. In regard to Ayurveda, mantras can be used to empower herbs, foods, or therapies. Relative to Vedic astrology, mantras can be used to bring in the sacred energy of the planets and the forces of time. Relative to Vastu, mantras can be used to sanctify the forces of space and directional influences. In the appendix of the book, more specific guidelines on the use of mantra have been provided.

Chapter 5:

Mantra, the Divine Word and Cosmic Manifestation

There are many profound philosophies of mantra and the Divine Word in the different spiritual traditions of the world. Western philosophy and theology has aimed at the Logos or Divine Word, as perhaps its prime inspiration, since the time of the ancient Greeks. The great yogic philosophies of India have been rooted in mantra, of which the ancient Vedic philosophy is probably the oldest and most comprehensive.

The *Vedas* teach how the entire universe in all its vastness arises from a single sound, just as the Big Bang theory of modern physics teaches how the entire universe arises from a single timeless and spaceless point. Yoga explains how our own psyche mirrors cosmic sound in the structure of our subtle body and its chakra centers, which are mantric formations.

Mantra can be said to be the highest form of philosophy because it provides the concentrated form of language necessary to embody the highest truths that go beyond our ordinary human language based on physical reality. Mantra is a deeper level of speech that reflects the laws of the universe, what is called dharma, 'that which upholds', in Sanskrit. Mantra is the 'language of dharma' that enables us to understand what dharma is and how it works. That is why in Mantra Yoga different sounds correspond to the natural and spiritual forces through which the universe operates, starting with *Oṁ* itself as the cosmic word.

Each object in the universe is an expression of the Divine Word and holds a specific message about the meaning and purpose of the universe as a whole. Nature itself is the first Book of Mantra or sacred sound, the outer reflection of the Divine Word. Yoga and all the Vedic sciences arose originally from an ability to understand the Divine Word, to read the language of nature that is mantra, and to unfold its secrets through Shakti, the hidden power of nature, whose origin is primal sound.

Speech and the Human Being

According to the *Upanishads*: "The essence of all beings is earth, the essence of earth is water, the essence of water is the plants, the essence of the plants is the human being, the essence of the human being is speech, the essence of speech is the *Rigveda*, the essence of the *Rigveda* is the Samaveda, and the essence of the Samaveda is *Oṁ*.[20] We as human beings are a manifestation of cosmic sound and have the ability to reflect the Divine Word in our own minds and hearts. Mantra is the language we need to learn in order to be able to do this.

Speech is the main faculty that defines our nature as human beings. Our special vocal organs are one of the main evolutionary developments that made the human species possible. We humans have the ability to make complex sounds with our tongues, mouths and throats that reflect the subtlety of what our brain can think and the intricacy of what our hands can fashion. Usually, the greater is our intelligence, the greater is our ability of communication through speech.

Our power of speech is originally an articulation of self, an expression of self-existence and individuality. The utterance of 'I' is the root of all other expressions. Speech is the expression of consciousness, its way of revealing itself and its powers of observation. It is because of our power of speech that we can recognize ourselves, name objects in the world, and reflect upon the meaning of our existence. The human 'I am' is a reflection of the Divine 'I am' through the unity of the human and the Divine Word.

Speech is the main motor organ that we use in life, through which we direct our other faculties. We are always speaking either with our mouth or with our minds. As our words precede our actions, speech is the basis of our power of action in general. This means that through control of speech we can control our karma and gain mastery over the entire movement of our lives. Yet besides our outer speech capacity there is an inner speech, the voice of the mind and heart, which proceeds through the power of mantra and sacred sound and contains our higher evolutionary potential in consciousness.

To understand mantra, we must first understand this underlying power of speech, which is ultimately rooted in consciousness itself, not just the vocal organ. Speech is a Divine potential that is part of the universal creative power. Speech is not simply a biological or species-based urge. Our human speech is not just used to express our basic life impulses; it has an additional power of poetry and philosophy. We can use the power of speech not only to communicate with other human beings, but to also communicate with the Divine powers that pervade the universe. Mantra is the means of this cosmic communication, though which we can become one with All.

Speech and the Goddess

Great spiritual traditions from throughout the world recognize the role of the Divine Word as the origin of the universe. The same is true of yogic thought, in which the Divine Word both creates the universe and is one with the Absolute beyond time and space. Yet in yogic thought, the Word is not simply God, the Word is the power of the Goddess.

As a creative power, speech has a feminine quality. It is the instrument of the great world Mother. Speech is the original form of the Goddess, who herself is the creative power of the silent Absolute hidden in infinite space. This power of speech, called

Vak or *Sarasvati* in the *Vedas*, is the force behind nature and holds all the powers of cosmic evolution.

The very body of the Goddess is made up of mantra, defined through the root sounds of the Sanskrit alphabet, through which she fashions all things, forming the myriad forms of creatures out of the vibratory power of the Word. The Goddess rules over the universe through her power of speech, which dictates the cosmic order and sets in motion all the laws of existence. Yet she herself is also the Word, and through it, she is herself all beings in the universe, which are aspects of her own self expression.

This Divine Word Goddess has entered into humanity and allows us to speak. She is the higher voice within us. Unfortunately, we seldom honor the Goddess by treating our speech as sacred. We too frequently use our speech in a destructive and egoistic manner. Such unsacred speech causes many problems in life, whether conflicts with others or emotional unrest within ourselves. However, once we reach the mantric level of language and reconnect with the Divine Word, our language once more becomes the expression of the Goddess and regains its healing and transformative capacity. Mantra requires that we let the Goddess speak through us. For mantra to really work, it should be employed as a means of worshipping the Goddess, not to gain something for ourselves!

Prana and Speech/ the Great God and the Great Goddess

The *Vedas* define the two fundamental forces in the universe as Prana or life-energy, which we experience mainly through the breath, and Vak, which is speech, articulation or expression overall.

Prana is the Great God or masculine principle – Shiva in Hindu thought – who represents the transcendent Prana or immortal life energy beyond life and death. This power was called Indra in Vedic thought, the foremost of the Vedic deities, who represents the ruling power of Prana as will, insight and the urge to transcend. Vak or speech is the Goddess or feminine principle, Shakti or the Devi (Goddess) relative to Shiva, and Indrani, the feminine aspect of Indra.

Prana is spirit, which is formless, while speech is the basis of form and matter through the naming process. Name and form arise through speech, while being and consciousness are sustained by prana. Prana and speech are intertwined, like husband and wife, or the right and left sides of the body. They always move together. Prana is the energy behind speech, which moves through the breath. Speech is the form or limitation that prana or the breath assumes. Speech is prana in action. Prana is the essence of speech, which communicates our life-energy, its intentions and its information. Prana or breath is the meaning behind speech, which is the sound created by the breath as it tries to express itself outwardly. Prana is the speaker, and speech is the instrument of speaking.

Prana and Vak are two facets of the same underlying reality. Prana is unmanifest speech, and speech is manifest prana. Prana naturally creates sound, which is the hissing sound of the breath.[21] Speech occurs through the outgoing breath and is, therefore, manifest prana. Our speech expresses our prana or our energy, not just our physical and vital energy but our mental and spiritual energy. Similarly, our prana or breath carries our thoughts as the seed of our words. Prana provides the impetus to speak, which at a higher level is the expression of inspiration.

This means that we cannot forget the role of prana in mantra. The power of the breath and the greater vital energy behind it vitalizes the mantra. Similarly, mantras can work to hold and sustain our prana. Prana, we could say, is the spirit of mantra. Mantra in turn is the expression of prana. Whatever most engages our prana or vital energy becomes the main subject of our speech.

Speech, Senses and Mind

Whatever we can perceive through any of our different senses, we can express through speech. Speech can relate what the eye sees, what the ear hears, what the nose smells, what the tongue tastes and what the skin touches. All the senses express themselves through the power of speech, apart from which they are mute and incapable of articulating themselves.

Speech therefore is the guide of all the other senses. Through the control of speech, we can control all our senses.[22] This means that mantras can help us master, energize and harmonize all our senses. Mantra connects our outer speech with the inner speech of the Gods, which can bring the Divine Will into our sensory functioning. Speech is more than a motor organ but connects to the speech of the mind, our deeper consciousness and the Divine word.

The mind is composed of thoughts, which are based on words and reflect our speech patterns. Thought itself is a subtle form of speech. We can observe this for ourselves. Our thoughts are a kind of internal conversation, our own mental talk, often framed as a soliloquy or an imagined dialogue. If we replace this mental speech with mantra, we can transform the energy of our minds and hearts. This higher speech of the mind is the basis of buddhi or higher intelligence in Yoga, which allows our thoughts and actions to flow with the Divine word.

Notice that you cannot see your mind or your thoughts, which have no visible form. The mind consists of sound which carries our memories, emotions and ideas. It is the power of sound that holds who we are, who we have been and who we wish to be. This is not just sound as one of the five elements but the primal sound vibration behind all the elements. Mantra as primal sound can change the nature of the mind down to the subconscious level. Through mantra, the control of both the mind and the senses becomes possible, not through the ego but through the Divine presence within us. Mantra can then open up our inner senses and higher levels of the mind that are otherwise very difficult to access.

Sound and Meaning

There are two factors in all words as 'sound' and 'meaning'. In yogic thought, the sound is said to be Shakti, the feminine principle of energy, and the meaning is said to be Shiva, the masculine principle of being. The sound is a vehicle for the meaning.

In our modern languages, the sound and meaning of words has little relationship. For example, there is no particular reason of sound quality why the English word 'tree' means 'a woody plant with a big stem'. The use of a particular sound for a particular object is based upon convention, rooted in historical usage, not in the power of sound. Another language can use a very different sound for the same object.

Yet we do seek to harmonize sound and meaning when it comes to literature, particularly poetry. The poet seeks to say something in a sound pattern that enhances the meaning. Uniting sound and meaning lends greater power to our language and allows the meaning to penetrate more deeply into our psyche.

Sanskrit rests upon an inherent relationship between sound and meaning. For example, the Sanskrit word for peace, shanti, comes from the root 'sham', meaning 'to calm'. The sound quality of the word shanti is peaceful. On the other hand, the English word peace, though having the same basic meaning as shanti has a sound quality that is harsher and does not serve as useful a vehicle for its meaning. *Repeat these two words shanti and peace for a few minutes and see which of the two sounds makes you feel more peaceful!*

Of course, meaning is more important than sound. It is better to say something meaningful in a clumsy manner than to say something meaningless with style. But it is better if sound and meaning remain harmonized. Sound reflects speech and meaning reflects the mind. It is important that the two resonate with each other.

Primal Sound

There are subtler realms of both sound and meaning. Ordinary words like 'house' or 'tree' have specific and limited meanings in time and space, denoting particular objects of the senses. Such 'substantive nouns' reflect a physical view of reality and a utilitarian sense of value. They have little ability to connect us with the Divine or sacred presence in nature.

There are higher levels of meaning in our language. We have words for emotions, ideas and spiritual experiences that do not correspond to specific physical objects. At the highest level, we have terms for God or the Supreme Reality. There are also deeper levels of sound. We recognize not only the level of poetry but that of scripture, which adds a spiritual dimension to expression that is often poetic as well.

Mantra teaches us that there is an additional level of 'primal sound' that corresponds to root meanings behind all words, ideas and objects. This is the basis of bija mantras or seed syllables like *Oṁ* that is said to carry the Divine in both its manifest and unmanifest forms. Spiritual principles easily remain mere concepts or beliefs for us, not objects of our direct experience. Anyone can repeat the word God and know what it means at a conceptual level, but this does not mean that they know God or have experienced the Divine within their own hearts and minds. But mantras and Divine names can easily connect us to the deeper truth behind such ideas.

The primal sounds of mantras are not mere ordinary words with specific dictionary meanings. Nor are they meaningless, as some might believe. Mantras contain entire spectrums of meaning from the physical to the spiritual and reflect various qualities of energy. Seed mantras can serve as vehicles to perceive, experience and realize the reality of universal consciousness, not only in a general sense but in the changing forms of our individual life experience.

Primal sounds are connected to 'primal meanings', which go back to the universal sense of Being and Self. Such primal sounds and their primal meanings are the basis of the roots of the Sanskrit language and are mirrored in its development. Mantra is a vehicle to bring our minds, hearts and prana to the level of both primal sound and primal meaning, in which we can return to the original state of unity with all. This requires that we use mantras with an intention, focus and aspiration to reach the Supreme.

Sound and Light/ Time and Space

Sound and light are inherently connected. Sound is a creation of light and electrical energy, just as thunder manifests from lightning. There is an electrical force or glow inherent in infinite space, from which a mantric vibration is ever arising like a continuous series of lightning flashes, sustaining all forms and processes in the universe.

The higher word or mantra consists of both sound and light. It is the word of light. Sound is the vibratory quality of space, which itself is the field of light. Light relates to the meaning of words, their mental component. Words serve to convey knowledge, which is a condensation of the light of the mind. For example, when we see something, like a tree, the light of the mind perceives it, but it is sound in the form of words in our memory that holds our knowledge of having seen it. Light reveals knowledge but sound carries, preserves and embodies knowledge. Mantra brings light into our awareness, but also allows us to carry and sustain that light as knowledge.

Light and sound relate to space and time. Light creates space as its field of illumination and sound creates time as its field of movement. Ganapati Muni defines "the nature of time is the most subtle sound."[23] Mantra, therefore, can project the root powers of time and its universal energies, ideas and potentials. Through mantra we can gain mastery of all the forces of time and karma.

Through mantra, we can awaken the Divine light within us and expand beyond the limitations of space, direction and manifestation. Through mantra, one can learn to ride the waves of cosmic sound and light, going back to the Divine Word at the heart of the world. This is the cosmic form of Mantra Yoga known only to Yogis who have gone beyond the body and mind.

The Four Levels of Speech

Speech has four levels in yogic thought, which are the four different states of the Goddess or Divine Word:

Four Levels of Speech (Vak)			
1. Vaikhari	Audible speech	Throat	Waking state
2. Madhyama	Pranic speech	Heart	Dream
3. Pashyanti	Illumined speech	Navel	Deep sleep
4. Para	Transcendent (Turiya)	Root center	Samadhi

Vaikhari refers to the coarse or literal level of speech. It is the word as spoken with the vocal organs in the mouth and the throat. Our minds usually dwell on this level of audible speech and the conventional meanings of words. This is the level of speech as related to outer sensations, which relates to physical reality. At this level, the outer form of the word is the main thing. To affect this level of speech, we must audibly repeat the mantra.[24]

We enter into *Madhyama*, which literally means the 'middle level' of speech, when we think or feel deeply about something, when we ponder or wonder about things. This requires that our life-force and vitality is engaged in what we say. Most artistic thinking comes from this level, which reveals subtle forms and inner energy patterns. This is the astral form of speech connected to the dream world. All mantras can be employed at this level when we repeat them along with the breath.[25]

Pashyanti or 'perceptive' speech occurs when we perceive the underlying cosmic truths or archetypes, the dharmas behind any object or situation. Its nature is light or revelation, showing the seed forces at work in the universe. This is the causal level of speech related to the deep sleep state. To reach this level in the waking state requires deep meditation or as an act of grace. It corresponds to the one-pointed mind in Yoga. It has a luminous quality to it. The word at this level has light and reveals the truth. Many mantric prayers and hymns are best understood at this level, which engages our deeper contemplative nature.[26]

Para, which means 'transcendent', is the level of pure silence in which meaning is so full and complete that it cannot be broken down into limited words. It is the level of pure consciousness, the Divine Word of silence of 'I am all' and the great realizations of Vedanta.[27] This is the transcendent level of speech which leads beyond any particular expression or utterance. It corresponds to the nirodha or merged condition of the mind, the state of samadhi in Yoga practice.

The higher Self or Paramatman has its own natural language, which reverberates in silence. Its basic seed ideas are revealed in the great insights of Vedanta such as *Aham Brahmāsmi*, 'I am the Divine Self'. This speech of the Self is the highest or supreme stage of speech, Para Vak. It consists of such realizations, not mere thoughts but concretely felt understandings as "I am All", "All is One", "The Self is the Entire Universe," or just the expression of the breath as "I". Prana is the "I am I" as it projects the sense of individual life. Our sense of self is rooted in speech, which in turn is based on the Divine Word.

Descent of the Sound Current

The ordinary human level of existence occurs mainly at the lower, outer or Vaikhari form of speech, while the Self-realized state is the Para or transcendent form. Developing our speech capacity from Vaikhari to Para is the inner movement of Mantra Yoga. Then we can take the power of speech back to Vaikhari or the audible word, but holding the consciousness of the Supreme! A teacher who can bring the Para or transcendent level of speech into the audible Vaikhari level becomes truly great. His very words become mantras.

An understanding of these four levels provides an important insight for Yoga practice. The power of speech must be brought down to the base of the spine and the root chakra to allow the energy of consciousness to ascend upward in the form of Kundalini in order to awaken our higher potentials. Before we ascend, we must first descend. To bring the power of speech inward and downward is the work of the Yoga of sound, whether as music, nada or mantra. Unless we have first done this, we are unlikely to be in a position to open the chakras or bring our energy up the Sushumna whatever else we may try to do.

To bring the current of speech down to the base of the spine, the breath must also be made to descend. In Vaikhari, we speak and breathe through the throat. In Madhyama, we speak and breathe through the heart. In Pashyanti, we speak and breathe through the navel. In Para, the breath merges into the Sushumna or base of the spine from which it automatically ascends. Try focusing your mind on these four different centers as the source of your breath. Note how your consciousness will progressively deepen.

To bring the current speech down to the base of the spine, our minds must also turn within. The mind must be withdrawn from the sensory centers in the head and allowed to dive deep within until it reaches the base of the spine, where the power of the Goddess is held in the Earth of our being.[28] In this process of bringing the power of speech downward, the fire of speech or mantra develops and purifies the lower chakras, stimulating the Kundalini.[29]

Speech as Kundalini

Kundalini is the inner serpent power behind all higher Yoga practices, the energy of the subtle body or primary electrical force behind consciousness. In our ordinary state of awareness, the Kundalini lies dormant or sleeping at the base of the spine and only a small portion of its power serves to run our ordinary physical and mental activities. When awakened, the Kundalini ascends and merges the mind into the Absolute giving liberation and Self-realization. One connects directly into the cosmic energy or Shakti.

Kundalini is the portion of the universal power of speech that dwells inside each one of us. We use but a fragment of it for ordinary thought and communication. Yet Kundalini holds encrypted within itself the code of Self-realization, our higher evolutionary potential. This manifests when we develop higher powers of speech through mantra and the practice of silent communion during meditation.

Kundalini speech is energized mantra. In this regard, we must remember that Kundalini wears the garland of the mantras of the Sanskrit alphabet and ultimately the garland of all mantras.[30] Mantra is the main yogic method used to arouse the Kundalini, particularly mantra repeated along with pranayama, meditation and deep devotion.

Yet working with Kundalini, we must remember that Kundalini is a form of the Goddess. She is closely connected to Kali, the dark Goddess of Infinite Space who represents Kriya Shakti or the power of yogic action. Kali works to set in motion the inner process of Yoga or self-integration within us. This proceeds through the dissolution of our attachment to the external world. Through it the external world gets withdrawn into the tattvas or cosmic principles, taking us back step by step from the gross elements to the Purusha or pure awareness, the higher Self.

Part II

The Mantra Purusha and Shakti Mantras

Chapter 6:

Mantra and Sanskrit, the Language of the Gods

When Sanskrit is called the 'universal language' or the 'language of the Gods', it is no mere exaggeration.[31] Sanskrit reflects the primal sounds through which the entire universe is created, by which it is sustained, and into which it is eventually dissolved. These primal sounds of the universe are embodied in the Sanskrit letters.

Sanskrit is not just another human language invented for purposes of social convenience, but a cosmic language. The letters of the Sanskrit alphabet allow the human mind to interface with the primal energies of cosmic intelligence and receive its deeper insights. Sanskrit, as it were, allows us to think with the Gods as one of the Gods ourselves! Through a right understanding of the Sanskrit alphabet, we can unite our individual Self with the universal Self, and regain our inner voice in the world of eternity.

Truly learning Sanskrit is not just a matter of learning another conventional language but of learning the very language of mantra. It is not a mere academic study or a means of improving communication, but an inner practice to create the foundation for Mantra Yoga.

Without a clear knowledge of the Sanskrit alphabet, the use of mantras becomes problematical and mispronunciations are likely to occur. We can compare the importance of knowing the Sanskrit alphabet in Mantra Yoga with the importance of knowing anatomy and physiology in asana practices. The Sanskrit alphabet helps us learn the 'anatomy and physiology of sound', through which we can move our subtle body with flexibility and grace.

The letters of the Sanskrit alphabet hold the primary sounds behind all other mantras. They are said to be the Matrikas, which means 'prime measures' or 'mothers'. The Sanskrit letters are the mothers of our inner spiritual being, we could say! The letters are the root forms of Shakti and bring her energy into our minds, hearts and bodies. Reciting the alphabet constitute a complete 'mantric workout' for all aspects of our mind, prana and senses. If we chant the Sanskrit alphabet with concentration and awareness, its letters can awaken the Kundalini force within us and transform our entire being.

The fifty letters of the Sanskrit alphabet form a list of important mantras that provide the keys to the sequence and layering of cosmic evolution. Once we know how these letters are created and their inner significations, we can use them to unravel the deeper meanings of all other mantras.

Learning Sanskrit

Unfortunately, there seems to be a common idea that Sanskrit is an incredibly difficult language to learn. This is not at all the case, as a simple examination of the matter can quickly reveal. Sanskrit is a scientific and phonetic language that is logical and consistent in its pronunciation, spelling and grammar. It is easier to pronounce than English. Its script is much easier to learn than the Chinese characters and no more difficult than the Greek alphabet. Sanskrit grammar may be daunting, but it is not much more difficult than Russian grammar, and a knowledge of Sanskrit grammar is not required to use most mantras.

Learning the Sanskrit alphabet itself is not a difficult task and can be done in a weekend class if one is really serious. The Sanskrit alphabet is phonetic with one letter having one sound. English is much more variable in pronunciation, particularly in regard to vowels, with different letters sometimes pronounced in very different ways. Learning its fifty letters or fifty sounds is something anyone can do with a little effort and guidance.

Reciting the Sanskrit alphabet is not just an exercise in phonetics. Mantric recitation of the Sanskrit alphabet is an important method of balancing the mind. The Sanskrit letters can stimulate all the powers of the brain and the nervous system, improving our concentration, memory and perception on all levels. Chanting the Sanskrit alphabet is one of the main practices of Mantra Yoga and great depth can be brought into it. It is important not only for beginning but for advanced students of mantra.

However, to really use the Sanskrit alphabet as mantras, one needs to learn the inner power of the sounds, not just their outer pronunciation. We could say that anything that vibrates in the universe is chanting mantra and speaking Sanskrit, whether it is an atom, a human being or a star. Mantra is the very life blood behind all forms and processes in the world around and within us. The Sanskrit alphabet emulates these cosmic sound vibrations that we can connect to through a proper understanding and recitation of its letters.

The Three Basic Types of Sounds

The Sanskrit language is based upon a clear understanding of the science of sound, which forms the basis for mantra practice. Sounds contain many secrets in how they are pronounced and impact our vocal cords and nervous system. Each sound strikes a different chord within us, we could say. There are three basic types of sounds that occur in all languages and are recognized in Sanskrit.[32]

1. The vowels, which are open sounds like the A-E-I-O-U of English. These are called svara in Sanskrit or 'that which resonates', as they are open sounds that can be drawn out.
2. The consonants, which contact based sounds like B, P or K in English. These are called *vyañjana* in Sanskrit or 'that which colors or articulates'. Consonants are closed sounds that are used to project the energy of the vowels in different directions.
3. The 'intermediate principle' of the semi-vowels (Y, R, L, V) and sibilants (S, SH, H-sounds) that partake of the qualities of both vowels and consonants. They can be lengthened like vowels or combined with consonants in their pronunciation.

Semi-vowels are called antahstha in Sanskrit or 'what stands in between', reflecting their meditating role between vowels and consonants. Sibilants are called ushma, meaning 'what creates heat', reflecting their connection with the sounds of the breath.

The Sanskrit alphabet is phonetically based, with each letter corresponding to a single sound. Sanskrit letters, therefore, are always specific sounds. Sanskrit letters are named after the letter plus the short-A vowel like Pa for what in English we would call the letter-P. They are regarded as syllables, of which there are fifty,[33] which are divided into these three groups:

1. Sixteen Vowels - Svara
A, Ā, I, Ī, U, Ū, Ṛ, Ṝ, Ḷ, Ḹ, E, Ai, O, Au, Aṁ, Aḥ अ, आ, इ, ई, उ, ऊ, ऋ, ॠ, ऌ, ॡ, ए, ऐ, ओ, औ, अं, अ:
2. Four Semivowels and Five Sibilants or Nine Intermediate Sounds - Antahstha/ Ushma
Ya, Ra, La, Va; Śa, Ṣa, Sa, Kṣa, Ha य, र, ल, व, श, ष, स, क्ष, ह
3. Twenty Five Consonants or Five Groups of Five
Five Guttural Consonants - Ka-varga
Ka, Kha, Ga, Gha, Ṇa क, ख, ग, घ, ङ
Five Palatal Consonants - Ca-varga
Ca, Cha, Ja, Jha, Ña च, छ, ज, झ, ञ
Five Cerebral Consonants - Ṭa-varga
Ṭa, Ṭḥa, Ḍa, Dḥa, Ṇa ट, ठ , ड, ध, ण
Five Dental Consonants - Ta-varga
Ta, Tha, Da, Dha, Na त, थ, द, ध, न
Five Labial Consonants - Pa-varga
Pa, Pha, Ba, Bha, Ma प, फ, ब, भ, म

Each type of sound has spiritual and yogic implications. Vowels represent consciousness, Spirit, the Shiva principle in Tantric thought, and the Indra principle in Vedic thought.[34] Vowels are the essence of sound and vibration, continuous, independent and enduring in their resonance. You can take any vowel and intone it indefinitely. Many powerful Sanskrit seed mantras like *Oṁ* and *Aiṁ* are vowel predominant for this reason. They allow our energy to open, expand and ascend to higher levels.

Opposite in nature to vowels, consonants represent matter or nature, Prakriti or the Shakti principle through which all manifestation arises.[35] Consonants serve to focus the pure sound quality of the vowels into particular forms or directions. Consonants are contact based and require a vowel in order to express them. Try pronouncing a word that consists of consonants only. It is not possible. While consonants allow for a definitive expression, they also create illusion as sound becomes limited. While vowels represent eternal powers, consonants are the forms which manifest in the limited field of time, though they can reflect higher qualities.

There are not many consonant dominant bija or seed mantras in Sanskrit but many begin with consonants like the mantra *Klīṁ*. Consonants help focus our thought and energy. Most words are consonant based as they allow for a greater structure, complexity and intricacy of sound and meaning. Longer mantras, prayers and hymns are more consonant based and bring in a greater diversity and specificity of meanings, while vowel mantras hold a more primal and general affect.

The sibilants and semi-vowels are said to represent the five elements and the pranas in Tantric thought, and Prajapati or the creative principle in Vedic thought.[36] They stand between vowels and consonants in their properties and between consciousness and form, or Spirit and Nature, at a cosmic level. They are widely used in bija mantras.

Pronunciation of Sanskrit Vowels

Sanskrit has both short and long vowels. Long vowels are an extension of the short vowels and are counted as twice as long in terms of their metrical value. They usually expand the energy of the sound outwardly.

The Sanskrit A-vowel is pronounced deep in the back of the throat, like the English sound 'a' in as 'another'. It vibrates the neck, lungs, heart and body, drawing the energy down and in. The long Sanskrit Ā-vowel is pronounced like the 'a' sound in 'father' and requires a much more significant opening of the throat.

The Sanskrit I-vowel is pronounced in the middle of the mouth, like the vowel sound in the word 'pin', and vibrates the head, brain, senses and mind, holding the energy in the center and allowing it to move upward from there. The long Sanskrit Ī -vowel is like the 'ee' sound in 'need'.

The Sanskrit U-vowel is pronounced with the lips and vibrates the face or the outer manifestation, like the u-sound in the world 'fl*u*te', directing the energy outward in an implosive manner. The long Sanskrit Ū-vowel is like the 'oo' sound in 'mood', literally shooting our energy outward

Sanskrit recognizes four compound vowels brought about by the combinations of the basic A, I, U sounds. A + I equals E at the first level and Ai at the second level. A + U equals O at the first level and Au at the second level. The two sounds Ai and Au, therefore, represent the final result of all the Sanskrit vowel sounds.

For compound vowels, the Sanskrit E-vowel is pronounced like the English sound in 'came'. The Sanskrit Ai-vowel is made like the English sound in the word 'aisle'. These longer vowels serve to open the mouth more, particularly in its middle part of the palate. The Sanskrit O-vowel is much like the English in 'yoke'. The Sanskrit Au-vowel is much like the English in 'ouch'. These grant the largest opening of the mouth and lips of all the vowels.

Sanskrit Ṛ is a soft-R as in the English word 'macabre'. Its long form *Ṝ* is the same but held longer. In chanting the alphabet, however, the vowel-R sounds are usually rendered by the sounds *ri* and *rī*, though with the soft r–sound. In Sanskrit pronunciation in South India, *ṛ* is more commonly pronounced ru and in North India, it is commonly pronounced *re*.

The Sanskrit Ḷ is a soft-L as in the English word 'table'. The long vowel-Ḹ is the same sound held longer. In chanting the alphabet, however, they are usually rendered by the sounds *lri* and *lrī* , though rendered with a soft and liquid pronunciation. These long forms are rarely found in actual words but do serve to fill out some mantric correspondences. They do not occur in many Sanskrit and Hindi fonts for this reason.

Sanskrit recognizes two special sounds in the field of the vowels that are actually the seeds of other sounds. They represent two distinct manners of vibrating or closing the vowels and the throat. The *aṁ* and *aḥ* vowels are seeds of the M and

H-sounds. They can follow after any vowel but as letters of the alphabet are written with an antecedent short-A vowel and classified among the vowels.

Aṁ, called Anusvara or the 'means of resonance', consists of drawing the vowel sound down into the throat, then nasalizing the vowel sound, and finalizing closing it with a lip sound of 'mmm'. This is the sound that we find at the end of mantras like *Oṁ*. It is generally transliterated as an ṁ with a dot on top (sometimes at the bottom).

Anusvara is often represented as the English letter-M, though it is more complex. It is like the seed of the M-sound, and as M is the last of all the Sanskrit consonants, Anusvara carries the power of all the consonants with it. Sometimes it is represented as the letter 'ng' in English, owing to its vibration in the throat, though this is not strictly correct either. It can actually stand for any of the Sanskrit Na or Ma sounds in consonant combinations.

Aḥ, called Visarga or the 'means of release', is an aspirated repetition of a final vowel created by adding a short or quick h-sound to it, as in 'namaha'. Often it is not marked in the transliteration of words. Sometimes it is marked by an H-sound, though it is a soft H that repeats the vowel, not a hard aspirated H-sound. We can understand it as the seed of the H-sound.

Visarga pushes the energy out or opens it and is connected to expression, expansion and realization. It is opposite the Anusvara in its effects, which is connected to dissolution and mergence. It is generally translated as an H with a dot below it *Ḥ*.

Pronunciation of Consonants

The Sanskrit language contains twenty-five consonants, organized in five groups relative to the location in the mouth where they are produced.

1) The Ka-series is the gutturals, pronounced in the throat
2) The Ca-series is the palatals, pronounced in the palate
3) The Ṭa -series is the cerebrals, pronounced at the roof of the mouth
4) The Ta-series is the dentals, pronounced behind the teeth
5) The Pa-series is the labials, pronounced with the lips

Each series of five consonants contains a hard sound (*ka, ca, ṭa, ta, pa*) and a soft sound (*ga, ja, ḍa, da, ba*) both of which can come in additional aspirated (H-sound) forms (*kha, cha, ṭha, tha, pha*) and (*gha, jha, dḥa, dha, bha*). Each series also each have a corresponding N or M sound (*ṅa, ña, ṇa, na, ma*). The cerebral and dental are originally one series, the dental being the primary. That is why dentals change into cerebrals in certain sound combinations, while cerebrals rarely start any words.

Guttural letters like Ka and Ga are pronounced much like their English equivalents. They are made in the back of the throat and represent a deep or primal level of thought, feeling and sensation, affecting the vital nature, prana, the senses, and the subconscious mind. The gutturals show our pranic urges and impulses in life.

Palatal sounds use the back palate of the mouth. Of the palatal sounds, Ca is pronounced like the 'ch' in 'church', while the Sanskrit Cha is pronounced like the sound in the English word 'itch'. Ja is pronounced like the English equivalent. They are made in the upper middle of the mouth with the help of the tongue. They are softer sounds than the gutturals and have more motion to them. This often gives them an emotional force and creative or generative power.

Cerebrals (*ṭa, ṭha, ḍa, ḍha, ṇa*) are made at the roof of the mouth, like the T in 'true'. They have a denser and more interiorized sound than their corresponding dentals. Dentals (*ta, tha, da, dha, na*) are made by the striking action of the tongue on the back of the teeth, like the T in 'tip'. They are hard contact sounds and project a certain force. They resemble the beats of a drum, *ta-ta-ta, da-da-da*. Cerebrals and dentals give stability and form.

Labials (*pa, pha, ba, bha, ma*) require the movement of the lips. They are the most outward sounds made at the front of the mouth. They have a bursting or explosive effect like the blowing of bubbles. They allow us to express our energies into the external world, having a productive action to bring things into form. They are generally equivalent to our English sounds like P, B and M.

The aspirated forms of the consonants are the hardest for English speaking people to pronounce (*kha, gha, cha, jha, ṭha, ḍha, tha, dha, pha, bha*). The simplest way to do this is to first pronounce the unaspirated letter followed by a short–a sound and then the 'ha' sound. For example, first pronounce 'kaha'. Then try to shorten and remove the first vowel sound 'kha'.

Pronunciation of Semi-Vowels and Sibilants

Sanskrit semi-vowels are equivalent to the English letter, Y, R, L, V. Ya derives from the vowel-I and is palatal in nature. Ra is cerebral and is a hard rolled r-sound, a bit like the Spanish-r, as opposed to the soft unrolled r-vowel. La is dental, made with the tongue hitting the back of the teeth. Va is labial or made with the lips (usually pronounced like an English-w when it occurs after another consonant).

In the Tantras, the semivowel mantras of *Laṁ, Vaṁ, Raṁ* and *Yaṁ* relate to the four cosmic elements of Earth, Water, Fire and Air. The rule is that the semi-vowels govern the elements because the elements mediate between the formless realm of Spirit (vowels) and the formed realm of matter (consonants).

You will notice that you can hold the sibilant sounds H, S or Sh almost indefinitely like a vowel. You can hold the S-sound, like a hissing sound, longer than other consonants. Sibilants are usually placed in the same intermediate series of sounds as the semi-vowels, though sometimes they form a separate fourth category.

The sibilants are of the same nature as the breath and can be equated with Prana and its manifestations. They have more versatility in their combinations than other consonants. Sa is a dental sound, made by the tongue behind the teeth. *Ṣa* is a cerebral sound (like Vishnu) or the English word 'ship'. *Śa* is a palatal sound (like Shiva) or the English word 'shut'. *Kṣa* is a guttural sound combining Ka and *Ṣa*. Ha is as in the English letter-H. Though a sibilant, *Haṁ* is also said to govern the element of Ether and is used along with the semi-vowels for the chakras, though elsewhere it is connected to prana.

Turning the Alphabet into Mantras

A final ṁ-sound, the Anusvara, is added to each of these letters to make the Sanskrit letters into seed mantras like *Aiṁ*. In the case of consonants, semi-vowels and sibilants, the short a-vowel is added as well, like *Kaṁ, Yaṁ* or *Saṁ*. It is possible to recite the letters without the final Anusvara, but it is less common in the case of mantric usage. That is why in the following chapters the letters will usually be represented with the Anusvara. The Anusvara helps to draw the sound of the letter deeper into the head and into the mind.

Chapter 7:

The Vowels: the Prime Vibrations of Consciousness

It is not enough to use the sounds of words as a tool; we must understand the nature of the tool that we are using. Only then can we shape our speech in a creative and insightful manner. In the following chapters, we will examine each letter of the Sanskrit alphabet from the standpoint of mantra, starting with the vowels, looking for the connections between the nature of the sound, how it is pronounced, and its deeper meaning and effect upon us.

Usually we treat the sounds of our words mechanically and unconsciously. We do not reflect upon the quality of the sound itself, unless we are reciting poetry. The word is just a convenient vehicle to convey the idea or emotion that we have in mind. We are not aware of its sound power or intrinsic value. We use the sound of words to think about things, but do not actually think about the sound itself.

To understand mantra and the Sanskrit language, we must reconnect sound and meaning. In Mantra Yoga, we focus upon the sound directly, upon the inherent meaning of the sound apart from any object or idea that it may be ordinarily associated with in the outer world. We look at the sound itself rather than merely using it as an instrument. To shift our thinking in this manner can be difficult but is very rewarding. It puts us in touch with the poetry of nature and the resonance of the cosmic life.

In Sanskrit, the vowels are the most important sounds and the most consistent in terms of their higher meanings in traditional texts. Yet as primal sounds, vowels carry a range of indications that can vary depending upon the factors they are related to. We should aim at grasping their essential qualities and full spectrum of possible derivative connotations. We cannot look upon them as formed words but must understand them on the level of sound essences.

The following study reflects primarily the Shaivite tradition, the philosophies that view the supreme reality as Shiva, pure consciousness, and his feminine counterpart of Shakti as the energy of consciousness. The letters of the Sanskrit alphabet are said to arise from Shiva's drum, which he beats while performing his thunderous Tandava movement as Nataraj, the Lord of the cosmic dance of existence.[37] However, the meanings given here are rooted in older Vedic teachings, where their outlines can be found. Moreover, the mantric meaning of the letters can be found in their application as root sounds of Sanskrit words.[38]

The Three Prime Vowels

- Sanskrit recognizes 'three primal vowels' that are the basis of all other sounds and of all creation, which are A, I and U.
- The primal sound-A (a as in another) is the most basic sound that forms the root of all other sounds. It relates to the Absolute (Brahman), pure existence, the infinite, the void, the unmanifest, and the changeless. It is said to be the Supreme Shiva and pure light.[39]

- The primal sound-I (i as in pin) is the sound of contraction, focus and direction. While the sound-A indicates inarticulate sound, the sound-I is the basis of articulate sound. The sound-I relates to Shakti or energy, the One, the atomic, the point or bindu, the seed power of will and desire through which all creation proceeds. As the sound reverberating in the center of the mouth, the greatest number of letters is connected to it.
- The primal sound-U (u as in fl*u*te) made with the lips has an expansive power that is strong, harsh or even explosive, almost opposite the contracting or focused power of the sound-I. It relates to the Shiva principle in developed, expressed or articulated form, arising to pervade all things, in a successive and graduated manner. It is said to have the power of knowledge.

Intone these sounds yourself and feel their energy within you.

- Notice how the A-sound holds the energy deep inside you. It relates to your sense of self, life, being and deeper awareness.
- The I-sound draws the energy up and out in an almost linear manner, holding it at the top of the mouth. It is your basic power of expression and motivation.
- The U-sound allows it to expand outward through the lips and beyond the body. It allows your energy to manifest in the outer world.

Now intone their long forms Ā as in father, Ī as in need, Ū as in mood. This makes their vibrations clearer. The long vowels represent the same energy of the short vowels but as doubled in length. As such, they represent a deepening of their energy and follow the same basic force and meaning. Ā allows one to rest in one's being. Ī allows one's energy to move and accelerate. Ū sustains expansion and expression.

The short vowels are considered to be solar and masculine in nature and represent the Shiva principle or will power. The long vowels are considered to be lunar and feminine in nature and represent the Shakti principle, the field of repose, rest or expansion. Yet the long vowels are more often used for mantric purposes as they can be intoned for a longer period of time and so have greater resonance.

In this explication of the three vowels, I am following specifically the Nandikesha Kashika, a short Shaivite text on the meaning of the alphabet. For the explication of the sixteen vowels as a whole, I will also bring in the meanings given by the Kashmiri Shaivite tradition like the great guru Abhinavagupta[40] as well as that of Ganapati Muni. Let us examine a few verses from the Nandikesha Kashika, which after noting how the letters arise from Shiva's drum, makes the following commentary on the three primal vowels.

> **Verse 3.** The letter-A has the form of Brahman and is free of all qualities, dwelling in all things. Resorting to the letter-I, it takes the form of the world. The letter-U is Ishvara (the cosmic Lord).
>
> **Verse 4.** The letter-A is the first of all letters. It is pure light, the supreme Shiva. Combining the beginning and end of all letters (A and H), the Self (aham) arises.
>
> **Verse 7.** Through its proximity to the letter-A, from its having produced

the world, the letter-I among all letters, from its Shakti-power is said to be the causal force.

Verse 9. The letter-A is of the nature of perception. The letter-I is said to be the portion of pure consciousness. The letter U-is said to be Vishnu, and from its pervasive power, it is Maheshvara.[41]

The letter-A is the pure Being or Absolute beyond all time, space, causation and creation. The letter-I is the Shakti or causative power that produces the manifest world. The letter-U is God or Ishvara as the Cosmic Lord ruling over and guiding the manifest world. Combining these letters A plus I, the absolute plus Shakti, is *Aiṁ* which is the sound Adya Shakti or the primal feminine, energy or Goddess principle. Combining A plus U is *Auṁ*, which is Adi Purusha or the primal masculine, Self or God principle.

The Sixteen Vowels

With this background, let us examine each of the sixteen Sanskrit vowels in detail.

अ – The Short Vowel *A*

The Absolute, the Infinite, Pure Being, the Void

Sound	Pronounced *a* as in *a*nother
Energetic	Pure existence, simple affirmation/simple negation, light as bare illumination, unmanifest Self
Spiritual	Absolute, Pure Consciousness, Godhead – Parabrahman, the Supreme Shiva
Physical	Top of head, back of head
Psychological	Deeper consciousness, source of mind and prana, primal Self
Yoga	Promotes pratyahara, meditation, samadhi, detachment, crown chakra energies, Yoga nidra

The Sanskrit letter-A, the short vowel, is regarded as the first of all letters, just as the letter A is in other alphabets. The short A-vowel is the most primal of all sounds, the origin and source of all. It indicates the basic opening of the throat necessary to produce any type of sound, the root vibration of the vocal cords. It is the basis of the guttural group of letters beginning with the consonant-Ka. It is the basic sound of the prana or exhaling breath which produces all other sounds. The Sanskrit-A is the most neutral, basic and easy of all utterances that we can make.

There are two aspects to the primal sound-A. First, it is simple affirmation or being itself. It reflects or illumines things as they are. It is the basic resonance behind all things, the underlying note or tone. In this respect it resembles the verb is, which is presumed in all statements. It is ultimately our own self-existence that is presumed in all that we say and think. Following this idea the primal sound-A represents what is original, first, primary or most important.

The second aspect of the primal sound-A is negation. As the original and absolute sound, it transcends all that is derived, relative and manifest. It is the Absolute, beyond which there is nothing, the Void that is beyond all name and form. The letter-A in Sanskrit serves to indicate negation when it is placed at the beginning of a word. For example, *rupa* means form, *a-rupa* means formless.

Tantric yogis call short A-vowel as Anuttara,[42] meaning that from which there is nothing greater, the supreme ultimate. They also call it *Amṛta*,[43] the immortal and deathless, the immortal nectar that we are always imbibing as we partake of being. Sri Aurobindo states that the letter-A relates to absolute existence, of which other sounds are relative existence. The Vedas say that the letter-A is Brahman or the Absolute.[44] It is the first of all the vowels that constitute the spirit (Shiva or Purusha).[45] It indicates the center, origin, being, Self and Supreme.

At a physical level, the sound-A serves to ground and stabilize our being and all its processes down to a cellular level. It is the root or base tone behind all the other vibrations of our organism, which we return to in a state of deep sleep. Repeating this sound serves to attune, harmonize and balance our entire organic field. It brings us back into our body and deeper awareness, connecting to the root energy of the heart and the center of our being.

At a psychological level, the sound-A returns us to the ground of our being and helps us shut off our outer noise. It calms and silences the minds and senses and takes the pranas back to their core energy. It helps us settle, let go, detach and simplify. It connects us to our deepest Self and being.

आ – The Long Vowel *Ā*

The Absolute in Expansion as the Space of the Higher Self

Sound	Pronounced *a* as in f*a*ther
Energetic	Higher Self or Atman, Self-expansion and awareness of the Absolute
Spiritual	Power of bliss, the space of consciousness
Physical	Forehead, face, expansion and circulation of energies
Psychological	Outgoing and creative aspect of mind, conscious mind, conscious Self
Yoga	Promotes contemplation, meditation, happiness, contentment, creativity, space

Just as the short A-vowel represents the unbounded pure being of the Absolute, the long Ā-vowel represents its expansion into infinite space, *Ākāśa*. As the short A-vowel represents pure being or Sat, the long Ā-vowel represents its manifestation as bliss, *Ānanda*, which is the delight or contentment inherent in being. It also relates to the power of attraction, *Ākarśana*, and helps draw things to us and aids us in returning to the source, having a kind of magnetic energy.[46]

As the short vowel-A represents the absolute in a universal sense; the long vowel-Ā represents the Absolute in a manifest sense, the individual Self or *Ātman*.[47] As the short A-vowel is pure Shiva, its long form shows the energy of Shakti inherent in Shiva, the power of rest inherent in the Absolute. As the short A-vowel is the Self in its underlying nature, the long Ā-vowel is the Self in its outward expansion. In Vaishnava thought, as the short A-vowel is Vishnu or Krishna, long Ā-vowel is the serpent Ananta, on which Vishnu reclines.

At a physical level, the long Ā-vowel is releasing, relaxing and revitalizing. Repeat 'aa', like opening your throat to reveal your tonsils, and feel this for yourself. The sound expands and releases the prana. It has a similar effect at a psychological and spiritual level, allowing us to relax into the ground of our being but with a certain expansiveness. As the short A-vowel relates to the consciousness in its unmanifest form (which at a lower level includes the subconscious), the long Ā-vowel relates to consciousness as mind, expression, feeling in the broader sense.

इ – The Short Vowel *I*

The One, Point, Atom, God, Creator and Cosmic Lord, Divine Will

Sound	As in 'eat' but shorter
Energetic	Contraction, focus, point energy, unity
Spiritual	God as ruling consciousness, Cosmic Lord
Physical	Right eye, guiding energy of the body, motivating prana
Psychological	Perception, logic, judgment, will power, guidance, motivation
Yoga	Yoga of seeing, dharana, will power, discrimination, knowledge

Just as the letter-A represents the unlimited and has no boundaries, the letter-I represents unlimited contraction or concentration. The letter-I is the infinitesimal or atomic, the point that contains all time and space, which explodes through the Big Bang. This ultimate point is called the bindu in Tantric thought, meaning not only the point but also the seed, as what is concentrated must again expand.

As the letter-A is the Infinite, the letter-I is the One. The field of the infinite (A) must be contracted into a point (I) in order to create the universe. As the letter-A is God as the Absolute or Godhead in the formless or monistic sense, the letter-I is God as the cosmic ruler, the creator or God in the theistic sense, the lord of the worlds or Ishvara.

While the vowel-A is the background of all sounds, the vowel-I is the means through which all the other sounds are made. In this regard, it is the Mother or Shakti principle. It is connected to the palatal group of sounds beginning with the consonant-Ca, but also with the cerebral and dental groups of sounds using the Ta and Da sounds, making it the source of the largest number of sounds.[48]

The sound-I, starting as a point, moves in a straight line. It represents will, motivation, orientation, time and direction. It shows the application of force in a specific and determined manner in order to bring about a specific result, which is the creation of the universe. Tantrics call the letter-I as Iccha, which means will, desire or love. From Iccha-Shakti or will-power all other forces come into being.

As the letter-A is the spirit as the Absolute, the letter-I is the spirit as embodied. In this sense of directed versus undirected existence the letter-I indicates the individual soul (Jivatman) as the letter-A is the supreme soul (Paramatman). Sri Aurobindo relates the letter-I to relative existence, but it is only so in the sense as the original creative idea and force behind relative existence. As the letter-A is the Absolute, the letter-I is the causal force.

As the letter-A is the root power of existence, the letter-I is the power of vision, insight and imagination. It focuses this power of existence along a particular line, leading to a specific manifestation. The letter-I gives us life, energy, motivation and a goal to achieve.

At a physical level, the sound-I serves to set in motion and sustain all the organic processes within us. At a psychological level, it similarly increases our vision, motivation, focus, energy and determination. Its spiritual implications are of the same nature, allowing to us to connect with the Divine will and energy within us.

ई – The Long Vowel *Ī*

Will as Ruling Power, Divine Mother, Ishvara Shakti

Sound	As in d*ee*p
Energetic	Ruling power, executive and creative force in its expansion
Spiritual	Divine Mother, Divine Energy, Shakti, Mahamaya
Physical	Left eye, left energy of the body, power of love
Psychological	Creative vision, emotion, empathy
Yoga	Imagination, visualization, devotional concentration, dharana

The long Ī-vowel is phonetically represented by the sound 'ee'. According to the Tantras, it is the expansion of the short-I vowel, intensifying will (iccha) into ruling power (*Īśāna*). It is called *Shakti bija*, the seed of Shakti or *Maya bija*, the seed of Maya, as it shows the creative will in its extension.

As the short-I vowel represents *Ishvara* or the cosmic lord, the long Ī-vowel represents *Ishvara Shakti*, the Divine creative, originative and executive power, the Divine Mother. This is why so many Shakti or Goddess mantras have this sound (note *Hrīṁ*, *Krīṁ*, *Klīṁ*, *Strīṁ*). It magnifies the electrical energy of the short I-sound.

It is also called *Shanti-bija* or the 'sound of peace' because its forces bring unity, homogeneity and harmony to all things. It is said to be *Vishnu bija* as the power of the creator Vishnu. It is said to be the lotus because it holds the lines of all manifestation. It is said to pervade all things, like the current of energy (I) flowing in space (A).

At a physical level, the long Ī-vowel awakens our higher prana, stimulating the nervous system and improving our vision. At a psychological level, it helps us develop insight, vision, imagination and motivation. Spiritually, it has a similar electrifying effect that invigorates all our higher practices.

उ – The Short Vowel *U*

Vibration, Unfoldment, Creation, Power

Sound	As in fl*u*te
Energetic	Vibration, work, effort, action, development, progression
Spiritual	Expansive force and penetrating power, ascending to new dimensions
Physical	Right ear, hearing, audio-perception, circulation of energies
Psychological	Intuition, prana, comprehension, mental grasp
Yoga	Perceptive listening, knowledge, peripheral awareness, learning, formless meditation, meditation on the void

The letter-U represents vibration or nada. It shows the opening of the creative force (*Unmeṣa*) into the external world. As the letter-I represents the Divine will power holding the seed of creation, the letter-U represents the Divine force unfolding, blossoming or blooming and setting forth the pattern of creation, allowing the worlds to arise and take shape like a blowing of bubbles. It adds depth, dimension and form to the initial creative direction of the letter-I. The letter-I is the concentration of energies behind creation, U is the expansion of creative energies which follows.

The vowel-U has a circular and expanding effect, just as its pronunciation by the opening of the lips, and projects things into manifestation. It establishes a field in which energies are both sustained and protected; its round vibration creating the spheres, lokas or world systems. It projects the labial group of sounds (those made with the lips) and the consonants beginning with the sound-Pa.

The sound-U is the strongest of the three primal vowels and has definite force, if not possible violence behind it. While the sound-A is expanding in the sense of releasing, relaxing and liberating, the sound-U is expanding in the sense of energizing, creating and forming, but at the same time having a complementary effect to remove or destroy. The letter-U is thus dualistic. It both creates and destroys and thereby sustains a vibratory field. The letter-U creates suspense, drama and emotion. It often has a violent or harsh force connected with it.

As the letter-A is the Absolute and the letter-I is the Creative Will and executive force, the letter-U is the Creative power and personality. As the letter-I is the bindu or primal point, the letter-U is primal vibration, Nada. As the letter-I represents will, the letter-U represents knowledge. Will creates a field of knowledge in order to manifest itself.

At a physical level, the letter-U helps us improve work and effort, granting us strength, resistance and durability. At a psychological level, it grants similar qualities and gives us an emotional power and reliance. Spiritually, the letter-U allows us to apply our energy into our practices and open up new fields of discovery.

ऊ – The Long Vowel *Ū*

The Wave, the Vibratory Field

Sound	As in shoot
Energetic	Vibration, music, nada
Spiritual	Field of Divine force and action, development, transformation
Physical	Left ear, creative hearing, intuition
Psychological	Receptivity, openness, emotional vulnerability
Spiritual	Receptive listening, opening of the mind and heart, listening to the inner sounds or nada

The long vowel-Ū intensifies the U-dimension of opening or unfoldment as vibration. While the short-vowel-U means opening, the long-vowel-*Ū* creates sustained opening, which is vibration.

It represents the space of creation that holds all the forces, principles and tendencies to be manifest later. In this regard is it different than the space of the long vowel-Ā, which is more the unmanifest space. It gives protection. It weaves. It is said to be like a series of waves (*Ūrmi*). It brings about the unfoldment of all the worlds. Yet when we turn it within, it brings about the dissolution of the worlds.

At a physical level, the long vowel-Ū allows the waves of prana to envelop the body and promote healing energies. At a psychological level, it breaks down resistance and clears the subconscious mind. At a spiritual level, it promotes revelation and surrender to the higher forces.

The R and L Sounds as Vowels

Sanskrit recognizes two special vowel forms of the letters R and L and their short and long forms as well. These are mainly the soft forms of these sounds as we commonly know them. While these letters are not used much by themselves, they are necessary to define the other groups of consonants.

Adding these to the three pure vowels A, I, and U, it provides the Sanskrit language with five prime vowels. The vowel-Ṛ is the root of the cerebral series of sounds. The vowel-Ḷ creates the dental series. These vowels are the seeds of their semi-vowel forms, which are the letters that we usually know by these sounds. These two letters also exist in short and long forms, though the long forms are even rarer in their occurrence.

ऋ, ॠ –The Soft or Vowel Sound *R*

This is the soft or unrolled Ṛ, while the consonant Ṛ is the rolled form. You experience it on the top of the mouth. The transliterated form of this letter is an R with a dot below it (Ṛ).

Sound	Soft and unrolled R (as in maca*bre*), often followed by a short-i sound
Energetic	Fire, color, light, warmth
Spiritual	Dharma, Cosmic Law, principle order; Divine Father as ruler of Heaven
Physical	Nostrils, prana, motivation
Psychological	Mind, intellect, perception, judgment
Yoga	Heating forms of pranayama, solar energy, judgment, discrimination

The letter-Ra in itself is a semi-vowel. The vowel-Ṛ is its precursor and follows the same basic line of meaning. First there is a connection of the R-sound with the concept of order and truth (Ṛtam), the foundation of dharma in the universe. We find this meaning even in the English language r- words like right, rite, rhythm, and rectitude.

Second, the letter-Ra connotes heat, light and fire, particularly in manifest form. The vowel-Ṛ is the seed of fire, like a burning ember. We can use it to reach the core of the fire element. Cosmically, it also relates to the heavenly realm or realm of light. It is connected to the deity Rudra, who is the form of Shiva governing light and sound.[49] It relates to the Purusha or higher Self working through and governing the forces of manifestation.

At a physical level, the vowel-Ṛ stimulates the seed of fire and prana within the body, circulatory and nervous systems. At a psychological level, it promotes right thinking, judgment, perception, and right values. At a spiritual level, it connects us to our higher dharma.

There is a long vowel form of this letter Ṝ but it is rarely used and not significantly different in meaning. It has a more feminine energy, representing the field of light, and being oriented to the left side of the body and the left nostril. It is most commonly pronounced as a soft r with an ee sound afterwards (ree).

ऌ, ल्̥ –The Soft or Vowel Sound *Ḷ*

The vowel-Ḷ is a soft L-sound, as opposed to a voiced L-sound. It is a rare sound in actual Sanskrit, so much so that most Sanskrit fonts do not contain it. The vowels-Ṛ and Ḷ form a pair as the fire and earth elements, Heaven as the realm of light and Earth as the realm of form, God and Nature, Purusha and Prakriti. The two are Shiva and Shakti, as the mountain God and the valley Goddess. They represent the seed or causal principles and energies behind manifestation. They hold the entire manifestation in the root form.

Sound	Soft L as in tab*le*, yet commonly pronounced like 'lri'
Energetic	Descending formative energy
Spiritual	Joy, creativity; Divine Mother as the Earth
Physical	Cheeks, sense of touch, emotion
Psychological	Feeling, emotion, happiness
Yoga	Cooling forms of pranayama, lunar and earth energy, devotion, visualization, imagination

There is a long vowel of this vowel (Ḹ) but rarely used and not significantly different in meaning. It has a more feminine energy and connection with the left side of the body. It is more commonly pronounced like 'lree', but there are some variations in how different groups chant it.

Four Compound Vowels

The four Sanskrit compound vowels (diphthongs) reflect the meanings of the two shorter vowels that they are composed of. They are commonly used in Sanskrit mantras.

ए – The Vowel *E*

The Sanskrit E-vowel is composed of the combination of the Sanskrit sound-A and the sound-I and combines their meanings. It is called Yoni Bija, meaning the womb or the source of all. It indicates unity, eka. It shows the state of all primal forces in their original condition of unity before manifestation, in which their differentiation is implicit but not yet evident.[50] It is connected to the feminine principle as the premanifestation phase of Shakti.

Sound	Like the long vowel-a as in c*a*ke
Energetic	Unity, union, descending creative energy
Spiritual	Seed state of forces; the Divine Mother getting ready to create
Physical	Upper lip, initial phase of speaking
Psychological	Feeling, balance, harmony, receptivity
Yoga	Devotion, concentration, reintegration

ऐ – The Vowel *AI*

After *Oṁ*, *Aiṁ* is the most important of all the mantras. While *Oṁ* represents unmanifest speech or prana, *Aiṁ* represents manifest speech in its seed form. *Aiṁ* develops the focus, direction, vision and knowledge of the I-dimension of sound to its fullest extent. It electrifies the mind and speech for knowledge, teaching and creative expression. As such, *Aiṁ* is the Mantra of Adya Shakti or the Supreme Feminine power and helps invoke that power and grace within us. It shows the concentration of energies prior to their full manifestation. We will examine it in detail under Shakti mantras.

Sound	As in the word '*ai*sle'
Energetic	Focus, expression, motivation, calling
Spiritual	Intelligence and creativity in manifestation, guiding intelligence
Physical	Lower lip, tongue; improves flow of energy in the head, mouth and lungs
Psychological	Mind, intellect and creative intelligence
Yoga	Mantra Yoga, concentration, teaching, counseling

ओ – The Vowel *O*

Oṁ is probably the most famous and most important of the Sanskrit mantras. It is said to be the Word of God, the Word of the Guru, Atman, and Ishvara. It represents both the manifest and the unmanifest Brahman. It causes our energy to open, expand, ascend and unify. We will examine it more specifically under Shakti mantras.

Sound	Like the o in 'yoke'
Energetic	Shiva energy manifest and unmanifest, affirmative, ascending
Spiritual	Universal ruling power, guiding and expanding force
Physical	Upper jaw, prana, mouth; opens the prana in the head and spine
Psychological	Clears the mental and emotional field, connects mind and higher Self
Yoga	Knowledge, devotion, unity, pranayama, energizes all the Yogas

औ – The Vowel *AU*

Auṁ creates the most complete manifestation of the vowels. It takes the primal-A sound and expands it to its fullest extent with the open long-U sound. *Oṁ* and *Auṁ* are similar. *Auṁ* is just an extension of the *Oṁ* energy, giving it more energy. It is said to relate to the Adi Purusha or the prime cosmic masculine energy, having a power to fill, pervade and transcend.

Sound	As in '*ou*t'
Energetic	Full expansion of Divine energy and consciousness
Spiritual	Shiva principle in full expression pervading the universe
Physical	Lower teeth and jaw, primary prana of mouth and face in full expression
Psychological	Expansive aspect of mind and prana
Yoga	Promotes contemplation, affirmation, pranayama, samadhi

अं अः – Anusvara and Visarga, *Aṁ, Aḥ*

The Primal Energies of Contraction and Expansion

Most Sanskrit bija mantras end with Anusvara, which allows their sounds to vibrate within the mind and nervous system. Yet a few are done with the Visarga to help project the force of prana through them. A few mantras can be done with either Anusvara or Visarga, which changes their effect.[51]

Anusvara is often an extension of the primal short A-vowel sound and has the same general range of indications in Tantric thought. It allows all other sounds to merge into the pure essence of sound at the top of the head, the A-sound of the Absolute, Brahman. It is said to be the Shiva-bindu or the 'point of Shiva' that merges the entire universe back into pure unity. It is often related to the mind and the Moon.

Visarga is often connected to the long-A vowel in terms of its range of meanings. In addition, it is used by itself as the mantra '*aḥ*', which stands for the Self (aham), Prana, the Sun and the day. It gives light and power and connects with our inner being and source of energy and vitality. It is only used with a few mantras like *Sauḥ, Śriḥ, Hrīḥ*, as well as *Namaḥ* for giving additional expressive or creative energy to them. It imparts Shakti to sounds as manifest power.

Anusvara, *Aṁ*

Sound	Final nasal sound as in Oṁ, drawing in of a sound and merging it into the mind
Energetic	Holding, harmonizing, internalizing, dissolving within
Spiritual	Mergence in the Deity, Being or the Absolute, Shiva
Physical	Head, top of the head, upper palate
Psychological	Mind, deep feeling, profound knowing
Yoga	Promotes contemplation, mergence, internalization, detachment, samadhi

Visarga, *Aḥ*

Sound	Soft-H as in Namaḥ , release of sound through exhalation
Energetic	Releasing, expanding, expressing generating energy
Spiritual	Higher Self in transcendence, first pranic manifestation, Shakti
Physical	Face, forehead, lower palate
Psychological	Outgoing or expanding energy and self-expression, ego, prana
Yoga	Promotes meditation, Self-inquiry, awareness of original prana

Chapter 8:

Semivowels and Sibilants: Powers of the Elements and the Pranas

The semivowels and sibilants are extremely important sounds in Yoga and Ayurveda. They connect to the primal forces of prana and the five elements, which in turn relate to the sensory qualities (tanmatras) sense organs, motor organs, and tissues of the body. In pranayama practices and in Kundalini Yoga, the sounds of the semi-vowels and sibilants are central. They help awaken our inner prana and dissolve the elements back into their seed powers allowing us to return to pure unity.

The Four Semivowels

The semivowels represent a greater density of expression than the vowels from which they develop. The semivowels as intermediate sounds between vowels and consonants stand between spirit or consciousness (vowels) and matter or perceived objects (consonants). As such, the semivowels represent the five elements, which are the means through which spirit becomes matter and matter returns to the spirit. In this capacity, the semivowels govern the chakras, the energy centers through which consciousness takes form. The semi-vowels allow us to work on the corresponding faculties, powers and qualities that the chakras rule over. The sibilant Ha is added to the four semi-vowels to indicate the ether element.

- The semivowel-Ya develops the movement, energy, direction, velocity and motivation, the Shakti of the vowel-I. This connects it to the air element.
- The semivowel-Ra, like the vowel-Ṛ, reflects light and heat but on a level of greater density, indicating friction, combustion, conversion and transformation. This connects it to the fire element.
- The semivowel-Va develops the vibration, flow, adaptability, receptivity and pervasive power of the vowel-U. This connects it to the water element.
- The semivowel-La, like the vowel-Ḷ, reflects form and creation but at a grosser level, giving density, shape and substance. This connects it to the earth element.

Raṁ and *Laṁ* retain the basic division of their vowel equivalents as male and female, right and left side, heaven (fire) and earth, intellect and emotion, mind and body. Yet sometimes *Vaṁ* takes this role opposite *Raṁ* as water and fire, left and right, female and male.

Table of the Semi-Vowels in their mantric forms

1. Laṁ – लँ			
Energetic	Inertia, density, formation, joy, grace	Chakra	Root – Muladhara
Deity	Brahma, Creator	Element	Earth
Symbol	Yellow square	Tanmatra	Smell
Sense Organ	Nose	Motor Organ	Elimination/ Reproduction
Tissue	Muscle	Body Part	Heart to palate/ lower abdomen
Organs	Colon, reproductive[52] and excretory systems	Dosha	Kapha

2. Vaṁ – वँ			
Energetic	Vibration, flow, permeation, pervasion	Chakra	Sex – Svadhishthana
Deity	Vishnu, preserver	Element	Water
Symbol	White crescent moon	Tanmatra	Taste
Sense Organ	Tongue	Motor Organ	Urination/ Reproduction
Tissue	Fat	Body Part	Left side of chest
Organs	Kidney, reproductive, pancreas, water metabolism	Dosha[53]	Kapha

3. Raṁ - रँ			
Energetic	Heat, friction, coloring, digestion, ripening	Chakra	Navel – Manipura
Deity	Rudra, Destroyer/transformer	Element	Fire
Symbol	Red upward pointing Triangle	Tanmatra	Sight
Sense Organ	Eyes	Motor Organ	Feet
Tissue	Blood	Body Part	Right side of chest
Organs	Liver, small intestine, digestive system	Dosha	Pitta

4. Yaṁ - यँ			
Energetic	Motion, direction, velocity, motivation	Chakra	Heart – Anahata
Deity	Maheshvara, Cosmic Lord	Element	Air
Symbol	Grey six pointed star	Tanmatra	Touch
Sense Organ	Skin	Motor Organ	Hands
Tissue	Plasma	Body Part	Heart
Organs	Heart, circulatory system	Dosha	Vata

5. Haṁ - हं			
Energetic	Expressive, expansive, diffusive, pervasive	Chakra	Throat – Vishuddha
Deity	Sadashiva, transcendent form of Shiva	Element	Ether
Symbol	Dark blue dot	Tanmatra	Sound
Sense Organ	Ears	Motor Organ	Vocal cords
Tissue	Prana	Body Part	Throat
Organs	Lungs, respiratory system	Dosha	Vata

The semivowels strengthen their respective element and chakra correspondences shown in this table. For example, the mantra *Yaṁ* can be used to strengthen the heart, skin, hands, plasma and air element. We will explore these connections relative to the Mantra Purusha.

Other Indications of the Semivowels

The semivowels have other indications and applications than their correspondences to the elements and chakras, and should not just be considered to be 'the sounds of the chakras'. We should be aware of their broader implications.

Laṁ is a sound of bliss or Ananda, which is the basis of creation. It indicates love, sweetness and play as in forms of the Goddess like Lalita (She who plays). As the sound made directly with the tongue, it indicates the tongue and the power of speech in general, particularly relating to singing and dancing. In this regard, the sound La can help set the Kundalini force in motion, drawing it into its upward dance. It can cause the earth within us to shake, move and release its hidden energy of consciousness through our entire being. It can also help awaken the bliss potential in the crown chakra.

Laṁ is prominent in many important Tantric mantras. It has the power to stop, hold or stabilize things opposite *Raṁ* which sets things in motion. It connects to watery and earthy qualities and to soft and feminine qualities. It is curious to note that there are sometimes two La sounds. The first is the ordinary dental sound La made with the tongue placed behind the teeth, which relates more to the earth element. The second is a cerebral sound, made with the tongue placed at the roof of the mouth, and is connected more to the higher power of speech. It is sometimes used instead of *Kṣaṁ* as the bija along with *Haṁ* for the third eye. However, these two aspects of the La sound are not always differentiated.

Vaṁ is a sound of vibration in general and can also be connected to the air element (Vayu, Vata). It has the power to pervade and permeate, and can relate to Vishnu as the Pervader. It holds the power of manifestation and the matrix of life. Like *Laṁ* it can increase bliss, beauty and happiness.

Raṁ is not only fire but also light and color. It occurs in many mantras in this context. It can create passion, energy, and delight.

Yaṁ is not only air but also direction, motivation, work and application, as in the terms *Yama* and *Ni-yama* of yogic thought. It serves to connect, regulate and control.

Haṁ is not only ether but also prana and the Sun, projecting force and power. It is not a semivowel but a sibilant (Sanskrit ushma) but works along with the semivowels relative to the elements. Note its additional indications under the sibilants below.

The Five S and H Sounds or Sibilants

The Vedas tell us that the Sa and Ha sounds govern the breath and relate to prana in general.[54] We can observe this in ourselves; our breath has a natural hissing type sound and is released with a Ha-sound. Such pranic forces are the mythical serpents and dragons, which symbolize lightning and electrical energy. Through pranic mantras we can bring greater electrical energies into our minds and bodies.

According to Sanskrit etymology, the root Sa means to take in, to inhale, to energize, to hold, to take power, to sit, to rule, to endure, and to set in motion. The sound-Sa, therefore, is the natural sound of inhalation. Ha as a root means to give out, to exhale, to leave, to abandon, to negate, to ridicule, to cast out, to throw, and to ward off. The sound Ha, conversely, is the natural sound of exhalation. Quietly listen to your breath and you will discover that this is the case.

Saṁ in Sanskrit means to unite, concentrate or focus. It refers to being (Sat), stability and endurance. It represents the power of time, the eternal and sattva guna, the quality of balance and harmony. It creates unity, cohesion and concentration. It is often related to the Moon or even to the water element at an outer level.[55] *Haṁ* on a broader level means to expand, invigorate and to shine. It refers to space and the infinite. It is prana in the higher sense of the term. It is often related to the Sun.

We have already noted the existence of two *Sha* sounds in Sanskrit. Śaṁ is the more important of the two sounds. It is the seed sound or bija of peace, which is Shanti. It relates of Shankara, a main name of Shiva Mahadeva who is the giver or maker (kara) of peace (sham). Śaṁ is calming, harmonizing and balancing. It is generally cooling, slows us down and provides a sense of contentment. It means to quiet, stop, or dissolve, and also to beautify, shine, or diffuse. In this regard, we can relate Śa generally to the retention of the breath, just as Sa and Ha relate to inhalation and exhalation. Śaṁ is used in the *Vedas* to grant the blessings of the deities, particularly in *Shanti mantras* or Vedic peace chants.[56] Śaṁ is also the seed sound of Shakti and not only quiets things, but does so with a degree of force. It can indicate to put to rest and so can mean to destroy. It can reflect the fullness of power.

Saṁ is like Ṣaṁ in meaning but has more energy and air in its production, making it is more stimulating and harsher, causing effort and resistance. It indicates the gathering of force and energy in a state prior to any manifestation or eruption. Like

Śaṁ, it can be related to retention of the breath, but more in its later phase. In some Tantric teachings,[57] the three sibilants are the sounds of the three gunas with Saṁ as sattva guna, Śaṁ as rajas and Ṣaṁ as tamas.

There is a fifth sibilant in some alphabet sequences, *Ksaṁ*, which is other times regarded as a compound of two letters K and *Ṣa*. It has a curious duality to its meaning. On one hand, it indicates patience, the ground, the Earth, forgiveness and endurance, which gives it some connection to Apana, the downward moving prana connected to the Earth. On the opposite side, it represents Shakti, turbulence, activity, setting things in motion. This second meaning comes out more when it combines with the vowel-U as in the root '*Kṣu*'.

These five sibilants energize our prana, directing the force of Shakti through the nervous system and the spine. Many Shakti mantras arise from them, particularly from the letters Ha and Sa. These sounds create heat and electrical energy, stimulating not only the breath but also the Kundalini Shakti. Ha and Sa together as in *Hsauḥ* create a powerful sound for energizing the serpent power. The Sa-sound has a special combination with the Ta and Tha consonants, particularly in the root 'Stha' meaning 'to stand'. Sa and Ta sounds connote stability and extension and are important in various mantras for this purpose.

At the highest level, the sibilants govern pure being, the Self or Brahman. This is their role as representing the immortal prana, which is the inner experience of 'I am all'. Through contemplating them at a deep level, one can enter into pure consciousness, much like through an understanding of the vowels.

Below is a table of some of the common yogic correspondences, applications and meanings of the sibilants. They reflect a number of systems, considerations and correlations, including to the five Pranas, an important consideration in Ayurvedic medicine.

Table of the Sibilants in Mantric Form

Śaṁ – शँ	
Energetic	Calming, harmonizing, slowing down, stopping, silencing, ending
Correspondences	Prana, space, Shakti
Mental	Peace, stillness, consolidation, composure
Pranic	Samana (balancing energy), retention (earlier phase)
Physical	Bones – energy flow heart to right hand flow of energy

Ṣaṁ – षँ	
Energetic	Stimulating, friction, effort, motivation
Correspondences	Prana, Shakti, motivation
Mental	Sets mind in motion, energizes will and endurance
Pranic	Vyana (expanding energy), retention (later phase)
Physical	Nervous system – energy flow heart to left hand

Saṁ - सँ	
Energetic	Uniting, integrating, balancing – lunar
Correspondences	Eternal, time, Being, wholeness
Mental	Concentration, balance, harmony, sattva guna
Pranic	Prana (internalizing energy), inhalation, inspiration, left nostril
Physical	Reproductive system, Ojas – heart to right foot

Haṁ - हँ	
Energetic	Dispersing, expanding, controlling – solar
Correspondences	Prana, space, light, Sun
Mental	Energy, expression, detachment, transcendence
Pranic	Udana (ascending energy), exhalation (first phase)
Physical	Prana, vital energy – energy flow heart to left foot

Kṣaṁ - क्षँ	
Energetic	Stabilizing, grounding, empowering, manifest Shakti
Correspondences	World principle, heaven and earth
Mental	Intelligence, patience, forgiveness, intensity of emotion, mental force
Pranic	Apana (stabilizing energy), exhalation (later phase)
Physical	Immune system, endurance, Ojas – energy flow heart to top of head

Chapter 9:

The Twenty Five Consonants

The Powers of Manifestation

Consonants are the main powers through which sound is diversified and a variety of words, statements and expressions of ideas becomes possible. The twenty five consonants have their particular energetics as described in Sanskrit texts. However, there is less agreement on their overall correspondences than there is with the vowels.[58] Consonants, owing to their diversity, allow for a broad range of meaning, which is also modified according to the vowels and other consonants they are conjoined with.

Each of the five sets of Sanskrit consonants (guttural, palatal, cerebral, dental and labial) consists of a hard sound (*k, c, ṭ, t, p*) and its aspirated or h-form (*kh, ch, tḥa, th, ph*), a soft sound (*g, j, ḍ, d, b*) and its aspirated or h-form (*gh, jh, dḥ, dh, bh*), as well as the corresponding n/m sound (*ṅ, ñ, ṇ, n, m*). The aspirated forms are secondary sounds that are not commonly found in Sanskrit words (with the exceptions of bh and dh). They usually have a stronger or harsher energy, like ga meaning 'to go' versus gha meaning 'to strike'. The n/m sounds are softer and more stabilizing in effect.

Guttural Consonants

Guttural sounds made with the back of the throat have a strong contact in their production and a pointed energy in their expression. Relative to the guttural consonants, the Ka-sound serves to stimulate, originate, or set in motion, representing the initial point or impetus behind things. As the vowel-A is the first of the vowels and indicates unmanifest existence, the consonant-Ka as the first of the consonants indicates manifest existence, the prime energy of life. It relates to the primal forces of time, space, action, desire, motivation and identity and has a wide range of meanings.

Ka is sometimes identified with Prakriti or primal matter, other times with the Purusha or pure consciousness, though more often in its manifest form as the individual Self. It is connected to Lord Brahma, the Creator, and Prajapati, the lord of creatures. It represents origins, prime nature and the causative force. The letter-Ka often relates to the heart and sets in motion the prana of the heart.[59] Other times it is related to water as the element of life.

Not surprisingly the letter-Ka is the most important consonant in Shakti mantras. Kaṁ itself is the seed sound of desire (Kama), which is often related to the subtle or the causal body. The Ka-sound occurs in *Krīṁ* and *Klīṁ*, the basic Shakti powers of energization and attraction, the electric and magnetic energies behind the universe.

In the variant of *Kuṁ*, it indicates the Earth, the Goddess, the altar, Kundalini, the fire in the Earth, the Divine child of Fire (the deity Skanda), even the planet Mars, the war God. It has a stimulating, deepening and sometimes agitating effect.

Kha is an intensification of Ka which relates to space but more in the manifest or circumscribed form. It occurs in the *Upanishads* as *Oṁ Khaṁ Brahma*, '*Oṁ* Space Absolute'[60], which probably refers to the small space within the heart.

The Ga-sound indicates movement, expression, achievement, accomplishment, structure and order, much like the deity Ganesha to which it commonly relates. Ga in Sanskrit indicates to go, to get, to achieve, to express, to count and to control. It increases our level of skill, functionality, dexterity and expertise.

Chanting *Oṁ Gaṁ Ganeśāya Namaḥ* allows our work and action to move forward and to become properly applied in order to reach their goal. The letter-Ga also has its place in *Guṁ*, the mantra for the Guru, giving guidance and motivation but also granting weight, authority and preeminence. As the Sanskrit root Gi or Gay, it indicates singing, resonance, and the transformational movement of sound.[61]

Gha is an intensification of that energy which can be forceful or even violent. It is connected to the fierce forms of Shiva like Bhairava. The *Ṅa* (ng) letter occurs rarely and is mainly used to vibrate the energies of other guttural letters, drawing them deeper into the throat.

Palatal Consonants

Palatal sounds have a soft and yet airy quality about them. Relative to the palatal consonants, the Ca-sound indicates motion, vibration, speed and emotional response. It is a feminine counter part of Ka, serving as a field to hold the forces of time, space and causation. We can contrast Ka as action with Ca as reaction or emotion. Ca is often connected to fierce Goddesses like Chandi, owing to the passion and emotion it can hold. It is also the seed sound of the Moon as Chandra. The Cha-sound adds more prana and rhythm, force and vibration to this movement, as in the word Chandas, the Vedic term for meter or prosody.

The Ja-sound indicates birth, production, speed and generation. Its most common mantric variation is *Jūṁ* (pronounced Joom), which grants a quick, vitalizing energy. The living soul is called *Jiva*, deriving from this consonant. The Jha-sound intensifies the meaning, creating a rush of energy like a waterfall (jhara). The *Ña* -sound is rare and serves mainly to hold the vibration of other palatal sounds.

Cerebral and Dental Consonants

Cerebral and dental sounds are made by striking the tongue to the roof of the mouth or to the back of the teeth. The Ta and Da sounds of both cerebral and dental types represent the basic structural forces or building blocks of all things. Ta-sounds indicate movement along a horizontal plane, while Da-sounds indicate upholding a vertical energy. Ta-sounds carry such root meanings as to extend, to level, to cross, to strike, to propel, to flatten, lay down or to resist. Da-sounds carry such root meanings as to give, to control, to hold, to cut, to stand, to support, to divide, to apportion, even to bite. The Na-sound relates to bowing, moving, resonating, to a range, sphere or realm of expression.

The dental series (*ta, tha, da, dha, na*) provides more stability to this structuralizing expression, the cerebral series (*ṭa, ṭha, ḍa, ḍha, ṇa*) provides more energy to it but can be heavier and cruder in effect. In the Sanskrit language the dental series predominates, with the cerebral series rarely used except in the middle of words or as a modification of the dental series. The ta and da sounds reflect the beating of a drum and are used to mark, measure or create rhythm in Indian classical music.

Ta occurs in Tat, a mantric sound which means 'That', referring to the extension of the infinite space of consciousness. *Ṭha* as a sound or mantra relates to the Moon, Shakti and to the Goddess, as does sometimes Tha.

Daṁ is a seed syllable for self-control and for the guru Dattatreya, who combines the energies of Brahma, Vishnu and Shiva. In the form *Duṁ*, it relates to the Goddess Durga who has control of all the forces of nature as the great world Mother. Dha is the basis of words like Dhāma or Dharma that provide support and indicate the natural law or domain. Na is important for indicating negation, much like the word 'no' in English, but also relates to vibration and resonance as in the root *Nu*.

Labial Consonants

Labials develop the expansive energy of the U-vowel vibration. They project force and energy and can be the strongest of the consonants. The Pa-sound indicates protection and power, both pushing out and drawing in. It is the sound of the male, the father, protector and provider. It is connected to the Purusha or higher Self. It holds such additional Sanskrit meanings as to drink and refers to water, perhaps connecting to the movement of the lips. Pha intensifies that energy, creating energy, assertion or even an explosive effect, becoming a weapon as it were.

The Ba-sound indicates circular expansion and development outward, being softer and rounder in its effect than Pa. The Bha-sound intensifies this with prana and indicates creation and manifestation in the broadest sense, being the basic sound of the world spheres (lokas) and their development. It projects a field of light. Mantras for the three worlds like *Bhu* and *Bhuvaḥ* are based on this letter.

The Ma-sound indicates the mother, the measure, the source, the origin and the end. As the last of the twenty-five consonants, it indicates dissolution. It draws things back to ourselves and helps us return to the source. Like the mother, it is softening, nourishing, cooling and calming to the body, mind and nervous system. It also refers to Self, mind and our internal nature.

Ma is very common in mantric formulas, not just as connected to the final or Anusvara but as indicating the mind, Self, heart and center. Sometimes the two consonants Ka and Ma are used to represent all the consonants, which fall between them in the order of the alphabet.

Consonants in Combination

Consonants can be combined with vowels, semi-vowels or sibilants. Generally the A-vowel sustains the basic meaning of the consonant. Its value is mainly indicative. The I-vowel directs the meaning of a consonant along a particular line. The U-vowel gives the consonant more force and sustenance, setting it in motion in an expansive manner. For example, Ha refers to cast out, Hi to throw or cast in a specific direction, and Hu to ignite, expand and explode.

The semi-vowel La adds a stabilizing effect to consonants, while Ra adds a fiery energy. The sibilant Sa gives stability, while *Śa* and *Ṣa* have a softening or muting effect. Stha or Sta is a common Sanskrit and English root meaning to stand or be stable. Consonants can also combine and share their energies with each other in various ways.

Consonant Mantras

Tantric Yoga practices use several consonant based mantras that are very powerful for stimulating our internal energies. These usually predominate in the semi-vowels and sibilants, rather than pure consonants with the exception of Ka and Ma. They create friction and heat. For example, the Bhairavi (fire Goddess) mantras, *Hsraiṁ Hsklrīṁ Hsrauḥ*! Another example is *Ḍrlkshaiṁ*, a powerful Dakini mantra. The Dakinis represent the specific Shaktis of the chakras, necessary for their individual activation.[62] Such potentially harsh mantras require specific guidance in their application.

Chapter 10:

Shakti Bija Mantras

Besides the mantric power of letters of the Sanskrit alphabet, there is another series of powerful bija or single-syllable mantras, which consist of several vowels or consonants. These come under the term 'Shakti mantras', as they are commonly used in the worship of Shakti, projecting various Shaktis or types of cosmic energies. *Oṁ* is usually the foremost of these Shakti bija mantras. With it there are said to be eight total such primary bija mantras, with *Aiṁ, Hrīṁ, Klīṁ, Krīṁ, Śrīṁ, Trīṁ,* and *Strīṁ*, as mentioned in the *Mantra Yoga Samhita*.[63] They are several more such mantras that are commonly found in bija mantras, particularly to the Goddess. We have examined most of these below.

Shakti bija mantras are probably the most important of all mantras, whether for meditation, worship of deities, energizing prana or for healing purposes. They carry the great forces of Nature such as the energies of the Sun and Moon, Fire and Water, electricity and magnetism, not simply as outer factors but as inner potentials of Divine Light. They project various aspects of force and radiance for body, mind and consciousness. They hold, resonate, and propel the Kundalini force in specific and transformative ways. Below is a simple table of the main energies (Shaktis) of the Shakti mantras.

Prime Shakti Mantras

Pranic energy	Oṁ	Energy of sound	Aiṁ
Solar energy	Hrīṁ	Lunar energy	Śrīṁ
Electric energy	Krīṁ	Magnetic energy	Klīṁ
Power of fire	Hūṁ	Power to stop	Hlīṁ
Power to stabilize	Strīṁ	Power to transcend	Trīṁ

Shakti mantras relate to the primary forms of the Goddess or Divine Mother and are commonly used in her worship. There are special Shakti mantras for each of the great Goddesses, through which we can commune with them and gain their grace. Shakti mantras are prime mantras used in Tantric Yoga, in which they are combined in various ways to bring about different results. They have a great capacity for transformation that can extend to the deepest layers of our consciousness and prana. They should be approached with deep concentration, reverence and respect as the very life blood of the Goddess.

Most Shakti mantras contain the vowel-Ī, the vibratory ee-sound, which is the main primal sound of Shakti. Most contain the consonant-R, which is the seed of fire, heaven, light, order and dharma and has a stimulating and energizing effect. Some contain the consonant-L, which is the seed of earth, water, joy and bliss and has a calming and stabilizing effect. Many begin with either the letter-H, which indicates prana, light and the Sun, or the letters S or Sh, which indicate the Moon, the mind and water. Some like *Auṁ, Aiṁ* or *Īṁ* consist of vowels only.

Application of Shakti Mantras

Shakti mantras can be used to create, sustain or dissolve various forms, patterns and forces within us. They have particular affinities with certain locations in the body or with specific chakras – like *Hrīṁ* and the heart – but also have a broader effect to promote certain types of forces, like *Hrīṁ* as solar energy that can be applied on many different levels.

The application of Shakti mantras, like other mantras, depends upon the goals of life that we are using them for (dharma, artha, kama, moksha), which gunas we are energizing them with (sattva, rajas, tamas), or their application through Yoga, Ayurveda, Vedic astrology or Vastu. In this way, the same Shakti mantra can be used in many different applications. Yet at the deepest level, Shakti mantras are meant to arouse and support the Yoga Shakti or inner power of Yoga within us.

For example, the mantra *Śrīṁ* at an outer level connects us to the abundance of our dharma and artha, our career and financial gains, and the fulfillment of our kama or desires. For Yoga practice, it grants devotion to guru and deity. In Ayurveda, it promotes healing, growth, and nourishment. In Vedic astrology, it is the mantra of the Moon and can be used for strengthening benefic Venus and Jupiter as well. In Vastu, it promotes well-being, prosperity and happiness in the dwelling.

Used with a sattvic intention, *Śrīṁ* has a nourishing and harmonizing force; with a rajasic intention, it has a power to promote outer development and achievement; and with a tamasic intention, it can gain a destructive or crushing capacity. At an outer Lakshmi (Goddess of Prosperity) level, *Śrīṁ* can grant us the abundance of the material world; while at an inner Lakshmi level, it can grant us the abundance of the spiritual life, which is devotion, bliss and the beauty of perception.

Oṁ and *Auṁ* – ओँ / औँ

Oṁ is the prime mantra of the Purusha, the Cosmic Being, the Atman or higher Self. As such, it attunes us with our true nature and higher reality. *Oṁ* is the sound of Ishvara, the cosmic lord, the creator, preserver and destroyer of the universe, who is also the inner guru and prime teacher of Yoga. It reflects both the manifest and the unmanifest Brahman, sustaining the vibration of being, life and consciousness in all worlds and all creatures.

Generally, *Oṁ* is divided threefold as A, U and M, with A referring to creation, the waking state and Brahma, the creator; U as sustenance, the dream state and Vishnu the preserver; and M as dissolution, the deep sleep state and Shiva the transformer. More specifically, *Oṁ* relates to Shiva, the cosmic masculine force.

Oṁ serves to open and clear the mind for meditation. It brings about an ascension and expansion of our energy. It promotes the higher prana and inner light and takes us into the formless realm. It draws the sound current up the spine, through the chakras and out the top of the head. *Oṁ* also means 'yes' and is said to be the sound of assent. It allows us to harmonize with the forces of the universe externally and with our own nature internally. It attunes us to the cosmic reality and the sacred vibratory patterns that arise from it.

Auṁ has the same general effects as *Oṁ* but with a greater force and prana, particularly for drawing our energy upwards. *Oṁ* extended becomes *Auṁ*, which has greater power to expand and pervade, allowing the Divine consciousness to permeate all things.

Relative to Ayurvedic medicine, *Oṁ* helps harmonize the body, prana, mind, and senses with the higher Self, Atman or Divine presence within. It connects us with the cosmic healing prana. It brings a deep healing energy into the subconscious mind to remove negative emotions, addictions and compulsions. Relative to Vedic astrology, *Oṁ* is the sound of the Sun and of the higher light behind all the stars and planets. In Vastu, *Oṁ* can clear the energy in the home or dwelling and bring in Divine light, grace, and knowledge.

Relative to other mantras, *Oṁ* is often used to begin them. It clears the mind for other mantras to work, opens us up to the higher consciousness, and brings a deeper prana into the mantra. Without first chanting *Oṁ*, it is said that other mantras may not be effective. Whole Upanishads and entire books have been written about it.

Aiṁ – ऐँ

After *Oṁ*, *Aiṁ* (pronounced 'aym') is the next most common bija mantra. *Aiṁ* is the feminine counterpart of *Oṁ* and often follows *Oṁ* in various chants. *Oṁ* and *Aiṁ* are the two main compound vowel mantras, A plus U making *Oṁ* (and *Auṁ*) and A plus I making *Aiṁ*. As such, together they comprehend all sounds.

As *Oṁ* is the unmanifest or expansive aspect of primal sound, *Aiṁ* is the manifest or directed form. As *Oṁ* serves to clear the mental field, *Aiṁ* helps us focus the mind and heart in a particular manner. As *Oṁ* is the word that is heard, *Aiṁ* is the word that is seen. As *Oṁ* is the supreme Purusha or cosmic masculine force, *Aiṁ* is Adya Shakti, the supreme Shakti or cosmic feminine force. That is why we find the mantra *Aiṁ* in so many different mantras to the Goddess or Divine Mother.[64]

More specifically, *Aiṁ* is the seed mantra of Sarasvati, the Goddess of knowledge and speech, the consort of Lord Brahma, the Creator in the Hindu trinity of great Gods. As such, *Aiṁ* aids us in learning, art, expression and communication and is good for promoting learning and education generally.

Aiṁ is also the mantra of the guru and helps us access all higher knowledge. It can be used to call or to invoke wisdom and understanding. It indicates motivation, direction and will-power. It can orient us toward whatever we are seeking. It increases concentration of mind and awakens our higher intelligence (Buddhi). Relative to other mantras, *Aiṁ* is often used to direct our awareness or intention to the deity, to function as our call to draw in the higher knowledge so the mantra can work.

In terms of Ayurveda, *Aiṁ* strengthens the voice and the vocal chords. It helps open the lungs and clear the senses. Astrologically, *Aiṁ* connects to the planet Mercury and to some extent the Moon, both planets that govern speech and expression. For Vastu, *Aiṁ* will bring creativity and learning into the dwelling, particularly for studies, libraries and classrooms.

Hrīṁ – ह्रीँ

After *Oṁ* and *Aiṁ*, *Hrīṁ* (pronounced 'hreem') is probably the most commonly used bija mantra. It is composed of the sound-Ha, which indicates prana, space and light, with the sound-Ra, which indicates fire, light and dharma, and the sound-Ī, which indicates energy, focus and motivation.

Hrīṁ is the prime mantra of the Goddess in all of her three main powers of creation, preservation and destruction, and so is the main Shakti mantra, with a more specific application than *Aiṁ*. It is said to be the Shakti bija and to be equivalent to *Oṁ* for the Goddess. More specifically, it relates to Parvati or Shakti, the consort of Shiva, who is the destroyer/transformer among the great trinity of deities.

Hrīṁ is a mantra of magical force, captivation and empowerment. It can be used relative to any deity or object whose presence we wish to access at the level of the heart. It brings about joy, ecstasy and bliss. *Hrīṁ* both purifies and exalts us in our inner quest, humbling us before the Divine power so that it can enter into our hearts.

Hrīṁ is a specific mantra for the heart (hridaya in Sanskrit) on all levels, whether the spiritual heart, the heart chakra, the emotional heart or the heart as a physical organ. It energizes the heart, provides warmth, and allows for both deep feeling and deep thought.

In terms of Ayurveda, *Hrīṁ* can be used to counter heart disease of all types, aiding in longevity and rejuvenation. More specifically, it helps promote the pranic and functional aspect of the heart and with it the power of circulation of the blood, the lungs and the nervous system. It has generally Pitta (fiery) energy but some Vata (air) energy as well, stimulating the higher pranas and emotions. In terms of Vedic astrology, *Hrīṁ* relates to the Sun, the planet of the heart, and helps promotes solar energy, expression and charisma.

Hrīṁ is usually a soft mantra but can also be harsh. As a soft mantra, it increases the finer energies of the heart. As a harsh mantra, it can be used to hypnotize or captivate, to dissolve or carry away.

Śrīṁ – श्रीँ

Śrīṁ (pronounced 'shreem') is one of the most commonly used mantras because it is probably the most benefic of all sounds, drawing to us all that is good, helpful and promoting of positive growth and development. More specifically, *Śrīṁ* is the seed mantra of Lakshmi, the Goddess of prosperity and abundance, and the consort of Lord Vishnu, the preserver in the Hindu trinity of great Gods, and brings Lakshmi's many blessings. *Śrīṁ* is also called 'Rama bija' and is used in the worship of Lord Rama, the avatar of dharma.

Śrīṁ is the mantra of faith, devotion, refuge and surrender. It can be used to take refuge in or express devotion to any deity, helping us to gain its favor and grace. *Śrīṁ* relates to the heart in its feeling aspect, whereas *Hrīṁ* relates to the pranic or functional aspect of the heart.

Śrī means splendor in Sanskrit, like the beautiful light of the Moon. *Śrīṁ* is often used along with *Hrīṁ*. As *Hrīṁ* is solar, *Śrīṁ* is lunar. *Śrīṁ* relates to the Moon in Vedic astrology and promotes a kind of lunar energy, Soma and beauty overall. Yet it is also used for other benefic planets like Venus and Jupiter, promoting their positive energies.

Relative to Ayurveda, *Śrīṁ* is mainly a Kapha (watery and earthy) mantra for improving health, happiness, fertility, love and calmness of mind. Yet it does have some secondary Pitta (fire) qualities and improves our glow, luster and light. It is particularly important for women's health and brings proper function and circulation to the female reproductive system. *Śrīṁ* has a soothing effect on the mind and emotions, allowing us to surrender to Divine grace and take refuge in the higher powers.

Halīṁ and Halrīṁ - हलीँ / ह्लीँ

Halīṁ (pronounced 'hleem') is a derivative of *Hrīṁ* which replaces the fiery and stimulating Ra-sound, with the watery and stabilizing La-sound, bringing the seed sounds of space (Ha) and earth (La) together. As *Hrīṁ* serves to energize and direct the power of prana, *Halīṁ* serves to hold and stabilize it.

Applied at a soft level, *Halīṁ* is a mantra of ecstasy and joy, a sound of Ananda (bliss and ecstasy). Applied at a harsh level, which is its most common usage, *Halīṁ* serves to neutralize or destroy. *Halīṁ* holds the Sthambhana Shakti or the power to stop things, particularly to stop subtle energies that have already been set in motion. In this regard, *Halīṁ* relates to the Goddess Bagalamuki among the 'Ten Wisdom Goddesses' (Dasha Mahavidya), who helps us restrain any negative speech that is directed against us. It is also called Raksha bija or the 'seed sound of protection' and can be used to seal off our energy from negative influences.

Halīṁ grants control of the body, senses, mind and prana, which it brings to a state of stillness. As such, it is an important mantra for the practice of Yoga. It helps us to stop the prana from its ordinary agitation and so aids in pranayama. It helps us to stop the mind and so is called Brahmastra, the 'weapon of Brahman' that puts all thought to rest. However, *Halīṁ* can be strong and should be used with care. Yet it is often better to slow down one's energies with Shanti or peace mantras before trying to bring them to an immediate halt, which this mantra can do.

Relative to Ayurveda, *Halīṁ* can be used to slow down and stop excess speech or pranic movement. In astrology, it has primarily a Saturn and Rahu influence to stop things but also a Mars influence to neutralize negativity.

Halrīṁ combines the Ha, La and Ra sounds: the sounds of space, earth and fire. It has yet more energy to remove negativity than *Halīṁ*, though it is not as effective in slowing things down. It projects the Kundalini force as a weapon to protect us from unspiritual influences.

Krīṁ - क्रीँ

Krīṁ (pronounced 'kreem') is the first and most important of the consonant mantras, the mantras that begin with a hard consonant rather than a vowel or sibilant. *Krīṁ* begins with Ka, the first of the Sanskrit consonants that indicates manifest prana and the initial phase of energy. To this it adds the Ra-sound or seed of fire, the Ī-sound or focusing power as in the other Shakti mantras. It creates light and intention like *Hrīṁ* and *Śrīṁ* but of a more specific, stimulating, and manifesting nature.

Krīṁ relates to Vidyut Shakti or the basic electrical energy behind all things in the universe – the Kriya Shakti or power of action on all levels. *Krīṁ* rules over all manifestation including time, space and action (causation). Through it, we can gain control of our karmas and also move beyond them.

Krīṁ is the seed mantra of Kali, the Goddess of time and transformation, the consort of Lord Shiva, the Destroyer/Transformer in the Hindu trinity of great deities. Through it, we set Kali's power in motion within us. It serves to energize things to the highest level, which is to raise their level of vibration to the point where we can return to the source.

Krīṁ is a mantra of work, yoga and transformative energy, and is said to be *Yoga bija* or the 'seed syllable of Yoga practice'. Its inner application is to awaken the Kundalini Shakti to merge our outer nature back into the higher Self. *Krīṁ* stimulates higher perception and higher prana, promoting the yogic process of pratyahara (internalization of mind) and giving greater power to concentration, meditation and Samadhi. The mantra can connect us with the inner power of any deity we wish to connect to.

In terms of Ayurveda, *Krīṁ* combines Vata (wind, electrical) energy with Pitta (fire) for an adrenaline type effect. It has a powerful electrical force and stimulates all the pranas and Agnis (biological fires), the circulatory and nervous systems, particularly the heart and the liver. In Vedic astrology, *Krīṁ* relates primarily to the planet Mars, which is the planet of work and effort. *Krīṁ* is generally a harsh or strong mantra, particularly as used with *Hrīṁ*, and so should be recited with care.

Klīṁ – द्यहए७

Klīṁ (pronounced 'kleem') is the softer, watery or more feminine aspect of *Krīṁ*. As *Krīṁ* is electrical or projective, *Klīṁ* has a magnetic quality that draws things to us. It can also be used to hold or fix things in place.

Klīṁ carries the *Akarshana Shakti* or the 'power of attraction'. It relates to Krishna, who grants bliss (Ananda) as a deity, and to Sundari, the Goddess of love and beauty. *Klīṁ* is the seed mantra of desire (Kama Bija) and helps us to achieve our true wishes in life. *Klīṁ* can be used relative to any deity we would like to access to fulfill our wishes. *Klīṁ* is the mantra of love and devotion, increasing the love energy within our hearts. For this reason, it is one of the most benefic mantras, and one of the safest and most widely used.

Relative to Ayurveda, *Klīṁ* is mainly a Kapha (water)-promoting mantra and is particularly good for the reproductive system and for the plasma and skin. It promotes *Kledaka Kapha* (the digestive fluids of the stomach), increasing our capacity for nourishment. Most importantly, it is specific for *Tarpaka Kapha*, the Soma of the brain that promotes well-being, soothing the nerves and calming the heart. It strengthens the immune system and brings contentment to the entire being. *Klīṁ* is not specifically an astrological mantra, but is sometimes used for Venus or the Moon. For Vastu, it can bring the energy of Divine love and beauty into the dwelling.

Klīṁ can have a harsh side as well. It can be used to fix, to stop or to nail down, or to hold things under the power of wishes, though such usage is not as common as its benefic application.[65]

Strīṁ and *Trīṁ* – स्त्राँ / त्रीँ

Strīṁ (pronounced 'streem') contains the Sa-sound of stability, the Ta-sound which gives extension, and the Ī-vowel that provides energy, direction and motivation. It is connected to root meanings such as to stand, to spread, to take a step, to rise or traverse from one level to another. It brings about an expansion and spreading of energy that can follow a horizontal expansion, a vertical ascent, or a spiral movement.

Strīṁ is said to be *Shanti bija* or the 'seed syllable of peace' and carries the Shakti of Sat or Pure being. *Strī* in Sanskrit also means a woman. The mantra *Strīṁ* provides the power of the Divine feminine (Stri-Shakti) to give birth, to nourish, to protect and to guide. It is similar to *Śrīṁ* in sound qualities but stronger and more stabilizing in its effects. It can be used to increase Shakti or feminine energy in oneself or in one's outer activity.

Strīṁ is another general mantra of the Goddess, particularly in her higher knowledge form. *Strīṁ* can be used relative to any deity whose energy we wish to expand or project in a creative manner. It grants poetic and artistic powers, as well as powers of argument, debate and law.

Strīṁ is the seed mantra of the Hindu Goddess Tara (not the Buddhist Tara, who is a different deity approached with different mantras). Hindu Tara is connected to Durga, who is often called Durga-Tara, as a protective and fiery form of the Goddess. She is the high priestess and represents the inner knowledge and the insight of the guru, particularly the power of the Word. Tara controls the weapons of the Gods, particularly the *Trishula* or trident of Lord Shiva. Tara also relates to the mantra *Oṁ*, and *Strīṁ* is the means through which *Oṁ* takes us across all difficulties.

Tara in astrological symbolism is the wife or feminine form of Brihaspati, the planet Jupiter. She is the great star Goddess associated with the star Aldeberan (the Vedic star Rohini), the bright red star of the constellation Taurus. As Brihaspati/Jupiter is the high priest or guru of the Gods, Tara is the high priestess of the heavens. *Strīṁ* as the mantra of the Star Goddess attunes us to the benefic powers of the stars and Nakshatras and gives us astrological knowledge.

In terms of Ayurveda, *Strīṁ* is important as a healing and empowering mantra for women, and can aid in childbirth and can promote women's health generally, strengthening the heart, reproductive system, circulatory system and bones.

Trīṁ (pronounced 'treem') is another version of the Tara mantra, but more specifically a mantra of Tejas or fire. Without the Sa-sound, it has more an energy of crossing over and ascending. Tri relates to the number three in Sanskrit and to the bridging of dualities. *Trīṁ* is also the seed mantra of the Trishula, the trident of Lord Shiva, which is his most powerful weapon.

The mantra *Trīṁ* is good for taking us across difficulties and overcoming inimical forces. It has a strong Pitta (fire) energy and also allows us to ascend in awareness. It is said to be the sound of Tejas, or the subtle essence of Pitta, which relates to valor, courage, daring and fearlessness. Otherwise, its indications are similar to that of *Strīṁ*.

Huṁ and *Hūṁ* – हुँ / हूँ

Hūṁ (pronounced 'hoom') is one of the most important Sanskrit mantras along with *Oṁ*, *Aiṁ* and *Hrīṁ*. It is said to be the Pranava or primal sound of Lord Shiva, the transformative aspect of the Divine Trinity.

Huṁ (short vowel as in fl*u*te) is the main Agni or fire mantra and can help enkindle fire in all of its forms from the digestive fire to the Pranic fire to the fire of the consciousness. It refers to a gaseous type of fire and so can be connected with lightning and to the power of prana and the breath. *Huṁ* is also a weapon and protection mantra and can be used to destroy negativity with its lightning fire. It can used to direct a fiery explosive energy with other mantras. It is also called Krodha bija or the 'seed sound of wrath'. It is the mantra that Lord Shiva uses to project the fire from his third eye that destroys all negativity and burns up all desires.

Hūṁ with a long vowel sound has a similar meaning but a more feminine and Shakti quality. It relates to fierce forms of the Goddess like Kali, Chandi and Chhinnamasta. It has the power to cut off and indicates the sword. However, *Hūṁ* has a soft potential as well. It is said to be the *Dhenu bija*, the 'seed sound of the Mother cow', calling its calf back to it. It calls out and invokes, while at the same time challenging and warding off. Both the long and short versions of this mantra *Huṁ* and *Hūṁ* are used for raising the Kundalini, particularly combining the mantra with the breath, and the fixing of the gaze at the navel, the seat of the digestive fire.

Relative to Ayurveda, both *Huṁ* and *Hūṁ* increase Prana, Tejas and Pitta, setting all our fiery energies in motion from the digestive fire to the fire of the mind. Both strengthen the immune system particularly against any active pathogenic attacks, but as harsh mantras require some care in application.

Astrologically, *Huṁ* and *Hūṁ* relate to fiery planets like the Sun, Mars or Ketu and increase their fiery properties. They are particularly good for bringing in the higher perceptive power of Ketu, which is a great aid in astrological research, spiritual healing and Yoga. Relative to Vastu, they can be used to create a protective energy shield around one's dwelling.

Hauṁ and *Hoṁ* – हौँ / होँ

Hauṁ combines the *Auṁ* sound with the Ha-sound, which gives strength and prana to the Divine Word. *Hauṁ* is an important mantra for Shiva and for the highest prana. *Hauṁ* can be regarded as an expansion of *Hūṁ* and carries similar powers. *Hauṁ* develops and expands our energy and awareness and has a revitalizing effect. It is one of the most powerful mantras for reviving a person's prana or mind, helpful even when the life is in danger.

Hoṁ is a related bija mantra with a similar meaning, but not quite as expansive in energy. It gives strength, both prana and Ojas (vital essence of Kapha) and so is a powerful healing sound.

Sauṁ and *Sauḥ* – सौँ / सौः

Sauṁ combines the *Auṁ* sound with the Sa-sound, which gives stability and strength to it. *Sauṁ* indicates Shakti, particularly as the original power of existence, Sat-Shakti. *Sauṁ* relates to Soma and the Moon, the mind and the principle of bliss or Ananda. In fact, it means 'what relates to the Moon' (Soma) and strengthens the lunar flow of energy within us.

The form *Sauḥ* has more an expressive energy. It is the prime heart mantra in the tradition of Kashmiri Shaivism, where it refers to the highest reality and can be as important as *Oṁ*. *Sauḥ* allows the nectar of Soma from the crown chakra to flow into the heart. It promotes contentment and happiness in the brain and nervous system. In this function, it is widely used in Shakti mantras, particularly those of a lunar nature, like that of the Goddess Sundari, *Aiṁ Klīṁ Sauḥ*, opening up the region of the Moon and the descent of the Soma. It is sometimes called Shakti bija or the sound of Shakti because of its power to get Shakti to move.

Hasauḥ – हसौः

This mantra combines the sounds *Hau* and *Sau* into a single mantra. It is very powerful for energizing the inner prana and electrifying the nervous system, stimulating the Kundalini Shakti. *Hsauḥ* is like the hiss of a serpent, stimulating the prana of the senses, mind and nervous system. It is strongly revitalizing but can be disturbing, if not applied in a calm state of mind.

Duṁ and *Dūṁ* – दुँ / दूँ

Duṁ (pronounced short as in flute) is a Durga mantra, projecting the energy of the protective form of the Divine Mother who saves us from difficulties. It is another powerful Agni or fire mantra like *Huṁ* with a weapon like effect. Whereas *Huṁ* creates an airy or pranic type of fire, *Duṁ* creates an earthy type of fire, like burning wood. It can be used to eliminate sorrow, obstacles or barriers. It has a martial energy to overcome opposition and grants self-control and self-discipline as well. Durga is the head of the Divine army, one should note, riding a lion, whose power this mantra sets in motion.

Dūṁ with the long vowel sound has a similar meaning and usage but a more feminine quality. It is more commonly used in Shakti mantras. These mantras can neutralize any negative force projected at us. Relative to Ayurveda, they strengthen the digestive fire and can be used to burn away toxins or Ama, working more at a tissue level. In astrology, Durga holds a solar energy, particularly as directed to the earth, and her bija can help bring out the feminine aspect of solar energy.

Īṁ – ईँ

Īṁ is the prime bija mantra of the older Vedic tradition in the *Rigveda*, said to be the Vedic Pranava or primal sound before *Oṁ* became predominant in that role. *Īṁ* indicates the power of seeing, ruling and directing power. It illumines, indicates, energizes and transforms. It represents the eyes in the Mantra Purusha, but extends to inner powers of vision, discrimination, visualization, creation and imagination.

In terms of Shakti mantras, *Īṁ* is the mantra of the central point or bindu of the famous Sri Yantra diagram, where it is repeated twice as *Oṁ Īṁ, Īṁ Namaḥ*, which is said to be like a streak of lightning.[66] It grants all the special powers of Sri Yantra, which extend to the crown chakra and the entire cosmic structure. We will discuss this mantra more under Vedic mantras.

Special Single Letter Shakti Mantras

There are instances in which mantras include a series of letters, without the closing Anusvara or ṁ-sound. Most common in this regard is the famous *Panchadashi* Mantra, said to be the most powerful of all the Shakti mantras and existing in several variations.[67] It relates to the Goddess as Tripura Sundari, to the crown chakra and the full scope of the Sri Yantra and Sri Chakra worship of the Goddess, which is one of the most important Tantric Yoga practices.[68] Entire sadhanas are built around it and its variant forms.

Ka E Ī La Hrīṁ, Ha Sa Ka Ha La Hrīṁ, Sa Ka La Hrīṁ
क ए ई ल ह्रीं, ह स क ह ल ह्रीं, स क ल ह्रीं

Other Important Bija Mantras

Glauṁ – ग्लौँ

Glauṁ is a special bija mantra for Ganesha. It takes the sacred *Auṁ* bija and adds the Ga-sound, the power of movement and accomplishment, along with the stabilizing and harmonizing energy of the La-sound. As such, *Glauṁ* holds and deepens the *Auṁ* vibration, allowing it to expand our being without a loss of focus. It helps remove obstacles and clear our path so that we can move forward with the mantra *Gaṁ*, the other prime Ganesha mantra.

Kṣrauṁ – क्ष्रौँ

Kṣrauṁ relates to *Narasimha*, the Man Lion that is the main fierce or protective form of Lord Vishnu, who is usually worshipped in benefic forms like Rama or Krishna. The sound has the power to twist, crush and uproot negativity. It is usually used in a harsh sense to purify the ego and reduce the animal desires within us.

Rāṁ – राँ

Rāṁ (pronounced with the long a-sound as in *fa*ther) is the mantra of Lord Rama, God in his protective, saving and compassionate form. The mantra provides warmth, rest, relaxation, comfort, happiness and joy. It relieves fear, agitation, pain and suffering. It is particularly good for calming children and helping them sleep, reducing Vata dosha and its nervous energy. It opens the higher light and power within us but in a way that is gentle, kind and compassionate.

Note that this is a different mantra than *Raṁ* (short-a) indicating the fire element as *Rāṁ* has a long-Ā vowel, which softens its fiery energy.

Mā – मा

Mā, which means mother, is an important Shakti mantra for invoking the Devi or Divine Mother, *Śrī Mā* or *Śrī Mātaji*. The sound *Mā* has a soothing, softening and nurturing effect upon us, drawing the Divine Feminine grace into our lives. It helps us let go of anger and aggression, conflict and hatred. It allows us to surrender to the Mother and her love. Yet it can also help improve our emotions, calm the mind and give greater mental powers. Some devotees simply chant *Mā Mā Mā Mā* to energize their devotion and open the heart. It has a Kapha, mothering energy on our physiology, increasing growth and nourishment within us.

Additional Sounds to Bija Mantras

Several special mantric sounds are often used along with bija and Name mantras for greater power or for certain effects.

Astra or Weapon Mantra: *Huṁ Phaṭ Svāhā* - हुँ फट् स्वाहा

Astra means a weapon, particularly something that is thrown, like a spear. This Astra mantra uses the short vowel form of *Huṁ*, which is specifically an Agni or fire mantra. The bija *Phaṭ* takes this mantric fire energy and directs it, like a strike to remove negative forces. *Svāhā* gives additional fire energy. Often the longer vowel form *Hūṁ* is used instead of *Huṁ*, particularly relative to Shakti Mantras. In Yoga practice relative to the chakras, the Astra mantra serves to dissolve the gross elements into the subtle, taking us back to pure unity. It purifies and removes the ego and all of its weaknesses.

On a health level, the astra mantra creates a weapon for destroying negative forces in body and mind. In the body, it can be used to counter pathogens, toxins or excess doshas. It stimulates the immune system to cleanse the body, much like an elevation of body temperature helps burn away toxins. In the mind, it wards off negative emotions, particularly those directed to us by others on a subconscious level, including the forces of anger, jealousy and envy.

The Astra mantra is added to the mantras for Tara (*Oṁ Hrīṁ Strīṁ Hūṁ Phaṭ Svāhā*) and other Goddesses. It can be added to any mantra to turn it into a weapon or a purifying force. It has mainly a fire (Pitta) energy but some air (Vata) as well. It increases Tejas and Prana, the inner energies of fire and air, in their purifying role. It breaks down resistance, dissolve barriers and remove deep-seated tamas.

However, one should not use such weapon mantras to attack others, or the destructive energy may reverberate back upon us. Use them only for protection or for removing negativity within yourself, particularly that of your own ego. Sometimes other mantras like *Hrīṁ* are used with *Phaṭ Svāhā*. Or *Phaṭ* may be used by itself to strike or remove negative energies.

Haṁsaḥ So'haṁ – हंसः सोऽहं

The mantras *Haṁsaḥ* and So'*haṁ*, the natural sound of the breath, are often combined with Shakti mantras like *Hūṁ* or *Hrīṁ*. They affirm our unity with the higher Self or *Ahaṁ*. They both set in motion the higher solar and lunar energies and keep them in a state of balance. They unite the dualities within us, particularly at a pranic level. We will discuss them in detail later in the book under Pranayama.

Namaḥ – नमः

Namaḥ is the mantra of reverence and surrender as in *Namas-te*, 'reverence to you'. It is used with name mantras to honor and surrender to the deity, like *Oṁ Namaḥ Śivāya*. It may also follow a name mantra like *Oṁ Gaṁ Ganeśāya Namaḥ*. It is very common in all layers of Sanskrit mantras from the earliest Vedic texts. It is the term that most characterizes not only Hindu chanting but also the Buddhist and Jain.

Svāhā – स्वाहा

Svāhā is said to be the wife or feminine counterpart of Agni or fire. She further energizes mantras with fire, adding more Shakti to them. *Svāhā* is repeated after mantras at Yajnas (fire sacrifices) while one is offering grains or anything else into the fire. Yet it is also used after mantras that one wants to project more fire energies with, like Kali and Tara mantras.

Jai and *Jaya* – जै / जय

Jai is a particle that means 'victory to' or 'glory to'. It is often used with name mantras to the deity like Jai Ma Kali! or to the guru like Jai Gurudeva! *Jaya* is the longer version of the same.

Hari Oṁ – हरि ओँ

Hari is a term that derives from the root *Hri* and is connected to the mantra *Hrīṁ*. It indicates light, particularly golden light, devotion, exaltation, vitality and preeminence. It is particularly associated with Lord Vishnu and Sri Krishna.

The Language of Shakti Mantras

A single Shakti mantra can be used as a meditation mantra in order to draw the mind into deep awareness. One repeats the mantra prior to meditation to bring the mind into a meditative state. Then one keeps the mantra going in the back of the mind as long as the meditation proceeds, to help sustain the process. Several Shakti bija mantras can be also used together as meditation mantras, often in groups of three to seven bijas.

Shakti mantras can function as names of deities to invoke them, like *Oṁ* and Shiva, or *Aiṁ* and Sarasvati. But they are more commonly used in conjunction with Divine names, like *Oṁ Aiṁ Sarasvatyai Namaḥ*!

Shakti mantras reflect various types of invocation. For example, *Oṁ Aiṁ Hrīṁ Śrīṁ*, means *Oṁ*; I invoke (*Aiṁ*); open my heart to (*Hrīṁ*); and take refuge in (*Śrīṁ*). Or *Oṁ Krīṁ Hūṁ Hrīṁ* means *Oṁ*; I energize (*Krīṁ*); enkindle (*Hūṁ*); and open my heart (*Hrīṁ*). Shakti mantras allow us to energize our thoughts and feelings at a deeper level with the force of higher awareness. They can be used with chakra mantras or with the Mantra Purusha sounds, bringing in their particular energies, as we will discuss under those topics.

Chapter 11:

Mantra Purusha: The Body of Sound

Besides our gross, form-based physical body, we have another subtle energy body made up of sound. Our higher Self or inner being, the Purusha of yogic thought, is connected to the physical body through this body of sound. Mantra Yoga contains a very important teaching through which we can harmonize this body of sound to insure the right flow of energy into the physical body. Each of the fifty letters of the Sanskrit alphabet corresponds to a certain portion of the physical body called the Mantra Purusha, the Cosmic Being or Person (Purusha) made of mantra.

This subtle body of sound vibration relates to the mental body[69] and to the subtle or astral body in general, the site of the seven chakras. It creates and sustains the physical body, supporting health and well-being within it. Through changing the frequencies of the subtle body of sound, we can bring healing into the physical body and remove negativities from the mind. For this reason, the Mantra Purusha is an important method of Mantra Therapy as well as a means of opening our higher awareness. It is perhaps the best mantric tool for Ayurvedic medicine.

Structure of the Mantra Purusha

The Mantra Purusha relates the primary groups of sounds as vowels, consonants, semi-vowels and sibilants to particular regions of the body. First, we will present the most simple and direct set of correspondences. Then we will present the details in a second set of tables.

- The sixteen vowels relate to the sixteen main regions and faculties in the head, including the senses.
- The twenty five consonants relate to the main joints on the arms and legs (five per arm and leg) and the five regions of the abdomen.
- The nine semivowels and sibilants relate to the tissues and primary constituents of the body, from the plasma to the mind.

Mantra Purusha – Basic Form			
Head			
Aṁ	Top of head	Āṁ	Forehead
Iṁ	Right eye	Īṁ	Left eye
Uṁ	Right ear	Ūṁ	Left ear
Ṛṁ	Right nostril	Ṝṁ	Left nostril
Ḷṁ	Right cheek	Ḹṁ	Left cheek
Eṁ	Upper lip	Aiṁ	Lower lip
Oṁ	Upper teeth	Auṁ	Lower teeth
Aṁ	Upper palate	Aḥ	Lower palate
Arms			
Kaṁ	Right shoulder	Caṁ	Left shoulder
Khaṁ	Right elbow	Chaṁ	Left elbow
Gaṁ	Right wrist	Jaṁ	Left wrist
Ghaṁ	Right base of fingers	Jhaṁ	Left base of fingers
Ṅaṁ	Right fingertips	Ñaṁ	Left fingertips
Legs			
Ṭaṁ	Right leg	Taṁ	Left leg
Ṭhaṁ	Right knee	Thaṁ	Left knee
Ḍaṁ	Right ankle	Daṁ	Left ankle
Ḍhaṁ	Right base of toes	Dhaṁ	Left base of toes
Ṇaṁ	Right tip of toes	Naṁ	Left tip of toes
Abdomen			
Paṁ		Right abdomen	
Phaṁ		Left abdomen	
Baṁ		Lower back	
Bhaṁ		Navel	
Maṁ		Lower abdomen	
Tissues			
Yaṁ	Plasma	Raṁ	Blood
Laṁ	Muscle	Vaṁ	Fat
Śaṁ	Bone	Ṣam	Nerve tissue
Saṁ	Reproductive tissue	Haṁ	Prana
Kṣaṁ	Mind		

Mantra Mantra Regions and Marma Points

In the Mantra Purusha, each letter of the Sanskrit alphabet functions as a 'locational indicator' for a particular part of the body. These 'mantra regions' often reflect special marma or 'energy regions' used in Yoga and Ayurveda. Marmas are not simply points, like acupuncture points, but zones that can extend from half an inch to four inches (finger units) in size. Marmas are discussed in many Ayurvedic texts, so we ask the reader to consult these for more details on their names, locations and usage.[70]

Many Mantra Purusha regions correspond to classical marmas. In other instances, they relate to secondary or less commonly used marmas. In some instances, Mantra Purusha sounds cover a larger region than marmas and can be correlated with more than one set of marmas. This 'mantra-marma' connection is very important for healing purposes and one of the most significant applications of mantra, particularly at a physiological level.

Mantra Purusha regions also relate to certain nadis or subtle channels, which have their openings or apertures at their locations, like the right eye and the Pusha Nadi, which ends there. They reflect the psychological and spiritual faculties and energies associated with their bodily locations. Similarly, the Mantra Purusha sounds correlate with the qualities of their respective letters in the Sanskrit alphabet, as already described.

In the more elaborate version of the Mantra Purusha below, I have added specific marma regions for each sound, as well as psychological effects, nadi and organ correspondences. In the case of the sibilants and semivowels, I have added their energy flows along the body. The semi-vowels govern the regions around the heart, while the sibilants govern energy flows from the heart to the extremities of the body. *Note the appendix for more detail on how the Mantra Purusha sounds connect with classical marmas.*

Mantra Purusha, Detailed Form	
Mantras for the Mind, Senses and Organs in the Head Prana Vayu, the motivating force among the five Pranas	
Top of head Crown chakra, Adhipati marma at top of the head, pineal gland Aperture of Sushumna nadi, which runs from base of the spine to top of the head Inner and higher mind, consciousness, Self, Prana, transcendence	Aṁ अँ
Forehead Third eye, point in center of forehead, pituitary gland Connecting point of the head nadis in the Sushumna, outer mind, mental perception, thought, feeling, expression	Āṁ आँ
Right Eye Right Apanga marma at lower corner of right eye Aperture of Pusha nadi which flows from third eye to right eye Direct perception, judgment, discrimination, motivation	Iṁ इँ
Left Eye Left Apanga marma at lower corner of left eye Aperture of Gandhari nadi which flows from third eye to the left eye Creative imagination, visualization, desire	Īṁ ईँ
Right Ear Right Vidhura marma below corner of right ear Aperture of Payasvini nadi which flows from third eye to the right ear Direct hearing and listening, comprehension, grasp of the whole	Uṁ उँ
Left Ear Left Vidhura marma below corner of left ear Aperture of Shankhini nadi which flows from third eye to the left eye Creative hearing and sound based imagination	Ūṁ ऊँ
Right Nostril Right Phana marma at base of right nostril Aperture of Pingala nadi which flows from third eye to the right nostril and governs the energy flow on the right side of the body generally Power of exhalation and right pranic flow, reason, will power	Ṛṁ ऋँ
Left Nostril Left Phana marma at base of left nostril Aperture of Ida nadi which flows from third eye to the left nostril and governs the energy flow on the left side of the body in general Power of inhalation and left pranic flow, emotion, responsiveness	Ṝṁ ॠँ
Right Cheek Right Shringataka marma at center of right cheek Expressive power of touch and feeling	Ḷṁ ऌँ
Left Cheek Left Shringataka marma at center of left cheek Receptive power of touch and feeling	Ḹṁ ॡँ

Upper Lip Point above center of upper lip, Urdhvoshta Connected to Sarasvati nadi which ends at tip of tongue Tongue, speaking ability	Eṁ एँ
Lower Lip Point above center of lower lip, Adharoshta Connected to Sarasvati nadi which ends at tip of tongue Tongue, taste ability	Aiṁ ऐँ
Upper Teeth Point above center of upper teeth, Urdhva Dantapankti Prana in the mouth and face Speech, singing ability, expressive	Oṁ ओँ
Lower Teeth Point above center of lower teeth, Adho Dantapankti Prana in the mouth and face Speech, singing ability, receptive	Auṁ औँ
Upper Palate Point at upper back of throat Relates to the mind, the moon, emotions, resonance, responsiveness, stimulates flow of Soma	Aṁ अँ
Lower Palate Point at lower back of throat Sense of Self and self esteem, self-projection, solar energy	Aḥ अः

Mantras for the Right Arm Vyana Vayu, the expansive force among the five Pranas Yashasvati nadi which flows from heart and navel chakras to the right hand and right foot Power of action generally	
Right Shoulder Right base of arm, Dakshina Bahumula Right Kakshadhara marma Power of will, initial motivation	Kaṁ कँ
Right Elbow Right Kurpara marma Power of will, stronger energy	Khaṁ खँ
Right Wrist Right Manibandha marma Power of expression, initial motivation	Gaṁ गँ
Right Base of Fingers Right Hastanguli Mula Power of expression, stronger energy	Ghaṁ घँ
Right Fingertips Right Hastanguli Agra Point of connection to the cosmic Vyana Vayu Manual dexterity and articulation	Ṅaṁ ङँ

Mantras for the Left Arm Vyana Vayu, the expansive force among the five Pranas Hastijihva nadi which flows from heart and navel chakras to the left hand and left foot Power of reaction generally	
Left Shoulder Base of Left Shoulder, Vama Bahumula Left Kakshadhara marma Power of emotion, initial motivation	Caṁ चँ
Left Elbow Left Kurpara marma Power of emotion, stronger energy	Chaṁ छँ
Left Wrist Left Manibandha marma Power of reaction, initial motivation	Jaṁ जँ
Left Base of Fingers Vama Hastanguli Mula Power of reaction, stronger energy	Jhaṁ झँ
Left Fingertips Vama Hastanguli Agra Point of connection to the cosmic Vyana Vayu Manual artistry and grace	Ñaṁ ञँ

Mantras for the Right Leg Vyana Vayu, the expansive force, and Apana Vayu, the downward force among the five pranas Yashasvati nadi which flows from the heart and navel chakras to the right hand and right foot Power of support and movement generally	
Right Hip Dakshina Padamula Power of support, primary focus	Ṭaṁ टँ
Right Knee Right Januni marma Power of support, adaptation	Ṭhaṁ ठँ
Right Ankle Right Gulpha marma Power of movement, primary focus	Ḍaṁ डँ
Right Root of Toes Dakshina Padanguli Mula Power of movement, adaptation	Ḍhaṁ ढँ
Right Tips of Toes Dakshina Padanguli Agra Power of movement, articulation Point of connection to the cosmic Vyana Vayu and Apana Vayu	Ṇaṁ णँ

Mantras for the Left Leg Vyana Vayu, the expansive air among the five pranas Hastijihva nadi which flows from heart and navel chakras to the left hand and left foot Power of support and movement generally	
Left Hip Left Padamula Power of support, primary focus	Taṁ तँ
Left Knee Left Januni marma Power of support, adaptation	Thaṁ थँ
Left Ankle Left Gulpha marma Power of movement, primary focus	Daṁ दँ
Left Root of Toes Left Padanguli Mula Power of movement, adaptation	Dhaṁ धँ
Left Tip of Toes Left Padanguli Agra Power of movement, articulation Point of connection to the cosmic Vyana Vayu and Apana Vayu	Naṁ नँ

Mantras for the Abdominal Region[71] Samana Vayu, balancing force among the five Pranas and Apana Vayu or downward moving force among the five Pranas Power of digestion and elimination generally	
Right Side of Abdomen Dakshamsha Prana and solar energy right side of abdomen Liver, digestion of solid food	Paṁ पँ
Left Side of Abdomen Vamamsha Prana and lunar energy left side of abdomen Stomach, pancreas, absorption of water, liquid food and sugar	Phaṁ फँ
Lower Back Nabhi marma on back of body Prana of the back side of abdomen Vishvodhara nadi, which radiates out from the navel to the organs of the digestive system	Baṁ बँ
Navel Nabhi marma on front of body Prana of the front side of abdomen, central location of Samana Vayu Vishvodhara nadi, which radiates out from the navel to the organs of the digestive system Small intestine, seat of digestive fire	Bhaṁ भँ
Lower Abdomen Basti marma (bladder) Apana Vayu or downward moving air Kuhu nadi that runs from the sex chakra to the urinogenital organs Reproduction, support, emotion	Maṁ मँ

Mantras for the Upper Body, Chest and Bodily Tissues Mainly govern various aspects of heart function and energy flows from the heart	
Heart, Center of Chest Hridaya (Heart) marma Varuna Nadi which arises from the heart chakra and permeates the body Circulatory system, plasma (Rasa Dhatu) Air energies, control of all pranas	Yaṁ यँ
Right Side of Chest Solar energy of right side of chest, heart lungs Blood (Rakta Dhatu) Fire energies of heart and lungs	Raṁ रँ
Heart to Top of Palate or Lower Chest Muscles (Mamsa Dhatu) Earth energies, strength, Ojas	Laṁ लँ
Left Side of Chest Lunar energy of left side of chest, heart, lungs Body fat (Meda Dhatu) Water energies of heart and lungs	Vaṁ वँ
Heart to Right Hand Energy Flow Upper right side of heart Right Talahridaya marma in center of right palm Bone tissue (Asthi Dhatu) Outward movement of Vyana Vayu	Śaṁ शँ
Heart to Left Hand Energy Flow Upper left side of heart Left Talahridaya marma in center of left palm Nerve tissue and bone marrow (Majja Dhatu) Outward movement of Vyana Vayu	Ṣaṁ षँ
Heart to Right Foot Energy Flow Lower right side of heart Right foot Talahridaya marma in center of sole of foot Reproductive tissue (Shukra Dhatu) Downward movement of Vyana and Apana Vayus	Saṁ सँ
Heart to Left Foot Energy Flow Lower left side of heart Left foot Talahridaya marma in center of sole of left foot Downward movements of Vyana and Apana Vayus Atma or Soul	Haṁ हँ
Heart to Belly Energy Flow Bottom of heart Connection of circulation and digestion and their respective fires, as well as the lower chakras Paramatman or Higher Self	Laṁ[72] लँ
Heart to Top of Head Energy Flow Top of heart Connection of heart to brain and mind, higher chakras Sushumna nadi, upper portion Pranatman or Self of Prana	Kṣaṁ क्षँ

Chapter 12:

How to Use the Mantra Purusha

The Mantra Purusha has many important applications relative to meditation, Yoga therapy, and Ayurvedic medicine. Like the human body overall, it can serve as a blueprint for the forces of the greater universe. This chapter will explore a number of the most important usages.

Reciting the Alphabet through the Mantra Purusha

The simplest way to use the Mantra Purusha is to recite the entire Sanskrit alphabet starting with the letter-A at the top of the head, directing our prana and attention to each mantra location along the way. This serves as a complete mantric workout of the entire body and its pranic field. You can touch the respective bodily locations as well.

To Strengthen Particular Locations in the Body

Mantra Purusha sounds work on their respective organs and body parts. If we wish to strengthen any of these sites, we should repeat their respective mantras while focusing on bringing prana to the location.

We can use the mantra points on the head to improve their related functions through the mind and senses. We can use the Mantra points on the arms and legs to treat their respective joints. We can use the Mantra points on the abdomen and chest to strengthen the corresponding internal organs.

For example, the Mantra *Aṁ* can be repeated while focusing on the point at the top of the head in order to strengthen our primary prana, sense of Self and power of deeper awareness. The mantra *Iṁ* can be used to strengthen the eyes, the sense of sight and our power of perception, judgment and discrimination. The mantra *Uṁ* can be used to improve our inner and outer sense of hearing, receptivity and overall comprehension. We can use the long form of the vowels to target the left side of the body. We can also use them to address the powers of the mantra location overall because *the long forms of the vowels create stronger resonance.* For example, we can use the long vowel *Īṁ* to strengthen the sense of vision overall.

The mantra *Kaṁ* can be used to strengthen the right shoulder, arm, overall strength of the body and power of action. The mantra *Caṁ* can be used to strengthen the left shoulder, arm, overall responsiveness of the body and power of emotion. The same logic can be extended to all the bodily parts, organs and tissues represented by the Mantra Purusha sounds.

Mantra Purusha and Asana Practice

We can use Mantra Purusha mantras during asana practice to focus our attention on the particular joints or body parts that they indicate. One can use the Mantra Purusha sounds for the arms while extending the arms in order to increase the attention and pranic flow through the arms, for example.

- *Oṁ Kaṁ, Khaṁ, Gaṁ, Ghaṁ, Ṅaṁ* for the right arm to hands.
- *Oṁ Caṁ, Chaṁ, Jaṁ, Jhaṁ, Ñaṁ* for the left arm to hands.

Similarly, one can use the Mantra Purusha sounds for the legs while extending the legs or while holding a standing pose in order to increase the pranic flow through the legs.

- *Oṁ Ṭaṁ, Ṭhaṁ, Ḍaṁ, Ḍhaṁ, Ṇaṁ* for the right hip to the right foot.
- *Oṁ Taṁ, Thaṁ, Ḍaṁ, Dhaṁ, Naṁ* for the left hip to the left foot.

Another powerful method is to go through all the sixteen mantra points on the head while in a sitting pose, doing pranayama and meditation to clear the energy of the head one point at a time. One can press or touch these mantra locations during the process.

Oṁ Aṁ	Top of head	Oṁ Āṁ	Middle of forehead
Oṁ Iṁ	Right eye	Oṁ Īṁ	Left eye
Oṁ Uṁ	Right ear	Oṁ Ūṁ	Left ear
Oṁ Ṛṁ	Right nostril	Oṁ Ṝṁ	Left nostril
Oṁ Ḷṁ	Right cheek	Oṁ Ḹṁ	Left cheek
Oṁ Eṁ	Upper lip	Oṁ Aiṁ	Lower lip
Oṁ Oṁ	Upper teeth	Oṁ Auṁ	Lower teeth
Oṁ Aṁ	Upper palate	Oṁ Aḥ	Lower palate

Mantra Purusha and Pranayama

We can use the Mantra Purusha sounds to hold the prana at their respective locations. For example, one can repeat the mantra *Īṁ* along with the breath in order to bring the prana into the eyes. Or, one can repeat the mantra *Kaṁ* along with the breath, while focusing on the right shoulder, to bring more energy into that location.

The same principle can be extended to all Mantra Purusha sounds and their respective locations. In addition, we will examine mantra and pranayama in a separate chapter, and show how to use the sibilants and semivowels relative to the breath in order to modify its energies.

Mantra Purusha and Pratyahara

We can use the Mantra Purusha sounds to withdraw the mind and prana to the locations indicated by the sounds. *In fact, the recitation of the Mantra Purusha overall is mainly regarded as a pratyahara method.* It helps us draw our awareness and prana into the body and through these points into the chakras. It helps us withdraw from body consciousness and consecrate our body as a vehicle of Divine consciousness. To do this is a matter of releasing any tension that may have accumulated at any of the Mantra Purusha locations, which can be done on exhalation. By relaxing all these mantra points, we can relax the body, prana, senses and mind.

Mantra Purusha and Dharana

We can use the Mantra Purusha sounds to hold the mind at their respective locations. This requires that we have developed a power of attention already. If we have done this, the Mantra Purusha sounds can be very important dharana locations. Holding our attention will stabilize the prana at the locations we focus on. This can be more easily done if we use the gaze to direct our attention, directing the vision to these points inwardly (not necessarily looking at them outwardly!).

For example, one can use the sound *Aṁ* to hold one's attention at the top of the head, to link and stabilize our body and awareness in the Absolute. Or one can hold the attention at any point that one wants to improve, like using a dharana of the mantra *Kaṁ* to strengthen the right shoulder. Dharana of any Mantra Purusha point will bring healing energy to that location. For example, Dharana of the ears along with the mantra *Ūṁ* will help heal the ears and open up higher powers of hearing. Pranayama, pratyahara and dharana of these mantra points can go together for a stronger effect.

Mantra Purusha with *Namaḥ*, and *Svāhā*

We can add other mantras to the Mantra Purusha sounds to give them more power or to vary their effects. We can chant the Mantra Purusha mantras after *Oṁ* in order to clear and energize them. After the Mantra Purusha mantras, we can chant *Namaḥ*, the mantra of consecration, in order to stabilize their energy or *Svāhā*, the mantra of energization, in order to stimulate it further. Examples:

- *Oṁ Aṁ Namaḥ*, to stabilize the energy at the top of the head.
- *Oṁ Aṁ Svāhā*, to increase the energy at the top of the head.
- *Oṁ Īṁ Namaḥ* to stabilize the energy in the eyes.
- *Oṁ Īṁ Svāhā*, to stimulate the energy in the eyes.

With Shakti Mantras

We can combine the Mantra Purusha sounds with Shakti mantras to bring about different effects at particular locations in the body and brain. *This is probably the most important approach to use.*

One method is to use a single Shakti mantra while reciting the entire Mantra Purusha, focusing on the respective parts of the body. This allows us to bring the power of the Shakti mantra and its specific energies to the entire body and pranic field. Note the following example:

- *Hrīṁ Aṁ* (top of head), *Hrīṁ Āṁ* (front of head), *Hrīṁ Iṁ* (right eye), *Hrīm Īṁ* (left eye), *Hrīṁ Uṁ* (right ear), *Hrīṁ Ūṁ* (left ear), *Hrīṁ Ṛṁ* (right nostril), *Hrīṁ Ṝṁ* (left nostril), *Hrīṁ Ḷṁ* (right cheek), *Hrīṁ Ḹṁ* (left cheek), *Hrīṁ Eṁ* (upper lip), *Hrīṁ Aiṁ* (lower lip), *Hrīṁ Oṁ* (upper teeth), *Hrīṁ Auṁ* (lower teeth), *Hrīṁ Aṁ*, (upper palate) *Hrīṁ Aḥ* (lower palate)

- *Hrīṁ Kaṁ* (right shoulder), *Hrīṁ Khaṁ* (right elbow), *Hrīṁ Gaṁ* (right wrist), *Hrīṁ Ghaṁ* (right base of fingers), *Hrīṁ Ṅaṁ* (right fingertips)

- *Hrīṁ Caṁ* (left shoulder), *Hrīṁ Chaṁ* (left elbow), *Hrīṁ Jaṁ* (left wrist), *Hrīṁ Jhaṁ* (left base of fingers), *Hrīṁ Ñaṁ* (left fingertips)

- *Hrīṁ Ṭaṁ* (right leg), *Hrīṁ Ṭhaṁ* (right knee), *Hrīṁ Ḍaṁ* (right ankle),

Hrīṁ Dḥaṁ (right base of toes), *Hrīṁ Ṇaṁ* (right tips of toes)

- *Hrīṁ Taṁ* (left leg), *Hrīṁ Thaṁ* (left knee), *Hrīṁ Daṁ* (left ankle), *Hrīṁ Dhaṁ* (left base of toes), *Hrīṁ Naṁ* (left tip of toes)

- *Hrīṁ Paṁ* (right abdomen), *Hrīṁ Phaṁ* (left abdomen), *Hrīṁ Baṁ* (lower back), *Hrīṁ Bhaṁ* (navel), *Hrīṁ Maṁ* (lower abdomen)

- *Hrīṁ Yaṁ* (plasma), *Hrīṁ Raṁ* (blood), *Hrīṁ Laṁ* (muscle), *Hrīṁ Vaṁ* (fat), *Hrīṁ Śaṁ* (bone), *Hrīṁ Ṣam* (nerve), *Hrīṁ Saṁ* (reproductive), *Hrīṁ Haṁ* (prana), *Hrīṁ Kṣaṁ* (mind)

In this practice, one brings the power of *Hrīṁ*, the Divine light and prana of the heart, to the entire body, filling the body with light. It is also possible to repeat each mantra more than once, for example, three times: *Hrīṁ Aṁ, Hrīṁ Aṁ, Hrīṁ Aṁ; Hrīṁ Āṁ, Hrīṁ Āṁ, Hrīṁ Āṁ; Hrīṁ Iṁ, Hrīṁ Iṁ, Hrīṁ Iṁ,* and so on through the entire alphabet and Mantra Purusha. This creates a stronger practice.

Another method is to focus on a single Shakti mantra relative to a particular point in the body and its Mantra Purusha sound. This provides many options to explore. A few examples:

- *Hrīṁ Aṁ* – to stimulate the flow of prana at the top of the head

- *Hrīṁ Yaṁ* - to stimulate the flow of prana to the heart

- *Klīṁ Yaṁ* – to promote contentment and happiness, the inner energy of water and Ojas, in the heart

- *Śrīṁ Aṁ* – to cool and nurture the energy of consciousness at the top of the head.

- *Krīṁ Kaṁ* – to stimulate the energy, work capacity and pranic flow at in the right arm.

- *Hūṁ Bhaṁ* – to increase the energy of fire and stimulate the region of the navel.

- *Strīṁ Maṁ* - to bring the feminine energy to the lower abdomen.

Mantra Purusha Kavacha

A Kavacha is a special protective field created by the mantra, of which there is a great variety in yogic texts. The most common Shakti mantra for this purpose is *Hūṁ* because it reflects the power of protection and wards off negativity.

One can use the *Hūṁ* mantra with each letter of the Mantra Purusha in order to create a protective shield around the body, strengthen the immune system and ward off negative emotions. This Mantra Purusha Kavacha is one of the longest and most powerful. For this, one focuses the mind or touches the particular bodily part while reciting the mantra.

Oṁ Aṁ Hūṁ, Oṁ Āṁ Hūṁ, Oṁ Iṁ Hūṁ, Oṁ Īṁ Hūṁ and so on through the alphabet.

Combinations of Shakti Mantras with the Mantra Purusha

Combinations of Shakti mantras bring about yet more powerful effects to the Mantra Purusha. These are a more complex and deeper level of practice. Examples:

- *Hrīṁ Śrīṁ Klīṁ Aṁ Aṁ Aṁ Aṁ* – to increase the flow of grace, contentment and healing power at the top of the head.
- *Hrīṁ Krīṁ Hūṁ Aṁ Aṁ Aṁ Aṁ* – for purification, cleansing, heating and protection at the top of the head.

The Mantra Purusha sounds for the tissues, elements and chakras are particularly useful and can be modified in the same ways. Note the following examples:

- *Oṁ Yaṁ Śrīṁ Namaḥ* - to bring the lunar, water or Kapha energy into the plasma and heart chakra.
- *Oṁ Yaṁ Krīṁ Namaḥ* - to stimulate the flow of prana through the plasma and the heart chakra.
- *Oṁ Yaṁ Hūṁ Namaḥ* - to stimulate heat, fire and the Agni of the plasma and to promote sweating.
- *Oṁ Yaṁ Hrīṁ Namaḥ* – to stimulate the circulation from the heart through the plasma and lymphatic system.

The Mantra Purusha with Your Primary Mantra

Whatever your primary or personal mantra may be, you can recite it relative to the Mantra Purusha. For example, if *Namaḥ Śivāya* is your main mantra, you can chant it with every letter of the alphabet and location of the Mantra Purusha:

Oṁ Aṁ Namaḥ Śivāya, Oṁ Āṁ Namaḥ Śivāya, Oṁ Iṁ Namaḥ Śivāya, Oṁ Īṁ Namaḥ Śivāya, and so on throughout the Sanskrit alphabet and the Mantra Purusha locations.

In this way, you can use the power of your personal mantra to consecrate your entire being. Or you can direct your primary mantra specifically to certain locations in the body that you want to emphasize or that may be sites of pain or disease.

The recitation of the alphabet is most commonly connected with the deities Ganesha, Sarasvati and Matangi, the Tantric form of Sarasvati, who is sometimes regarded as a female counterpart of Ganesha. For example, relative to Ganesha, one can chant his bija *Gaṁ* and his name relative to each letter and its Mantra Purusha correspondences.

Gaṁ Aṁ Gaṇeśāya Namaḥ, Gaṁ Āṁ Gaṇeśāya Namaḥ, Gaṁ Iṁ Gaṇeśāya Namaḥ, and so on throughout the alphabet.

This 'Ganesha Mantra Purusha' will help remove obstacles and obstructions, including physical and psychological diseases in every part of the body and mind. It can cause Ganesha to appear in the form of your own body!

Mantra Nyasa – The Mantra Purusha as a Consecration of the Entire Body

Nyasa is a common practice in Hindu devotional rituals. Nyasa mainly consists of mantras, but rituals, gestures and mudras are often combined with them. Nyasa can also be a kind of Prana-pratishta or 'installing the prana' or spirit of the deity into the body. Through it, we make the prana of the deity our own prana. Nyasas relate mainly to Bhakti Yoga, in which we consecrate ourselves to a particular deity.

The Mantra Purusha in Yoga is most commonly used as a Nyasa, which is a means of consecrating the body to the deity or the higher Self. In this procedure, one recites the Mantra Purusha while dedicating each corresponding part of the body to the deity or the higher Self. It is a process of spiritualizing one's body and taking us beyond body consciousness.

The Mantra Purusha is the main form of Nyasa for the entire body. It is also called the Matrika Nyasa or the consecration of the letters of the alphabet. There are shorter Nyasas for only the five fingers or the six main parts of the body, as well as Nyasas for the planets, directions, Nakshatras, and other factors that are performed regularly as part of Hindu pujas. Even if we are using the Mantra Purusha for health purposes, we should remember its sacred nature as a Nyasa.

To get these mantras to really work requires that we have developed concentration of mind and prana. Just knowing the right mantras for particular body parts is not itself enough. However, we can also use these mantras to help develop such concentration.

Part III

Special Methods of Mantra Yoga and Mantra Therapy

Chapter 13:

Mantra and Pranayama:

The Yoga of the Sun and the Moon

Pranayama and mantra naturally go together and work best in combination. Using a mantra along with pranayama unites the mind and prana, drawing our attention and awareness into the breathing process. It can turn pranayama into meditation, as well as bring energy, vitality and wakefulness into the repetition of the mantra. Uniting prana, our power of action, with the mind, our power of knowledge, integrates us back into the source of our being. Prana gives Shakti to the mantra and makes it alive and vibrating within our entire body.

The sound of the breath is our most natural and constant outer mantra, we could say. The sound of our heart beat, which is connected to the sound of the breath, is our most natural internal mantra. An important goal of mantra practice is to get one's mantra to resonate with the breath, so it is naturally repeated, strengthened and deepened along with every breath that we take – and then to get it to resonate with every heart beat, so that our heart beat is the beat of the mantra.

There are many ways of using mantra with the breath. The following chapter emphasizes repeating bija mantras along with the breath, though longer mantras can be used as well. Bija mantras have the greatest affinity with the breath and are said to be "prana predominant"; whereas longer mantras are "meaning predominant" and require more contemplation in their usage.

We will examine alternate nostril breathing and breathing through both nostrils along with the use of bija mantras. We will focus on the sibilants (s and h-sounds), semi-vowels (ya, ra, la, va) and Shakti bijas to enhance and transform the practice of pranayama.

More specifically, we will explore the balancing of solar and lunar, male and female, Shiva and Shakti energies known as the "Yoga of the Sun and the Moon". This balancing of solar and lunar energies within us is the basis of traditional Hatha Yoga in which "*Ha*" means the Sun and "*Ṭha*" means the Moon. Traditional Hatha Yoga is the 'Yoga of the Sun and the Moon', using mantra and pranayama to balance the two forces and bring about transformation. It is not an asana centered practice such as the term is used for today.[73] As such, traditional Hatha Yoga is the foundation of deeper Tantric Yoga practices.

Using Mantras to Count the Breath

Regardless of the type of pranayama that one follows, mantras repeated mentally can be used for counting the breath. Bija mantras like *Oṁ* or *Hrīṁ* can be repeated a certain number of times along with the breathing process, like 8 repetitions on inhalation, 4 on retention or 8 on exhalation, or multiples thereof. Longer mantras can be used in the same way. For example, the Gayatri mantra of 24 syllables can be repeated with the first 8 syllables on inhalation, the second 8 syllables on retention and the third 8 upon exhalation.

It is better to use mantras to count the breath rather than to use numbers as some groups do. Numbers lack the resonance of mantras and can put the mind into a dull or mechanical state. Repetition of mantras increases our mental energy while that of numbers tends to reduce it. The mantra can be energized with the power of devotion or knowledge, which a number cannot.

Aham Pranayama: the Sound of the Self

In Tantric philosophy, inhalation as an open sound relates to the vowels, specifically to the vowel-A, the first and most important of the Sanskrit vowels. Exhalation as a closing sound relates to the consonants, semivowels and sibilants, specifically to the letter-Ha, which is the last of the Sanskrit letters and governs prana as a whole. Extending this principle, the sound "*A*" relates to inhalation, while the sound "*Ha*" relates to exhalation. Try this for yourself. Mentally repeat the sound "*A*" on inhalation and "*Ha*" on exhalation and feel the energies involved.[74] This means that the entire Sanskrit alphabet is inherent in your breath.

The word *Ahaṁ* means "*I*" in Sanskrit. Repeating the *Ahaṁ* mantra along with the breath (A for inhalation and Ha for exhalation), we naturally attune ourselves to the ultimate sound of the breath which is "*I-I*", meaning "I am I "or "I am the Self of all beings." This utterance of *Ahaṁ* or I is the original and highest level of speech.[75] All words, all thoughts and the breath itself naturally begin with the sense of I. The sense of Self, which is the root of consciousness, comes first, then the mind comes into being and through it we can see the outer world.

Ahaṁ is reflected on all levels of our nature. Speech is *Ahaṁ*, with A as the first letter and *Ha* the last letter of the Sanskrit alphabet. Breath is *Ahaṁ*, with A as inhalation and Ha as exhalation. Thought is *Ahaṁ*. The I-thought or *Ahaṁ* is the root of all thoughts. The I-thought reflects the original prana that rises from the heart, of which it is a manifestation. Our true Self consists of the nature of *Ahaṁ* beyond speech, breath and mind. Through the *Ahaṁ* mantra, everything is comprehended.

Ahaṁkara or the "I process" is the Sanskrit word for ego, as opposed to the Self which is *Ahaṁsvarūpa* or the Self-nature. *Ahaṁkara* at a cosmic level is the main power of external creation through which the mind, five sense organs, five motor organs and five sense qualities (tanmatras) are differentiated. The *Ahaṁkara Tattva* or cosmic principle in Yoga philosophy is defined in terms of the Sanskrit alphabet.[76] Division arises through sound which proceeds through the alphabet. This means that through reciting the Sanskrit alphabet, or just repeating the *Ahaṁ* mantra, and turning within, one can integrate all the cosmic principles as well as all aspects of mind, senses and pranas and return to pure unity.

Practice the *Ahaṁ* mantra along with a silent meditation on pure being or pure consciousness, the eternal presence. Contact the current of the Self as the I-thought, the origin of breath and speech in the heart. "*Ahaṁ* Mantra Meditation" is one of the most direct means of Self-realization.[77] It keeps the energy of the breath in the hridaya or spiritual heart that encompasses all that is.

Balancing Solar and Lunar Energies on the Right and Left Sides of the Body

The basic ignorance and suffering inherent in human life occurs owing to the fact that our minds and prana are caught in dualistic and contrary forces. These dualities consist of the various attractions and repulsions, likes and dislikes, desires and fears that keep us disturbed and agitated. Yoga requires balancing these dualistic forces, to lead us to a state of unity where there is lasting peace within us.

This duality of thought and emotion is reflected in the body as a division of solar and lunar energies, the right Pingala and left Ida nadis or subtle channels, fire and water, Prana and Apana (ingoing and outgoing aspects of prana), and Pitta and Kapha doshas, the biological fire and water humors in Ayurveda.

- The right solar or Pingala nadi relates to the right nostril and right side of the body, and is accordingly warming, drying, stimulating and detoxifying in its effects.
- The left, lunar or Ida nadi relates to the left nostril and the left side of the body and is accordingly cooling, moistening, calming, nourishing and tonifying in its action.

In addition, in Tantric Yoga, lunar energy generally relates to inhalation, which has a similar nourishing effect as the Ida nadi, particularly for the sense organs that like inhalation serve to take in prana. Solar energy relates to exhalation, which has a similar expressive force as the Pingala nadi, particularly for the motor organs that like exhalation consist primarily of pranic discharges.[78] But this is a matter of degree. There are solar types of inhalation and lunar types of exhalation, among the many different types of Tantric Yoga pranayamas.[79]

Our energies fluctuate between these dualistic forces, though one side usually predominates overall. Pitta dosha people, those with a fiery temperament in Ayurvedic thought, will have the breath more commonly flowing through the right nostril. Kapha dosha people, those of a watery temperament, will find the breath to flow more through the left nostril. Vata dosha types, those with airy temperaments, will more commonly find their breath fluctuating back and forth between the right and left nostrils.

Pranayama can be used to balance the two forces, particularly alternate nostril breathing called Nadi Shodhana in Sanskrit or "cleansing the channels". The solar and lunar divisions of the breath can be connected with bija mantras of a solar or lunar nature for a greater effect.

Lunar	Solar
Left side of body	Right side of body
Ida nadi	Pingala Nadi
Absorbing	Discharging
Tonifying	Reducing
Saḥ or So	Haṁ
Śrīṁ, mantra of the Moon	Hrīṁ, mantra of the Sun
Vaṁ, mantra of water	Raṁ, mantra of fire
Shakti	Shiva

So'haṁ Pranayama

So'haṁ Pranayama is probably the most common form of Mantra Pranayama. It consists of letting the sound So resound naturally on inhalation and the sound *Haṁ* on exhalation, following them in the sound of the breath itself. Adding the vowel-O, whose energy is opening and expansive, to the consonant-Sa, which draws energy inward, allows the inhalation to be wide and expansive. So inhalation increases the lunar nurturing energy of the breath. Haṁ as exhalation sends energy outward into the realm of action and increases the solar stimulating aspect of the breath. In the most basic form of *So'haṁ* Pranayama, one allows the breath to naturally deepen, while mentally repeating these mantras and listening to them in the sound of the breath.

The mantra *So'haṁ* is a great statement of spiritual knowledge. So or Sa means "He" as the higher Self, the Atman. *Haṁ* is short for *Ahaṁ* meaning "I", myself. This natural sound then is saying that" He (the higher Self) am I" or "I am God or pure consciousness". In this way, our breath becomes our inner guide and guru, ever teaching us our oneness with all. Many Yogis have gained Self-realization through the *So'haṁ* mantra alone. One can also use the *So'haṁ* mantra to draw the prana up the chakras one by one, chanting the mantra at each chakra step by step from the root chakra to the crown chakra.[80]

Haṁsaḥ Pranayama

Vedic thought contains many wonderful and cryptic symbols. One of the most poignant and beautiful is the image of the hamsa, which outwardly means a swan. The hamsa symbolizes the bird of the soul. It is said to be golden in color and to reside in the heart. It is identified with the Sun, which is a symbol of both the soul (Atman) and prana. This bird of the soul rests upon the breath. Its two wings are exhalation and inhalation, Ha and Sa.

The *Upanishads* state, "With the sound Ha, one moves outward. With Sa, one moves in again. The individual soul repeats the mantra *Haṁsaḥ, Haṁsaḥ,* all the time, 21,600 times in the course of the day.[81] This is called the spontaneous Gayatri (ajapa Gayatri), which ever grants liberation to the Yogis."[82]

We can look at the *Haṁsaḥ* mantra as *So'haṁ* in another form, with Ha as exhalation and Sa as inhalation. However, some Yogis reverse the natural order of *So'haṁ* and use Ha for inhalation and Sa for exhalation. While *So-haṁ* for inhalation and exhalation naturally deepens the breath, *Haṁ-saḥ* for inhalation and exhalation adds additional fire to the breath.

Haṁsaḥ So'haṁ Pranayama

We can combine these two prana mantras together as *Haṁsaḥ So'haṁ*. This helps balance the solar and lunar energies in the body and mind. It also affirms the unity of the individual soul with the supreme Self.

- The *So'haṁ* mantra works better with alternate nostril breathing, inhaling with the left nostril and exhaling with the right.
- *Haṁsaḥ* works better with inhaling with the right nostril and exhaling with the left.

In this practice, one breathes in through the left nostril with the mantra-So, and then out through the right nostril with the *mantra-Haṁ*. Then one breathes in through the right nostril with the *mantra-Haṁ* and out through the left nostril with the *mantra-Saḥ*. One can also use the mantra So to take the lunar energy up the spine on inhalation, and *Haṁ* to bring the solar energy down the spine on exhalation, followed by using the mantra *Haṁ* to take the solar energy up the spine on inhalation and *Saḥ* to take the lunar energy down the spine on exhalation. The *Haṁsaḥ So'haṁ* mantra has many other applications in deeper Yoga practices, several of which will be discussed later in the book.

Hrīṁ and *Śrīṁ* in Pranayama

Hrīṁ and *Śrīṁ* are prime Shakti mantras with important correlations to the breathing process and its solar and lunar aspects. *Hrīṁ* is the bija mantra of the Sun at an astrological level. *Śrīṁ* is the bija mantra of the Moon. The two sounds relate to the heart in terms of function (*Hrīṁ*) and substance (*Śrīṁ*), thought (*Hrīṁ*) and feeling (*Śrīṁ*). They also relate to the solar and lunar nadis (Ida and Pingala, the solar and lunar sides of the body, and the right and left eyes. Instead of using the sounds Sa and Ha, one can use the mantras *Śrīṁ* and *Hrīṁ* for a similar effect. This practice connects the energy of the breath with that of the heart.

Mantras for the Five Elements and Pranayama

Another important Mantra Pranayama method is to use the seed mantras of the five elements (la, va, ra, ya, ha). While the sibilants work more on the energy of the breath, the semi-vowels affect more the circulation of the blood that the breath sets in motion. The mantras *Laṁ* for earth, *Vaṁ* for water, *Raṁ* for fire, *Yaṁ* for air and *Haṁ* for ether, can be used along with alternate nostril breathing or with both nostril breathing. They can be employed to balance solar and lunar energies or for other purposes.

- *Haṁ* as the bija mantra of the ether element will tend to increase the ether energy through any nadi, chakra or marma that it is associated with, bringing in its inherent qualities of space, openness, receptivity and release.
- *Yaṁ* as the bija mantra of the air element will tend to increase the air energy through any nadi, chakra or marma it is associated with, bringing in its inherent qualities of stimulation, movement, change and increase of speed.
- *Raṁ* as the bija mantra for the fire element will tend to increase the energy of fire through any nadi, chakra, or marma it is associated with, bringing in its inherent qualities of heat, light and color.
- *Vaṁ* as the bija mantra for the water element will tend to increase the energy of water through any nadi, chakra or marma it is associated with, bringing in its inherent qualities of coolness, moistness, lubrication and nourishment.
- *Laṁ* as the bija mantra of the earth element will tend to increase the earth energy through any nadi, chakra or marma it is associated with, bringing in its inherent qualities of strength, stability, resistance and support.

Of these five element mantras, *Yaṁ* as the bija mantra for the air element from which prana arises, is probably most important. It aids in the flow of prana or air in any of the nadis or channel systems. Overall, it has a drying, cooling and lightening effect, reflecting the qualities of the air element. Because of the connection between prana and air, the air-mantra *Yaṁ* is widely used with pranayama to get the prana to move, as well as to dry up any blockages in the nadis. Because of the effect of wind to increase fire, *Yaṁ* can be combined with the mantra *Raṁ* to increase the energy of fire.

Raṁ and *Vaṁ*, the Bijas of Fire and Water for Balancing Solar and Lunar Energies

Raṁ is the bija mantra for the right side of the body, which has a fiery or solar nature. *Vaṁ* is the bija mantra for the left side of the body, which has a watery and lunar nature. Mentally repeating the mantra *Raṁ* while breathing through the right nostril will increase the fiery nature of the breath; mentally repeating the mantra Vaṁ while breathing through the left nostril will increase its watery effects. These mantras help increase the energies of the respective right and left, solar and lunar nadis.

Using the corresponding five element mantras with the appropriate nostril, like the mantra *Raṁ* with the solar nostril is a kind of "increasing or parallel therapy". One can also employ a "decreasing or opposite therapy", like using the mantra *Raṁ*, the fire mantra, with the lunar nostril that has a watery energy.

If we repeat the mantra *Raṁ* while breathing through the left nostril, which has a watery nature, we will tend to dry it out. This can be helpful when there is too much Kapha or water, or too much cold in the body, or when the left nostril is inhibited in its flow. Similarly, if we repeat the mantra *Vaṁ* while breathing through the right nostril we will tend to moisten it. This can be helpful when there is too much Pitta or fire in the body, or too much heat in the body or the right nostril is inhibited in its flow.

Similar strategies can be employed with the seed mantras of the other elements. If we repeat the mantra of the earth element *Laṁ* while breathing through either nostril, it will tend to slow down, stabilize, block or restrict the flow through the nostril by bringing the energy of earth into the flow. This can be good when the flow is too open or too rapid. If we repeat the mantra of the ether element *Haṁ* while breathing through either nostril, it will open and increase the flow. This can be good when the flow is closed or blocked.

Five Element Mantras with Both Nostril Breathing

We can also use the bija mantras for the five elements with both nostril breathing in order to increase the elements working during inhalation and exhalation. If your inhalation is heavy and restricted, for example, you can repeat the air mantra *Yaṁ* or the ether mantra *Haṁ* to open it up. If your breathing overall is too fast and ungrounded, you can repeat the earth mantra *Laṁ* to slow down and stabilize it. If your breath is cold or damp, you can repeat the fire mantra *Raṁ* to warm it up. If it is too hot or dry, you can repeat the water mantra *Vaṁ* to cool and moisten it.

You can also direct the breath up or down the spine with the mantras of the respective elements that you wish to increase, for example, drawing the fire energy up the spine with *Raṁ* and the water energy down the spine with *Vaṁ*. It is possible to balance the five elements through the breath with the help of these five element mantras. Such strategies will vary according to the condition of the individual and their pranic flows.

Five Element Mantras, Pranayama and the Chakras

The five element mantras can be used to direct energy to the respective chakras that they rule over. One can repeat the seed mantra of the chakra while holding the gaze and awareness at the site, breathing in and out. This grants power over the element and a mastery of the faculties and qualities associated with it. For example, one can repeat the mantra *Laṁ* while meditating on the root or earth chakra, allowing the breath to naturally deepen. This process should be done for some time, generally at least twenty four minutes per chakra. In this way, one can gain power over the earth element and chakra, granting strength, stability, groundedness and patience to one's being.

You can similarly repeat the mantra *Vaṁ* along with the breath, while concentrating on the sex or water chakra to develop the energy there, and so on through the other chakras with their respective seed mantras. For the third eye, you can use the bija mantra *Kṣaṁ*, the seed sound of the mind. For the crown chakra, you can use the mantra *Oṁ* or *Aṁ*. This process is called "Chakra Mantra Dharana" or concentrating on the mantra at the chakra.

Balancing Fire and Water Energies Above and below with Mantra and Pranayama

Agni and Soma in Tantra

Tantric Yoga emphasizes balancing Agni and Soma or fire and water, just as we find in the Vedas and in Ayurvedic medicine. In Tantric Yoga, Agni as the serpent fire relates the Kundalini force that dwells in the lower three chakras,[83] particularly the root chakra. Soma is the complementary nectar or amrit that dwells in the higher three chakras,[84] particularly the crown chakra, which is often referred to as the Soma. The goal of Tantric Yoga is to allow the Agni to ascend as the Kundalini fire and the Soma to descend as the complementary nectar or Divine grace, which allows for the full expansion of our inner being. Mantra is a key component and prime catalyst of this process.

We have discussed the importance of balancing the energies on the right and left sides of the body. Yet besides this, one must also strengthen the water and fire energies or Soma and Agni forces above and below in the body. This usually follows from balancing the energies on the right and left sides. Besides their general correlations with the three lower and three higher chakras, Agni and Soma have specific locations in the physical body that can be used to control their energies.

- The navel is the place of solar energy below in the body, preserved in the idea of the solar plexus and the navel or fire chakra.
- The soft palate of the mouth is the place of the lunar energy above in the body, reflecting the mind, which has a lunar character.

In Ayurveda, the belly is the location of the Jatharagni or "digestive fire", the main form of fire governing the physical body and its metabolic processes. It is also the location of Pachaka Pitta, the form of Pitta or fiery energy that governs digestion and supports the Jatharagni. Balancing the Jatharagni or digestive fire is the basis of physical health and is necessary for any dietary or herbal therapy to really work. Yoga asanas aim at balancing the Jatharagni as a key goal of practice.

The brain is the location of Tarpaka Kapha, the form of Kapha giving contentment and lubricating the brain and nervous system. Maintaining its proper flow is the basis of psychological and emotional health and well-being. The brain has the capacity to produce special secretions that promote calm and contentment and which allay pain, anxiety and fear. Modern medicine has various names for these like endorphins and has developed special drugs to increase them. In yogic parlance, these are our inner 'somas" or nectars (amrit) that can draw us into deeper states of meditation.

Yoga in the higher sense is all about developing the Soma within our minds. This Soma not only gives outer well-being but promotes inner happiness and peace leading to samadhi or the unitary state of mind and heart. Mantra, pranayama and meditation are among the main means of increasing it. Through mantra and pranayama, we can change our brain chemistry, promoting contentment, happiness and even bliss.

The key to physical health is to maintain a strong digestive fire energy in the navel below to protect the body. The key to psychological health is to maintain a strong lunar nectar in the head above to protect the mind. This is one of the keys to Ayurvedic medicine for both purification and rejuvenation. If the fire energy moves upwards adversely, it will burn up the lunar energy that is the basis of longevity, and harm our vitality. This is also one of the secrets of traditional Hatha Yoga. One must protect the Soma or the Moon above even when developing the Agni or fire below. Through such practices, great Yogis could prolong their life spans, promote rejuvenation and gain higher states of consciousness. Without developing the higher Soma, trying to arouse the Kundalini below can burn up the nervous system.

Mantra is one of the best means of balancing the lower fire and upper lunar forces of the navel and the head, particularly when combined with pranayama.[85] This also serves to balance Pitta and Kapha, the biological fire and water energies, which in turn aids in stabilizing of Vata dosha, the underlying force of air and prana, and the most important dosha clinically.

Balancing Solar and Lunar Energies and the Kundalini

According to a yogic understanding, the prana or vital energy does not normally flow through the Sushumna or central channel unless the solar and lunar energies are first balanced. Without first creating this balance, the chakras do not receive any direct prana or energization. The Kundalini Shakti remains asleep at the base of the spine and the chakras are not activated at a deep level. We can compare this to the state of an electrical system which is limited to a small battery, which does not have enough power to run much by way of equipment, whereas when the Kundalini Shakti is awakened, it is like connecting to a power grid that can run anything.

The prana ordinarily flows through the right and left, solar and lunar, the Ida and the Pingala nadis, shifting back and forth. The chakras only receive the limited prana conveyed by these two nadis. In the process, a small amount of nectar is conveyed by the lunar nadi to the Kundalini in the root chakra, which feeds and sustains the Kundalini so that it can uphold our regular physiological and psychological processes, but leaving it overall dormant.

This means that unless one first balances the solar and lunar nadis, any deeper work on the chakras will likely remain ineffective. Any talk of opening or awakening the chakras without first balancing these two forces, remains largely speculative.

To awaken the Kundalini and energize the chakras, one should do Yoga practices first that aim at stopping the flow of nectar through lunar or Ida nadi. Once that occurs, deprived of its nourishment, the Kundalini is forced to seek its nourishment by ascending through the central channel of the Sushumna to the ocean of nectar or Soma in the crown chakra, opening the chakras along the way.[86]

The Breath of the Digestive Fire for the Body

To accomplish this drying up of the Ida nadi, a special practice of alternate nostril breathing is used relative to the fire below. This procedure may be repeated for some period of time until a significant amount of purification occurs.

- First, one inhales through the left or lunar nostril along with the air mantra *Yaṁ*, repeating the mantra as many times as comfortable, drawing its energy into the navel.
- Second, one holds the breath along with the Shakti fire mantra *Hūṁ*, repeating the mantra as many times as comfortable, stimulating the fire in the navel to burn up any impurities in the abdomen and dry up the lower chakras.
- Third, one exhales through the right nostril along with the air mantra *Raṁ*, repeating the mantra as many times as comfortable, letting the impurities disperse.
- Then one reverses the process, repeating the fire mantra *Raṁ* along with inhalation through the right nostril, the Shakti fire mantra *Hūṁ* upon retention, and the air mantra *Yaṁ* along with exhalation through the left nostril.

Traditionally, inhalation is recommended for 16 counts, retention for 64 counts and exhalation for 32 counts. That requires very strong lungs and a good deal of previous pranayama practice to be able to do, which is quite rare. Shorter ratios should be used when the lungs are weaker. Even rations of 4/4/4 should be used to begin with, increasing the duration as the power of the breath increases over time. One should seek to increase the power of Prana naturally through slow, steady practice for the best results.

In this process sometimes a "dark man of sin" is imagined in the navel or to the left of the abdomen, symbolizing the ego, which is burned up or purified. Or from the standpoint of Ayurvedic healing, one can visualize the Ama or toxins in the body being burned up. It is important to hold the gaze and direct one's eyes inwardly to the navel center during this process, as the gaze aids in kindling the fire. This method arouses the Kundalini Shakti, which is connected to the digestive fire.[87]

The Breath of Soma for the Mind

Besides the need to increase the fire below is a complimentary need to increase the water or nectar above. Normally our brains and minds are overheated and over stimulated, which results in the depletion of the mind's nourishing lunar energy. This leads to stress, anxiety, agitation, fear and anger. Besides consolidating the fire energy below for purification purposes, one needs to consolidate the lunar energy above for revitalization.

- First, one inhales through the left or lunar nostril with the water mantra *Vaṁ*, repeating the mantra as many times as can be done comfortably, drawing the energy up into the head and the place of the Moon in the soft palate of the mouth.
- Second, one holds the breath with the Shakti lunar mantra *Śrīṁ*, repeating the mantra as often as can be done comfortably, forming a spiritual body or body of

nectar in the head.

• Third, one exhales through the right nostril with the earth mantra *Laṁ*, repeating the mantra as often as can be done comfortably, consolidating the spiritual body or body of nectar in the head.

• Then one reverses the process, repeating the earth mantra *Laṁ* along with inhalation through the right nostril, the Shakti lunar mantra *Śrīṁ* upon retention, and the water mantra *Vaṁ* along with exhalation through the left nostril.

One should hold one's gaze at the soft palate of the mouth, the upper back of the throat opposite the third eye during this practice. The procedure should continue until a significant amount of inner calm and well-being is created. Through this practice, one consolidates the Soma or nectar in the head so that it can balance the ascending Kundalini fire.

Note that these are basic versions of Agni and Soma mantra pranayamas. There are variations on how they can be done. Mantras for the other elements may be used as well as other Shakti mantras, depending upon the level of the individual practitioner.[88] By performing both practices, one strengthens the digestive fire below and the mental calm and coolness above. One burns up toxins in the body and spiritualizes the mind.

Matangi, Goddess of All the Powers of Sound

Chapter 14:

Tantra, Mantra, Chakras and Kundalini

Traditional Tantric Yoga consists of the use of mantras, deities, rituals, and meditation for achieving all the goals of life, particularly the ultimate goal of liberation. Tantra recognizes that we live in a universe full of Divine powers that we can communicate with in order to improve our lives. While these forces are present for everyone, only those who know how to contact their energies can fully benefit by them. Tantra teaches us this art of cosmic communication through the language of mantra.

Mantra is the central pillar of traditional Tantric Yoga. The mantra represents the "sound form" of the deity that is the key to the deity's energy and its grace. The mantra is allied to the yantra or "energy form" of the deity, the geometrical pattern that sets its energy in motion. The chakras themselves are internal yantras or energy forms. The term Tantra itself refers to the "teaching" about the deity and its worship, both externally and internally, which centers on the mantra.

Tantra contains extensive teachings about mantras including various correspondences of the Sanskrit alphabet with cosmic powers and principles. The Mantra Purusha is largely a Tantric teaching. Tantra gives much importance to Shakti mantras for the worship of different Goddesses. Kundalini Yoga and the use of chakra mantras is another important aspect of Tantra.

Tantric Yoga follows an integral approach, employing all eight limbs of Yoga from asana to samadhi, adding to it a sophisticated external ritualism. As a way of knowledge based on Vedantic philosophy, Tantra emphasizes Self-realization and the realization of Brahman as the ultimate goal of life. As connected to Vedic science in general, Tantra includes Ayurveda, Vedic Astrology, and Vastu in its own Tantric forms or "Tantric sciences".

The Sounds of the Petals of the Chakras

The Kundalini Shakti itself is the inner power of mantra, whereas the chakras are the energy fields created by its unfoldment. Mantra is the best means of arousing the Kundalini and energizing the chakras, which like the Kundalini remain dormant and asleep in the ordinary human state. Kundalini is defined according to the Sanskrit alphabet: "starting with the letter–A and ending with the letter-*Kṣa*, so is called the Kundalini."[89]

We have noted that it is not possible for the Kundalini to rise or the chakras to be opened unless the prana first enters the Sushumna, which requires the balancing of solar and lunar energies and the development of higher Agni and Soma forces. This process is aided by bringing the sound current downward to the root chakra through the power of mantra. Both of these practices rest upon the development of a higher consciousness and power of attention within us.

The petals of the chakras represent an unfoldment of primal sound through the fifty letters of the Sanskrit alphabet. The six lower chakras contain a total of fifty petals, each of which relates to one of the fifty letters of the Sanskrit alphabet. This is the "garland of letters" that shows the vibratory frequencies of the chakras. The thousand petal lotus or crown chakra indicates all possible sound combinations of these fifty letters. The letters can be recited as mantras along with the Anusvara-*ṁ* as chakra mantras.

1. Sixteen Vowels (Svara) – the sounds of the Throat chakra, Vishuddha, smoky brilliance in color
Aṁ, Āṁ, Iṁ, Īṁ, Uṁ, Ūṁ, Ṛṁ, Ṝṁ, Ḷṁ, Ḹṁ, Eṁ, Aiṁ, Oṁ, Auṁ, Aṁ, Aḥ
2. The Twelve consonants beginning with Kaṁ, the sounds of the Heart chakra, Anahata, red like coral in color
Kaṁ, Khaṁ, Gaṁ, Ghaṁ, Ṅaṁ , Caṁ, Chaṁ, Jaṁ, Jhaṁ, Ñaṁ, Ṭaṁ, Ṭhaṁ
3. The ten consonants beginning with Ḍaṁ, the sounds of the Navel chakra, dark blue in color
Ḍaṁ, Ḍhaṁ, Ṇaṁ, Taṁ, Thaṁ, Daṁ, Dhaṁ, Naṁ, Paṁ, Phaṁ
4. The three last consonants and three first semivowels – the sounds of the Water chakra, bright like lightning in color
Baṁ, Bhaṁ, Maṁ, Yaṁ, Raṁ, Laṁ
5. The last semivowels and three first sibilants – the sounds of the Root chakra, golden in color
Vaṁ; Śaṁ, Ṣaṁ, Saṁ
6. The last two sibilants – the sounds of the third eye, bright like the full Moon in color
Haṁ, Kṣaṁ
7. The Crown chakra contains the potential of all sounds and is snow white in color

The Sounds of the Chakra Petals and Mantra Purusha

While this sequence at first looks different than that of the Mantra Purusha, a deeper examination reveals many connections.

- The throat chakra governs the element of ether, which in terms of bodily structure is represented by the head. The sixteen vowels of the Mantra Purusha are the sounds of the head.

- The heart chakra governs the element of air and to the arms/hands as a motor organ. The Mantra Purusha letters of the guttural and palatal consonants relating to the right and left arms dominate the sounds of the heart chakra.

- The navel chakra governs the element of fire and to the feet as a motor organ. The majority letters for this chakra are those in the Mantra Purusha that relate to the right and left legs/feet.

- The sex or water chakra relates to the three last labial sounds (*Baṁ, Bhaṁ, Maṁ*), which relate to the lower abdomen (a region of water) and to the first three semi-vowels (*Yaṁ, Raṁ, Laṁ*) that govern the tissues of plasma, blood and muscle that are mainly watery in nature.

• The root chakra, which governs the earth element, relates to the last semivowel-Va and the first three sibilants (*Vaṁ, Śaṁ, Ṣaṁ, Saṁ*). These govern the tissues of fat, bone, marrow and reproductive, which are connected to the root and earth energies within us.

• The Third eye relates to the last sibilants of *Haṁ* and *Kṣaṁ*, which reflect prana and mind.

Recitation of the Sanskrit Alphabet through the Chakras

The process of recitation of the Sanskrit alphabet through the chakras consists of first drawing the energy of speech from the throat down to the base of the spine with the forty eight sounds of the Sanskrit alphabet. Then one draws the energy of speech up to the third eye where resides the two additional sounds *Haṁ* and *Kṣaṁ* that represent the powers of prana and mind. This recitation draws the sound current downward to the base of the spine in order to arouse the Kundalini and stimulate it to ascend. In this process, our speech is internalized and brought to the level of primal sound.

To practice this method, recite each of the letters of the alphabet while meditating upon the petals of the chakra where they occur, starting with the throat. In this process, one traces the energy of speech through the four levels.

• One begins with the sixteen vowels in the throat chakra that relate to the Vaikhari, the outer or audible form of speech.

• One continues with the first twelve consonants in the heart chakra as the Madhyama or middle, pranic level of speech.

• One continues with the ten consonants in the navel chakra as the Pashyanti or illumined level of speech.

• One continues with the ten remaining consonants, semivowels and sibilants in the sex and root chakras as the Para or transcendent form of speech, through which the Kundalini or higher sound energy awakens.

• Then the Kundalini Shakti rises up to the third eye carrying all the letters of the alphabet along with the two remaining letters *Haṁ* and *Kṣaṁ*, connecting the power of speech with that of prana and mind.

• This awakens all possible mantric powers and sounds in the crown chakra.

One can bring in additional Shakti mantras as taught for the Mantra Purusha, like adding the mantra *Hrīṁ* to each chakra petal sound for opening up its energy. One can also use a Devata (deity) mantra for the letter of each petal like *Oṁ Aṁ Namaḥ Śivāya*. This is a very powerful devotional practice.

Kundalini Chakra Mantra Yoga

This powerful method of Mantra Yoga emphasizes the central sounds of the chakras (the bijas of their respective elements) along with Shakti mantras. It does not consider the sounds of the petals of the chakras.

The Kundalini is aroused with the fiery mantra - *Hūṁ* - along with the mantra for the chakra. The awakened Kundalini fire purifies and dissolves the elemental powers of each chakra, allowing our awareness to ascend to the next chakra. It also purifies the corresponding sense and motor organs, dissolving our ego attachment to them. In this process, one goes through the chakras from below to above starting with the root chakra. However, one must be ready for such a process by purification of one's life style and emotional nature as a foundation for the practice to really work. Otherwise, such strong mantras can be disturbing.[90]

Oṁ Laṁ Hūṁ	Purifies the earth element in the root chakra
Oṁ Vaṁ Hūṁ	Purifies the water element in the sex chakra
Oṁ Raṁ Hūṁ	Purifies the fire element in the navel chakra
Oṁ Yaṁ Hūṁ	Purifies the air element in the heart chakra
Oṁ Haṁ Hūṁ	Purifies the ether element in the throat chakra
Oṁ Kṣaṁ Hūṁ	Purifies the mind in the third eye
Oṁ Oṁ Hūṁ	Purifies consciousness in the head chakra

One can also repeat the bija mantras silently along with the breath for greater effect, for example: *Oṁ Laṁ Laṁ Laṁ Hūṁ Hūṁ Hūṁ Hūṁ*!

After this procedure is completed, one can bring the consciousness of the Divine Self into each of the chakras, starting from above with the chakra mantra plus *Haṁsaḥ So'haṁ Svāhā*, the great Purusha mantra. This draws the Soma or lunar nectar down to balance the Kundalini fire's ascent. It also requires that one has placed one's sense of happiness, love and devotion in the Divine presence within.

Oṁ Oṁ Haṁsaḥ So'haṁ Svāhā	Energizes the consciousness of the Divine Self or Atman in the crown chakra and pure consciousness
Oṁ Kṣaṁ Haṁsaḥ So'haṁ Svāhā	Energizes the consciousness of the Divine Self or Atman in the third eye and mind
Oṁ Haṁ Haṁsaḥ So'haṁ Svāhā	Energizes the consciousness of the Divine Self or Atman in the throat chakra and ether element
Oṁ Yaṁ Haṁsaḥ So'haṁ Svāhā	Energizes the consciousness of the Divine Self or Atman in the heart chakra and air element
Oṁ Raṁ Haṁsaḥ So'haṁ Svāhā	Energizes the consciousness of the Divine Self or Atman in the fire chakra and the fire element
Oṁ Vaṁ Haṁsaḥ So'haṁ Svāhā	Energizes the consciousness of the Divine Self or Atman in the water chakra and the water element
Oṁ Laṁ Haṁsaḥ So'haṁ Svāhā	Energizes the consciousness of the Divine Self or Atman in the earth chakra and the earth element

One can add the lunar mantra *Śrīṁ* for greater effect as: *Oṁ Oṁ Śrīṁ Haṁsaḥ So'haṁ Svāhā, Oṁ Kṣaṁ Śrīṁ Haṁsaḥ So'haṁ Svāhā*, and so on down the chakras. This aids in the descent of Soma, which is a lunar power.

Deity mantras can be added to these chakra mantras (here counting from the root chakra up) like *Oṁ Laṁ Namaḥ Śivāya* or *Oṁ Vaṁ Namaḥ Śivāya*. Shakti bijas can be added like *Oṁ Oṁ Aiṁ Klīṁ Sauḥ, Oṁ Kṣaṁ Aiṁ Klīṁ Sauḥ* (here counting from the crown chakra down). These are but a few examples.

Such chakra mantras work better combined with the breath, for example, with one breath per mental recitation of the overall mantra. The number of mantra pranayama recitations per chakra can be gradually increased, with seven as a good number to begin with.[91] These secrets are passed on in individualized sadhana. This twofold process is similar to the energy balancing of the Fire below and the Moon above taught already, but occurs at a more internal level of practice, aiming at the Sushumna or central channel itself.

The Spiritual Heart (Hridaya), the Chakras and the Power of Sound

All six lower chakras and their various petals are contained in and comprehended by the thousand petalled lotus of the crown chakra. The thousand petalled lotus, in turn, is contained in and comprehended by the hridaya or spiritual heart. The hridaya or spiritual heart is not the heart chakra (Anahata) but the core of our being, the seat of the Atman or Purusha, in which all chakras, all worlds and all beings are comprehended.

The spiritual heart is sometimes visualized as a small space or cavern in the heart.[92] Sometimes it is seen as a flame, in the center of which is the lightning power of consciousness. Sometimes the entire body is visualized in that flame. It is often figured as a lotus of eight petals in the region of the heart in which either the Atman or the Ishta Devata, our chosen form of the Divine for worship, is meditated upon. These eight petals correspond to the eight directions of space (four cardinal and four intermediate directions) and to the eight causal powers of the five elements, ego, intelligence and great Nature.[93]

Certain approaches of Jnana Yoga, the Yoga of Knowledge, and Bhakti Yoga, the Yoga of Devotion, focus directly on the heart and may not regard the Kundalini or the chakras in a separate light.[94] They speak of opening the knots of the heart as the key to liberation.[95] They emphasize dwelling in the heart, not any ascent or descent of energies. However, this dwelling in the spiritual heart can bring about the proper harmonization, ascent and descent of energies, without a specific effort to do so.

The small space within the spiritual heart is the ultimate source of sound and mantra, of prana and mind, of Agni and Soma, Shiva and Shakti. In it dwell all beings, all worlds, all time and all space, but it is not in any way tainted or affected by these. One can also practice the "Mantra Yoga of the spiritual heart" or "Hridaya Mantra Yoga". One focuses on the mantra, the deity and the Self in the heart.

There are specific mantras for the spiritual heart, the most important of which is *Hrīṁ*. The heart is the location of the higher Self that is the supreme aspect of Prana, the hamsa. A good mantra for the heart is the mantra to the Supreme Light (Paramjyoti Mantra), which is also an important mantra for the Sun, with which the spiritual heart is connected:

Oṁ Hrīṁ Haṁsaḥ So'haṁ Svāhā

The mantra has a power similar to the Gayatri mantra to awaken our higher perception. It liberates the hamsa or bird of the soul, connecting us with the Divine prana in the heart. It is a universal mantra that can be recommended to anyone.[96] It does not have the potential complications of Kundalini mantras.

We can chant this mantra in all the chakras along with their respective chakra mantras in order to bring the light of the spiritual heart into all the chakras. For example relative to the root chakra, one can chant:

Oṁ Laṁ Hrīṁ Haṁsaḥ So'haṁ Svāhā

Shakti Mantras and the Chakras

Shakti mantras have general actions in all the chakras according to their energies, though they may be more helpful in certain chakras than in others. I have given a few of these possibilities below that can be combined with various practices. Combinations of these mantras can be used, particularly relative to deities, like the the Kali mantra *Krīṁ Hūṁ Hrīṁ* to bring energy and light to all the chakras or the Sundari mantra *Hrīṁ Śrīṁ Klīṁ* to bring bliss and contentment.

• The mantra *Hūṁ* brings a fire energy to all the chakras in which it is used, projecting its power. It is usually connected to the root chakra, the navel and the third eye, the seats of fire within us, and is probably most powerful in the navel. It is used to draw the fire energy up the chakras.

• The mantra *Śrīṁ* provides a nurturing and cooling lunar energy to all the chakras we direct its energy towards. It is usually connected to the heart and to the lunar aspect of the head. It is used to draw the Soma energy down the chakras from above.

• The mantra *Hrīṁ* brings a solar light and space to all the chakras in which it is used, deepening the experience of the chakra. It is usually connected to the heart but can bring light to all the chakras. It connects the chakras with the spiritual heart.

• The mantra *Krīṁ* with its electrical force helps open all chakras in which it is used. It is like an electrical charge that activates the chakras. It is often connected to the root chakra, the navel chakra and the third eye.

• The mantra *Klīṁ* brings magnetic or devotional energy to all the chakras in which it is used, helping to consolidate its energy. It also serves to draw the energy of water into the chakras. It is usually connected with the heart but also with the lunar region of the head.

• The mantra *Aiṁ* brings space and attention to all the chakras in which it is used. It brings guidance and knowledge into the chakra. It is usually connected to the throat, third eye and head, the seats of knowledge.

• The mantras *Strīṁ* or *Trīṁ* allow us to move up from one chakra to another. It also allows us to spread out the energy of the chakra to different parts of the body. It is most commonly connected to the navel chakra.

• Pranic mantras like *Hsauḥ* stimulate the Kundalini in the root chakra in a powerful way.

Chapter 15:

Mantra Deity and the Chanting of Divine Names

After the primal sounds or bija mantras, probably the next most important are special "name mantras". These consist of names, epithets, qualities or functions of the Divine in different forms, manifestations, or personalities. They are centered on one word, the name, which may have several syllables.

There is a tremendous power in the name, as we all know. In our ordinary communication, we use names in order to draw the attention of a person to us. If I know your name, for example, and call you by it you respond personally. If I address you by someone else's name, you will not respond at all. The same is true of the Divine and higher consciousness. If we know the Divine names, we can commune more readily with the Divine being. Our minds revolve around various names. When we repeat such Divine Names, our minds and hearts become purified and we begin to see the Divine in others.

A human name is an indication of a being, a person, a conscious Self. It is because we are endowed with being ourselves that we can recognize our own name and respond to its call. Similarly, it is because of the presence of the universal Being that we can name other objects and endow them with their own particular being. Ultimately, it is only because of eternal Being of the Divine that we can name anything. This means that the naming process contains a recognition of the universality of Being, which is the basis of the sacred or mantric name.

Unfortunately, our society does not honor the name as sacred but uses it for exploitation. We do not honor the person or the inner being but only the outer identity, face, label or credit card number. It is important that we bring back the sanctity of the Name back into our lives. This is one of the most important applications of mantra. Through the Mantra Yoga of Divine Names we can reclaim the sacred universe and make sacred all beings.

Reciting Divine names is a way of awakening Divine qualities within ourselves. Ultimately, Being is One and all names are Divine names. Sanskrit is a language of Divine names. It shows how all sounds manifest from the Divine Word as a Self-revelation. Through Divine Names we can reclaim our own Divine Being as the Self of all, taking us beyond separate ego identities of body and mind.

Namaḥ, the Great Chant of Devotion

Throughout the Hindu tradition since Vedic times, there has been the commonly reverberating chant of *Namaḥ* or *Namo* to various deities. We find the same *Namaḥ* chants in the Buddhist, Jain and other traditions from India. Perhaps no other term in the history of the world has served to promote so much devotion and honoring of higher consciousness.

Namaste is a greeting that has the same basis, honoring that Divine presence, which is then invoked with a Divine Name. It is important to chant our *Namaḥ* every day in order to honor the Divine within and without.

Divine Names and Bhakti Yoga

The Yoga of Devotion or Bhakti Yoga is perhaps the most important and foundational of all the Yogas. It provides the feeling, passion or motivation that carries us along our spiritual path, however we may define it for ourselves. In addition, Bhakti is the most accessible of all Yoga approaches because it relies more on internal feeling than external forms, techniques or mental powers.

Bhakti Yoga emphasizes chanting as its main method, with the repetition of mantras, particularly Divine Names, along with ritual worship, prayer, and devotional meditation. It uses the chakras, particularly the heart, as sites of internal worship and a shrine or temple as part of external worship. Divine names and mantras are part of both internal and external worship.

Names of important forms of divinity can be used like *Oṁ Namaḥ Śivāya* for Lord Shiva, the transcendent Being, or *Oṁ Namo Bhagavate Vāsudevāya* for Krishna, the avatar of Divine love. Divine names may be combined with seed mantras to the deities like *Oṁ Hauṁ Namaḥ Śivāya*, or *Oṁ Klīṁ Kṛṣṇāya Namaḥ* for yet other effects.

There are many collections of the names of Hindu Gods and Goddesses like the *Thousand Names of Shiva* (Shiva Sahasranama), the *Thousand Names of Vishnu* or the *Thousand Names of Lalita* (the Goddess). Reciting such thousand names helps stimulate the thousand petalled lotus of the head, which contains all possible sounds and meanings. There are also many hundred name chants and yet smaller numbers of names.

Stotras and Chants

Stotras are longer mantras, prayers, songs or hymns in Sanskrit, the verses of which form the basis of many Sanskrit chants. The term Stotra refers to a hymn of praise or affirmation. Such hymns of praise, propitiation or seeking favor of the deity are common in many spiritual and religious traditions. There are many famous Sanskrit *Stotras* chanted today and good recordings of them can be commonly found in India. In fact, *Stotras* are more common in the devotional context of India than are Kirtans. There are special books that one can buy that contain collections of *Stotras*. Most of these are in Sanskrit or in the regional languages of India, but a few are in English.

Stotras are generally aimed at specific deities as one of the main practices of Bhakti Yoga. There are formless or philosophical *Stotras* as well, though these do not always have the same devotional power. The idea is that the Stotra can gain the favor of the deity which rules over the particular issue involved and so resolve it at a level of higher consciousness. *Stotras* can be chanted for all the goals of life, including health and liberation. It usually depends upon the intentionality with which the Stotra is recited. One can chant a Stotra to seek Divine blessings and grace for whatever one truly needs in life. However, there are *Stotras* specific to particular aims or goals in life, like certain Lakshmi *Stotras* that give wealth.

There are many famous *Stotras* to Shiva, Devi, Vishnu, Krishna, Rama, Ganesha and other deities that can be used in their worship and as part of Yoga practice.[97] Certain *Stotras* to the Goddess as *Tripurasundari* reveal secrets of Yoga, mantra and the chakras that are otherwise hard to find. The alliteration and the cadence of the *Mahishasura-Mardini Stotra* can aid in the awakening of the Kundalini Shakti. The alliteration and the cadence of the *Shiva Tandava Stotra* can awaken the presence of Shiva within us. I personally chant many *Stotras* on a regular basis. It is one of the best ways of developing devotion and a mantric healing power. [98]

Prayer (Prarthana)

The propitiation of the deity to help us in our lives is called Prarthana in Sanskrit and prayer in English. There are many Sanskrit mantric prayers or Prarthanas. Sometimes these are part of *Stotras*.

According to the Vedic view, we live in a user friendly conscious universe. We can get anything that we truly desire, but we have to know how to ask. Prayer teaches us how to ask the Divine for the help that we truly need in life. All mantras are prayers of a kind. Mantra itself is a kind of "language of prayer" in which the sounds of the prayer reflect the Divine language, the language of mantra. Yet we must be careful what we are seeking in our prayers, aiming at what is best for ourselves and for all beings.

Forms of the Gods and Goddesses

Bhakti Yoga rests upon a personal connection with the Deity. This is not the external God of an institutionalized belief but the internal divinity within our own hearts, our inner Self. For the practice of Bhakti Yoga, we must create a personal relationship with the deity. This takes two main approaches, either as a type of relationship or as a particular representational form, which usually go together.

As a type of relationship, we can worship God as the Divine father, mother, brother, sister, friend, beloved, master or teacher - or in any other type of relationship that we are inclined to. Generally, father, mother or beloved are the main approaches preferred. In this way, we assume a deep personal connection with the Divine that can be the basis for meditation. Such a divine connection can also help us heal our human relationships and the psychological problems these may have caused for us.

As a particular form, there are many depictions of the Deity, usually in one of these relationship aspects, particularly as the Divine Father and Divine Mother, which become various Gods and Goddesses. We may choose to worship the Divine in a human form, in some natural form as a sacred animal, plant or mountain, or in symbolic forms like Shiva lingas or the geometrical Sri Yantra. It is a matter of our deeper yearning and natural inclinations.

Since our main attachment is to the human form, looking at the Divine in a human form can be a good way to focus our attention. Yet worshipping the Divine in the world of nature helps us to understand how consciousness pervades the entire universe. Ultimately, we must see the Divine in all beings.

Some people prefer to worship God, who is an infinite and eternal being, as formless. Yet they usually still look upon God in relationship terms as the father or mother, or as having some sort of personality, son or representative whom they honor. Others may worship God through Divine qualities like Divine love, compassion, fearlessness, strength and so on. These qualities can also be worshipped symbolically through different Gods and Goddesses that represent them, like worshipping the power of Divine love through Lord Krishna, the avatar of Divine love, joy and devotion. One must remember that the deeper mind and soul communicates more through symbols, images and mantras, than through literal words or abstract ideas.

At the highest level, we can use mantras to invoke our inner being or higher Self, the Atman or Purusha within us. We can use mantra to invoke the Absolute or the cosmic being into our lives. The true Divinity is not apart from us. And our true being is not apart from the Divinity. To find this, we need to surrender our ego self and discover our true nature as pure consciousness.

Ishta Devata

The form of God or manifestation of Divinity that one personally chooses to worship is called an Ishta Devata or "chosen deity" in Sanskrit. In the Yoga tradition, it is important to worship the Divine according to the form or approach that most appeals to one's heart. Yoga emphasizes having such an Ishta Devata as an inner guide, goal or aspiration. According to the *Yoga Sutras*, the power of concentration on God or surrender to Ishvara (Ishvara-pranidhana) is the best means to bring about samadhi.[99] For this, one should chose the form or approach that most appeals to one's inner being and deeper aspirations.[100]

An *Ishta Devata mantra* is our main personal devotional mantra or means of calling on the Divine. Whether we worship God as father or mother or as various deities or avatars, there are special mantras that we can take up in each case. The Ishta Devata is a matter of personal choice, but its mantra becomes more powerful if given by a guru or by tradition. *One can always feel free to use the mantra of one's Ishta Devata or chosen divinity for any life-purpose, including healing.* This is another reason why it is good to have such a deity.

Ishta Devata mantras consist of names of deities or gurus, generally given in the dative (to) case grammatically and with the term *Namaḥ* or reverence. Some include bija mantras as well.

Examples:

Oṁ Namaḥ Śivāya (for Shiva)
Oṁ Namo Bhagavate Vasudevāya (for Krishna)
Oṁ Gaṁ Ganeśāya Namaḥ - Reverence to Ganesha

Guru Mantras

There are special "guru mantras" used to contact various great teachers. One can use guru mantras for all life-purposes including healing. The inner guidance and influence of the guru helps calm the mind and control the senses. One repeats the mantra as a means of communicating with and developing devotion for the guru. Example:

Oṁ Namo Bhagavate Śrī Ramaṇāya (for Guru Ramana Maharshi)

Speech and the Forms of the Gods and Goddesses

The Yoga tradition abounds with an abundance of names, forms and approaches to Divinity, which all have their counterparts in Divine sound and mantra. There is a great trinity of deities that governs the cosmic processes of creation, preservation and dissolution (reabsorption of the universe back into the absolute). The three have masculine and feminine forms as Brahma/Sarasvati, Vishnu/Lakshmi, and Shiva/Kali. It is the feminine forms that are most connected to speech and mantra.

Generally, the Goddess Sarasvati, who relates to knowledge and to creative power, is the main Goddess of speech, communication, poetry and music. But the other two forms of the Goddess also relate to speech in different aspects. Lakshmi is the loving or nurturing form of speech, speech at a devotional level. Kali is the energetic or transformative form of speech, speech at a pranic level. As indicating the power of Shakti overall, Kali reflects higher forms of speech in which the Divine Word awakens within us and withdraws us back into the Absolute, revealing the beauty and bliss beyond time and space.

The Five Deity Lines

Hindu devotional worship recognizes five main sects or divisions relative to five great deities, each with its own special mantras.

1) Shiva and the Shaivite tradition

2) Vishnu and the Vaishnava tradition, including Rama and Krishna

3) The Goddess and the Shakta tradition

4) Ganesha or Ganapati tradition

5) The Sun (Saura) tradition and planetary deities

Much overlap exists between these five groups. Goddesses have their place in the Vaishnava and Shaivite lines, as well as the Shakta approach. Shakti is also worshipped along with Lord Shiva as part of the Shaivite approach. Lakshmi is also worshipped along with Lord Vishnu as well being part of the Goddess or Shakta line.

Skanda or Subrahmanya (Murugan in South India) is sometimes added as another line. Buddha is sometimes added, along with various Bodhisattvas and Buddhist deities. Mahavira, the main teacher of ancient Jainism, is sometimes added as another line along with other Jain deities.

Some complexity can exist among these lines. Relative to the Goddess, for example, there are ten great wisdom Goddesses (Dasha Mahavidya), nine forms of Durga (Nava Durga), eight aspects of Lakshmi (Ashta Lakshmi), and so on. We will examine the mantras for some of the most important deities below, but it is by no means a complete list. Note that the Sun and planetary deities will be included in the chapter on Vedic astrology.

In Tantric thought, all deities have Agni and Soma,[101] fiery and watery, solar and lunar forms. The fiery forms are generally regarded as harsh, destructive, protective or purifying in energy. The watery or lunar forms are soft, creative, nurturing or rejuvenating. For Lord Shiva, for example, Shiva or Shankara is the benefic or lunar form, while Rudra or Bhairava is the fierce or solar form. For the Goddess, Parvati or Sundari is the benefic or lunar form, while Durga or Chandi is the fierce or solar form.

Below are indicated some of the most important Hindu deities and a few of their many mantras, emphasizing the seed sounds or bija mantras.[102]

Shiva/ Rudra

Shiva is the deity of the universal life force and of the Supreme Being. He has control of Vayu and of Vata dosha, which he calms and harmonizes. His is the light of pure awareness. His energy controls the mind and helps counter emotional and psychological disturbances. His main bija mantras are *Oṁ* or *Hauṁ*. His main name mantra, which is probably the most famous of all name mantras, is: *Oṁ Namaḥ Śivāya*! Sometimes additional bijas are added to this like *Oṁ Hrīṁ Hauṁ Namaḥ Śivāya*!

Rudra is the fierce form of Shiva. He relates to Agni and to fire. He is the deity ruling over fevers and grants recovery from them, including all manner of infectious and contagious diseases. He is also the deity governing over Ayus or longevity. He helps us overcome death-threatening diseases, accidents or circumstances. His Vedic mantra is the Mrityunjaya (Tryambakam) mantra and the famous Rudram, a long set of chants from the *Yajurveda*.

Other important forms of Shiva include Yogeshvara, the Lord of Yoga, and Dakshinamurti, the great teacher of Self-knowledge. A shorter set of mantras can be used for these forms of Shiva as well: *Oṁ Hauṁ Jūṁ Saḥ!*

Ganesha

Ganesha, the elephant-headed deity, is an important deity in Yoga and in Vedic sciences in general. Ganesha rules over the forces of time and dispenses the fruits of karma. As such, he is specifically a deity for Vedic astrology, and his image is found on Vedic astrology charts. He works to destroy all obstacles and is propitiated before any major endeavor. This extends to healing as he destroys all obstacles to health or well-being. In addition he grants wisdom and skill, the two main qualities needed for any endeavor to succeed.

Ganesha is the first son of Shiva and Parvati, and is especially close to Parvati. He carries the grace of the Goddess. Through him the power of Shakti is dispensed to us, just as electricity is channeled into various currents and circuits. Ganesha is worshipped in the root chakra to stabilize the Kundalini force, which he turns into a force of knowledge. His Tantric bija mantra is *Glauṁ*. His main name mantra is:

Oṁ Gaṁ Gaṇeśāya Namaḥ! or *Oṁ Gaṁ Gaṇapataye Namaḥ*!

Skanda

Skanda is the second son of Shiva and Parvati. He relates more to Shiva as Ganesha does to Parvati. He is the Divine youth that destroys all negativity. He reflects Agni or fire as a cosmic principle and as our own inner fire or indwelling soul. He brings us the deepest Self-knowledge and the most direct Self-realization. His main mantra is: *Oṁ Śaravaṇa Bhava*!

Krishna

Krishna is the form of Vishnu that holds all yogic powers, including all healing energies for our emotional nature. He is the incarnation of Divine love, bliss and all higher Yoga teachings. Krishna represents the magnetic energy of Divine love to take us back to the source of life. Astrologically, he is connected to the Moon. Those seeking the unfoldment of Raja Yoga should worship him. The *Hare Kṛṣṇa* mantra for him is well known. An important mantra for him is: *Oṁ Klīṁ Kṛṣṇāya Namaḥ!* Also used is the name mantra *Om namo bhagavate vasudevaya.*

Rama

Rama is the incarnation of Vishnu as the ideal king and protector, the representative of dharma. Worshipping him protects us from all negativity externally and purifies our minds and hearts internally. His energy is of a solar nature, but its gentle and nurturing side, not its destructive heat. His energy is particularly good for children and for countering Vata disorders (disturbances of the nervous system). His seed mantra is simply *Rāṁ* or: *Jai Śrī Rāṁ*!

Vishnu

Vishnu is most worshipped through his incarnations as Krishna and Rama. Perhaps his most common mantra is the Narayana name mantra: *Oṁ Namo Narāyaṇāya*! Another important Vishnu mantra is *Oṁ Hrīṁ Hrīṁ Oṁ Viṣṇave Namaḥ*!

Hanuman

Hanuman, the monkey-faced God, is the son of Vayu, the wind God. He represents the higher force of prana behind Vata dosha. He promotes healing, rejuvenation and longevity. He also has the knowledge of and represents the power of all the healing forces of nature.

Hanuman is the ideal Yogi who grants skill in asana and pranayama as well as the supreme power of devotion. While he is devoted to Sita and Rama, he is often regarded as an aspect of Shiva. His main seed mantra is the prana mantra *Haṁ* or: *Oṁ Haṁ Hanumate Namaḥ*! *Hauṁ* is also used for him as Hanuman is regarded as an incarnation of Lord Shiva.

Dhanvantari

Ayurveda uses the form of Dhanvantari, an incarnation of the cosmic power of healing, as its main deity. His image is the most common image found in Ayurvedic schools and clinics everywhere. Dhanvantari is a form of Vishnu, who rules over the forces of preservation in the universe, which include healing. *Stotras* to him are commonly chanted before Ayurvedic classes and programs. Dhanvantari's mantra is: *Oṁ Dhaṁ Dhanvantaraye Namaḥ*!

Lakshmi

Lakshmi is the wife of Lord Vishnu, the cosmic preserver and protector. She grants health, wealth, beauty, fertility, happiness and abundance – all the good things of life that the great majority of people are ever seeking. She is a special deity for women and helps with women's health problems, gynecological disorders, fertility issues, menopause, and so on. She relates primarily to the water element but to some extent to earth as well (particularly as the Goddess Sita, the wife of Rama). Her Tantric form is Kamalatmika, who unfolds the higher grace of Divine bliss. Her main seed mantra is *Śrīṁ* or three syllabled as: *Śrīṁ Hrīṁ Klīṁ*!

Sarasvati

Sarasvati is the wife of Lord Brahma, the cosmic creator, and the Goddess of knowledge. She gives wisdom, intelligence and good memory along with skill in the fine arts, music, dance and literature. She is worshipped for learning and education. Her Tantric form is Matangi, who dispenses all the inner and secret knowledge of mantras, plants, and all the forces of nature. Her main mantra is the guru bija *Aiṁ*. Another good set of bijas for her is: *Hrīṁ Aiṁ Dhīṁ*!

Sundari

Sundari is a Goddess of love, beauty, delight and Soma. She is the deity of the mystic Moon which is also the energy of the crown chakra. Her grace is most sought after in the higher Yoga practices. She allows the immortal Soma nectar to flow from the thousand-petal lotus above, granting all higher powers of speech and mantra. Generally called Tripura Sundari or the "Beauty of the Three Worlds", she represents the benign aspect of Shiva's consort, whose fierce form is Kali.

Somewhat like Krishna, Sundari holds the magnetic power of attraction but more from the knowledge side. Other blissful forms of the Goddess relate to her including Lalita and Rajarajeshvari and even Lakshmi. Mantra Siddhi or perfection in mantra in the broadest sense is given by her. Her mantras are: *Aiṁ Klīṁ Sauḥ* as three syllabled, or *Hrīṁ Śrīṁ Klīṁ Aiṁ Sauḥ* as five syllabled.

Durga

Durga represents the Great Mother in her protective role. She rides a lion and carries the weapons of the Gods and leads the army of the Gods to destroy all negativity. Worshipping her is one of the best places to begin to honor the Mother. Kali is often regarded as her fiercer manifestation.

Durga rules over the universe and directs each soul to its real purpose, awakening the higher intelligence of nature within us. At a deeper level of Yoga practice, fiery

Durga represents the awakened Kundalini fire, controlled by the power of tapas or self-discipline, which turns it into a force of splendor and majesty. The Kundalini once purified, awakened and seated on the throne of the heart becomes Durga. If we honor Durga, she will guide our sadhana and transform us in the inner light. Durga's prime mantra is: *Oṁ Duṁ Durgāyai Namaḥ*! Another good mantra for her protection is: *Oṁ Hrīṁ Krīṁ Duṁ Durgāyai Svāhā*!

Kali

The Goddess Kali is one of the main deities of the practice of Yoga. She represents the reabsorption of the time bound universe back into its eternal source. She governs over the process of mergence. She is the power through which earth is dissolved into water, water into fire, fire into air, air into ether, ether into mind and mind into pure consciousness. She represents the movement back through the Tattvas to the Purusha beyond them. She grants the highest strength, energy and vitality, but one must be strong oneself in order to carry her indomitable force.

Kali relates to the great prana mantra *Krīṁ*. It also occurs as three syllables -*Krīṁ Hūṁ Hrīṁ* – or as seven syllables: *Krīṁ Krīṁ Krīṁ Hūṁ Hūṁ Hrīṁ Hrīṁ*. Another set of three syllables for Kali is: *Hrīṁ Śrīṁ Krīṁ*! Kali grants the prana of eternity that can overcome all the negative energies born of time.

Dattatreya

Dattatreya is a combined form of Brahma, Vishnu and Shiva, as well as a great ancient sage and yogi who was taught by nature. His mantra is very important because in the absence of a guru, one can pray to Dattatreya for guidance and for empowerment of mantras: *Oṁ Drāṁ Dattatreyāya Namaḥ*!

Other Deities

There are detailed teachings in the Puranas and Tantras about various deities, their worship and their corresponding mantras, names and rituals. The Buddhist and Jain traditions have similar teachings about Sanskrit mantras. Other spiritual and religious traditions have their own sets of Divine Names, including not only Biblical traditions but pagan and Native traditions of all types. We should always remember the connection between mantra, devotion and Divine names. Even bija mantras should be approached with reverence as representing Divine powers, as the seeds of Divine names.

Chapter 16:

Ayurvedic Mantra Therapy

Mantra is one of the most important healing practices in Ayurvedic medicine. Mantra therapy is the main tool used in Ayurveda for healing the mind, but it can aid in physical healing as well. In fact, mantra has been called the most important healing therapy in Ayurveda as a whole. This is because mantra brings in both the cosmic powers and the soul of the patient into the healing process. Even if we are applying outer Ayurvedic treatment methods like diet, herbs, massage or Pancha Karma, mantra can be used to make these more effective.

The use of mantra is the central practice of Yoga and Ayurvedic Sattvavajaya therapy or 'sattva-promoting therapy', which is Ayurveda's main psychological therapy emphasizing the development of sattva guna or mental clarity to calm the mind and emotions. Mantra is also a prime therapy for working on prana, enabling us to direct a healing prana in specific ways. Mantra has physical effects as well, strengthening the brain, senses and nervous system.

The rules of application for Mantra therapy are the same as those for Ayurveda as a whole. Mantras are not a substitute for other health measures, but have their place in aligning the mind of the person with the goals of the treatment. Mantras should be prescribed along with the right diagnosis and the appropriate support treatment methods like diet and herbs. However, just as certain herbs can be used as "home-remedies" even by those who may not be fully trained in Ayurveda, certain mantras can function like home-remedies to treat common diseases and to keep the doshas in balance.

Bija mantras are probably the main mantras used in Ayurvedic mantra therapy. In addition, there are mantras to certain deities to promote health or treat specific diseases. We have already discussed a number of mantric applications and their Ayurvedic relevance.

• The Mantra Purusha is perhaps the most important aspect of Ayurvedic mantric healing, particularly adding the appropriate Shakti mantras and looking at the related marmas. Ayurvedic practitioners should learn the Mantra Purusha as part of their healing tools.

• Shakti mantras like *Hrīṁ* and *Śrīṁ* direct powerful healing forces that have a wide application in Ayurveda for creating or balancing energy at a deep level.

• Chakra mantras like *Laṁ* and *Vaṁ* have important Ayurvedic applications through their correspondences between the doshas, elements and bodily tissues.

• Prana mantras like *So'haṁ* to balance the solar and lunar energies can be brought into Ayurveda for balancing the doshas along with the breath.

• Mantra practices for increasing the Fire below (Jatharagni) and the Soma above (Tarpaka Kapha) are very important, along with pranayama for balancing the doshas and healing the body and mind at a root level.

Knowing Your Own Sound Nature, Shabda Prakriti

Ayurveda emphasizes the unique constitution or nature (Prakriti) of a person, defined through various degrees and combinations of the three biological humors of Vata (air), Pitta (fire) and Kapha (water). Most books on Ayurveda contain doshic tests to help ascertain your Ayurvedic type.

Prakriti or Nature, we should note, consists of vibration which is primarily sound. So too, our individual constitution or "personal Prakriti" has its own vibratory sound pattern. This means that by changing the sound pattern within our minds and nervous systems, we can change the energy of our entire being and balance the constitutional forces or doshas within us. We can counter disease and debility and replace them with health and vitality through the right use of sound and mantra.

Just as each person has a unique constitution, so each person has unique sounds, vibrations and mantras. Your own mantras are the sounds, words, music and songs that most commonly resound within you, the resonance of your own mind and heart. These reflect our patterns of breathing, our heartbeat, our speaking and moving, which all generate sound.

The first thing is to become aware of this vibratory sound pattern at work in your nature, observe it and recognize its implications. Meditation is a good place to do this. As you sit quietly and turn your awareness within, the background sound pattern of your mind will be revealed down to a subconscious level. You may discover that your inner sound vibration is erratic, chaotic, fragmented, disturbed or even in a state of conflict. Through mantra therapy, you can heal the sound pattern of your entire being, letting the mantra take over for the agitation of your thoughts and bring wholeness and equipoise to your entire nature.

Energetics of Sound and the Doshas

Bija mantras, name mantras and extended mantras (prayers and chants) all have great healing powers.[103] Yet one must be careful in thinking that one can mechanically correspond mantras with particular diseases as defined according to a modern medical nomenclature – as if there were one specific Sanskrit mantra for cancer, another for arthritis, and so on. It is better to look at mantras according to the energetics of the elements, doshas, tissues and other factors of Ayurvedic medicine, as well as relative to Vedic astrology.

Mantras like foods or herbs have energetics that can be defined according to the five elements, heating and cooling factors, harsh or soft affects. Some of these qualities are inherent in the sounds themselves. However, root sounds are subtle and can often be applied in several ways. They represent tendencies, directions, tones or shades, not clearly defined outer objects or actions. Sound, which is the sensory component of the ether element, contains the potentials of all five elements in a seed form.

We can alter the energetics of a sound by the kind of force, emotion, meaning, or intensity that we energize it with. This means that sounds cannot be simply reduced to Vata, Pitta or Kapha in their properties, though they do have doshic tendencies that can be brought out by application or combination. Doshic correlations are more prominent in certain sounds like the semivowels.

For example, *Ra* is usually a Pitta sound as the vowel-*Ṛ* is the seed of Fire, while *La* and *Va* are usually Kapha sounds owing to their earth and water connections. *Ha* and *Ya* are largely airy sounds, with the *Ha* sound being more expansive and the *Ya* sound more focused. Aspirated sounds (like *kha* and *gha*) tend to bring in more Vata, with their additional air, though this does not necessarily change the overall energy of the consonant itself.

The I-vowel has an electrifying and motivating effect that is aligned with Shakti, but can sometimes agitate Vata dosha. The U-vowel often creates a harsh effect that can agitate Pitta dosha and Vata doshas, with *Huṁ* and *Duṁ* having a fiery energy, and *Kṣuṁ* having an airy energy. Stabilizing sounds like *Sa, Ta, Stha, Kṣa* and *Dha* can create or hold more Kapha, as do all *Na* and *Ma* sounds.

Shakti Mantras in Ayurveda

Shakti Mantras have doshic equivalents according to their energy. *Hūṁ* or *Hrīṁ* as corresponding to fire and Sun are more Pitta in nature. *Śrīṁ* and *Klīṁ* as relating to the Moon and water are more Kapha. *Krīṁ* as wind and electrical energy is more Vata in effect but has some Pitta through its lightning. These mantras are very powerful for changing the qualities of the mind and prana. Generally, we apply mantras of opposite nature to treat the doshas, just as we recommend foods of opposite nature to reduce them. For example, for reducing Pitta dosha, which is fiery in its qualities, cooling and lunar mantras are usually the most appropriate.

Shakti Mantras and the Doshas	
Vata Dosha	Soft mantras are best like Hrīṁ, Śrīṁ, Klīṁ, Strīṁ, Sauṁ Care is taken using harsh mantras like Krīṁ, Huṁ, Hlīṁ, Hsauḥ
Pitta Dosha	Cooling, lunar and soft mantras are best like Śrīṁ, Klīṁ, Aiṁ, Sauṁ Care is taken using harsh or fiery mantras like Krīṁ, Hūṁ, Hrīṁ, Dūṁ, Hsauḥ or Hlīṁ
Kapha Dosha	Warm and stimulating mantras are best like Krīṁ, Hūṁ, Hrīṁ, Dūṁ, Hsauḥ Care is taken using soft, lunar or watery mantras like Śrīṁ, Klīṁ, Sauṁ

Shakti mantras can be used to change the doshic energies in the locations indicated by the Mantra Purusha. For example, *Kaṁ Śrīṁ* can bring a lunar Kapha energy into the right arm. *Kaṁ Hrīṁ* can bring a solar Pitta energy into the right arm. *Kaṁ Krīṁ* can bring a pranic Vata energy into the right arm. Specific marmas can be targeted this way as well. Such treatment strategies are mentioned relative to the Mantra Purusha and do require some power of concentration to energize the sounds properly.

Mantras and the Three Vital Essences

Mantras work better to promote the three subtle essences behind the doshas, rather than to counter the doshas themselves. It is easier to use mantras to increase Prana, *Tejas* and *Ojas* than to reduce Vata, Pitta and Kapha. *Ojas*, the vital essence of water for Kapha dosha, promotes immunity, fertility, calmness and stability in the body and mind. *Tejas*, the vital essence of fire for Pitta dosha, increases heat, fire, courage, valor and fearlessness. *Prana*, the vital essence of air for Vata dosha, gives strength and aids in rejuvenation, as well as promoting creativity, adaptability and mobility in body and mind. While mantras can be used to promote any of these three vital essences, it should be remembered that mantra overall tends to generate heat or *Tejas*.

We generally benefit both health wise and spiritually from developing more of these three vital essences, while we usually need to keep the doshas from accumulating. However, care must be taken trying to increase the respective vital essence if its corresponding dosha is high. For example, when Pitta is high, one should be careful with mantras to increase *Tejas*, as they may cause the heat of Pitta to increase as well.

Mantras that Promote the Three Vital Essences		
	Mantras	**Letters**
Prana	Oṁ, Aiṁ, Krīṁ, Hrīṁ, Hsauḥ, Yaṁ, Haṁ Haṁsaḥ So'haṁ	Consonants like Ka, Kha, Ca, Cha, Ja, Jha, sounds dominant in the I-vowel
Tejas	Huṁ, Duṁ, Hrīṁ, Krīṁ, Trīṁ, Hsauḥ, Kroṁ, Raṁ Svāhā	Sounds dominant in R-sounds, as also by the U-vowel
Ojas	Hoṁ, Klīṁ, Śrīṁ, Strīṁ, Sauṁ, Vaṁ, Laṁ, Kṣaṁ Namaḥ	Sounds dominant in La, Na, Ma, Ta, Da, Sa and Śa

Pranic mantras like *Haṁsaḥ* or *So'haṁ* are powerful for increasing our positive Prana. *Namaḥ* or *Namaste*, through increasing devotion and humility, strengthens Ojas. *Svāhā* as the fire offering mantra increases *Tejas* and *Agni*.

The great Shiva death-conquering mantras, *Oṁ Hauṁ Jūṁ Saḥ* are excellent for Prana and all aspects of Pranic healing. The Kali Bijas, *Krīṁ Hūṁ Hrīṁ*, are powerful for Tejas, particularly in the root chakra and the heart. The Sundari Mantras, *Hrīṁ Śrīṁ Klīṁ* help with Ojas and overall strength.

Mantras, Deities and Elements

Deities reflect the cosmic forces both at outer and inner levels. As such, certain deities align with various elements and can be used to promote them. Generally, one would propitiate deities of opposite nature to a dosha in order to lower it, but any sincere devotion helps to keep the doshas in balance! However, in some instances one can seek out the deity that corresponds to the element in order to bring it under control.

For such purposes, simply chant the name mantra of the deity with reverence, seeking its healing blessings. The following correlations are only general. Many deities have various forms and in their higher aspects transcend the outer elements. You can note the chapter on Mantra and Divine Names for their name mantras and bijas, as well as the chapter on Vedic astrology for the mantras for the planets.

Sphere of Fire, **Agni-Tejas**	Durga, Rudra, Bhairavi, Skanda, Rama, Kali (martial form), Tara, Uma, Chinnamasta (Vajra Yogini) Sun, Mars, Ketu
Sphere of Air, **Prana-Vayu**	Hanuman, Kali (space form), Shiva, Buddha, Sarasvati, Matangi, Dhumavati, Bhuvaneshvari Saturn, Rahu, Mercury
Sphere of Water, **Ojas-Soma**	Lakshmi, Sundari, Vishnu, Krishna, Kamala, Ganesha, Ganga Devi, Bhumi Mata (Mother Earth) Moon, Venus, Jupiter

Stotras and Suktas to these deities can be chanted for health purposes just as these Divine names can. There are also specific healing *Stotras* like that to Shitali Devi, which aims at countering fevers and inflammation.

Mantras and the Seven Bodily Tissues

The Mantra Purusha sounds for the tissues have very important Ayurvedic applications, which we can build on for various purposes.

- *Oṁ Yaṁ* - for a healthy plasma or Rasa Dhatu
- *Oṁ Śrīṁ Yaṁ* – adds the Shakti bija *Śrīṁ* for beauty, health and vitality in the Rasa Dhatu

One can add the Sanskrit name of the tissue along with Shakti mantras. These can be found in the appendix under Mantra Purusha: Complete Sanskrit Nyasa.

- *Oṁ Śrīṁ Yaṁ Rasātmane Namaḥ* – adds *Rasātmane Namaḥ*, "reverence to the essence of the plasma (rasa dhatu)".
- *Oṁ Hūṁ Yaṁ Rasātmane Namaḥ*, to increase fire and reduce Kapha in the plasma or rasa dhatu.
- *Oṁ Śrīṁ Ṣaṁ Majjātmane Namaḥ*, to increase Kapha and reduce Vata in the nerve tissue.
- *Oṁ Hrīṁ Śaṁ Asthyātmane Namaḥ*, to reduce Kapha and Vata and increase Pitta and Agni in the bone tissue.

Mantras and Marmas

See the appendix on Mantra and Marmas for more detail on this important aspect of Ayurvedic Mantra therapy. We can bring all the methods of working with the Mantra Purusha sounds into marma therapy once we understand these correlations. This will greatly expand our usage of mantras in Ayurveda and Yoga.

Ayurvedic Teas for Mantra Practice

Yoga and Ayurveda recommend the use of certain special herbal teas during mantra practice to help facilitate Vak-Siddhi, the power of speech and mantra. Two primary herbs are used. The first is brahmi (Centella asiatica) and the second vacha (Acorus calmus).[104] These are usually used in various proportions, most commonly two thirds brahmi and one third calamus, taking about a teaspoon of the powder, cooked in warm milk with a little sugar (cane sugar), honey or ghee.

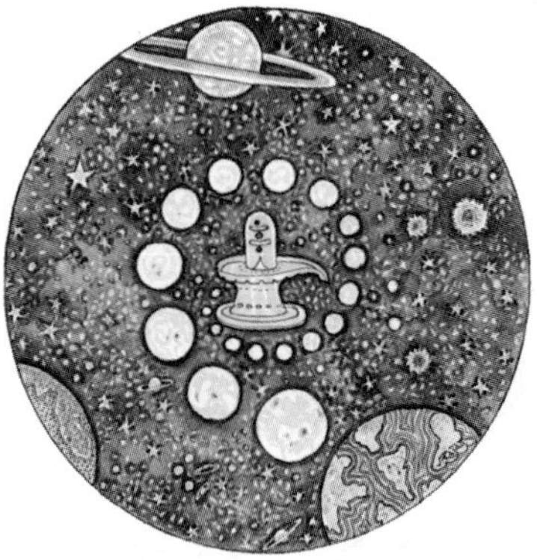

Chapter 17:

Vedic Astrology Mantras

Vedic astrology is the main Vedic science connected to Mantra Yoga. There are two reasons for this. First, Vedic astrology provides us with the keys to choose mantras and correctly time their usage. Traditionally in India, mantras and even the names of children are chosen based upon astrological considerations. Second, mantras work on a subtle level that reflects the same forces as the planets and stars. While astrological positions are patterns of cosmic light, mantras are patterns of cosmic sound. Most mantras are astrological in nature or application, and all mantras can be looked at from an astrological angle.

Specific astrological mantras, like those for the nine planets, are extremely helpful because the astrological chart covers all our karmas in life. Astrological mantras can be used for all the four goals of life of dharma, artha, kama and moksha. Astrological mantras, like Ayurvedic mantras, can also be used for healing body and mind. As spiritual, liberation or moksha mantras, astrological mantras can help us improve our Yoga practice or sadhana. *In this regard, planetary mantras are perhaps the most important and easiest to use of all mantras in any mantra therapy.*

Vedic astrology contains a well defined Mantra therapy, probably more so than any other Vedic science. Mantra therapy is an important remedial measure (upaya) in Vedic astrology. Vedic astrology has special mantras for the planets, the signs of the zodiac and the 27 Nakshatras (lunar constellations) to help us harmonize the astrological influences in our lives. Vedic astrologers commonly prescribe these for their clients and use them for themselves.

Vedic astrology can be called the "Vedic science of karma". It tells us what our karmas are likely to be and when they are likely to unfold during the course of our lives. Yet Vedic astrology does not simply leave us helpless before karma, it teaches us how to optimize, modify and transcend our karma. For improving our karmas, the main inner method used in Vedic astrology is the use of mantra. The main outer method used is planetary gemstones, but even these can only be effective if first empowered by mantras.

Timing of Mantras

Astrological timing is an important means of energizing and empowering mantras and making them more efficacious. Vedic astrology can tell us the best times to begin or change our mantra practice. All mantras are usually first given according to an auspicious time defined by the astrology. They are usually repeated with some regularity defined according to the rules of astrology relative to the time of the day, the phases of the Moon, the seasons of the year, or according to special timing factors relative to the birth chart of the individual.

Certain moments in time are what we could call "mantras in time". These are special junctures in time that determine the nature of what happens afterwards. At such key moments, time and mantra can unite to bring about great transformation. Such "mantric junctures in time" include sunrise, noon and sunset during the day, new and full moons during the month, equinoxes, solstices and eclipses during the year, and powerful planetary combinations at a yet broader level.

Relative to the individual birth chart, such key moments begin with the birth itself, and include beginnings of planetary periods and important planetary transits. Relative to life events, such special times include marriage, birth of children, starting of new ventures, entering a home and all the main events that color our existence. There are special ways to use mantras to improve our karmas at such moments.

Timing in Vedic astrology is part of "Horary astrology" or Muhurta. Muhurta considers the planetary energies operating on a daily basis, particularly those of the Moon. These factors are presented in a Vedic calendar or Panchanga, which emphasizes five main considerations. These are the 1) day of the week based upon which planet rules the day; 2) Nakshatra - Lunar constellation in which the moon is located; 3) Tithi - lunar phase or lunar day; 4) Karana - half of the tithi; 5) Yoga - specific distances of the Sun and Moon.

For choosing a mantra, a good Vedic astrologer will additionally consider the birth chart of the person, their relevant *Dashas* or planetary periods, transits to the birth chart, and the annual chart (Varshaphala). This can take some time and effort to examine correctly. One's astrological birth chart has its own resonances in cosmic sound that can be uncovered through the sounds of the planets, signs and Nakshatras. We will examine these below.

Name Mantras for the Planets

Vedic planetary mantras address the deity or power of consciousness behind the material energy of the planet and are not just an honoring of the planet in the outer sense. Vedic astrology has special mantras for the planets based upon their names. In addition to the main name mantras for the planets, each planet has its broader hundred names, its Stotra or hymn of praise and its Kavacha or hymn of protection. There are also special Vedic verses to the planetary deities and to the Nakshatras that are often used in rituals.[105] Most important are the following names of the nine planets and their seed syllables.[106]

Planet	Sanskrit Name	Mantra
Sun	Sūrya	Oṁ Sūṁ Sūryāya Namaḥ
Moon	Candra	Oṁ Caṁ Candrāya Namaḥ
Mars	Kuja	Oṁ Kuṁ Kujāya Namaḥ
Mercury	Budha	Oṁ Buṁ Budhāya Namaḥ
Jupiter	Bṛhaspati	Oṁ Bṛṁ Bṛhaspataye Namaḥ
Venus	Śukra	Oṁ Śuṁ Śukrāya Namaḥ
Saturn	Śani	Oṁ Śaṁ Śanaye Namaḥ
North Node of Moon	Rāhu	Oṁ Rāṁ Rāhave Namaḥ
South Node of Moon	Ketu	Oṁ Keṁ Ketave Namaḥ

Below is a special set of Tantric bija mantras for the planets that is often used as well.[107] Each set of mantras consists of a set of variations on one primary bija mantra that reflect the planet itself.

Planet	Seed Mantra	Extended Mantra
Sun	Hrīṁ	Oṁ Hrām Hrīṁ Hrauṁ Saḥ Sūryāya Namaḥ
Moon	Śrīm	Oṁ Śrāṁ Śrīm Śrauṁ Saḥ Candrāya Namaḥ
Mars	Krīṁ	Oṁ Krāṁ Krīṁ Krauṁ Saḥ Kujāya Namaḥ
Mercury	Brīṁ	Oṁ Brāṁ Brīṁ Brauṁ Saḥ Budhāya Namaḥ
Jupiter[108]	Grīṁ	Oṁ Grāṁ Grīṁ Grauṁ Saḥ Gurave Namaḥ
Venus	Drīṁ	Oṁ Drāṁ Drīṁ Drauṁ Saḥ Śukrāya Namaḥ
Saturn	Prīṁ	Oṁ Prāṁ Prīṁ Prauṁ Saḥ Śanaye Namaḥ
Rahu	Bhrīṁ	Oṁ Bhrāṁ Bhrīṁ Bhrauṁ Saḥ Rāhave Namaḥ
Ketu	Strīṁ	Oṁ Strāṁ Strīṁ Strauṁ Saḥ Ketave Namaḥ

Such mantras are usually recited at least 108 times on the days that belong to the planets: Sunday for the Sun, Monday for the Moon, Tuesday for Mars, Wednesday for Mercury, Thursday for Jupiter, Friday for Venus and Saturday for Saturn. For Rahu one can use Saturday, as Rahu is like Saturn in nature. For Ketu one can use Tuesday, as Ketu is like Mars in nature.

Instead of the bija mantras for the names of the planets, the Shakti mantras can be used instead, like *Oṁ Hrīṁ Sūryāya Namaḥ*! Or more than one bija can be used like *Oṁ Aiṁ Hrīṁ Śrīṁ Candrāya Namaḥ*. Such combinations should be learned and practiced with the appropriate guidance.[109]

Relative to Ayurveda, one should remember that most Vata disorders and most diseases in general are caused by Saturn and Rahu. Most Pitta disorders are owing to Mars and Ketu. Most Kapha disorders are owing to the Moon. Mantras for the planets can be used to counter diseases owing to the planets, as well as to strengthen the parts of the body that the planets rule over.[110] Besides planetary name mantras, there many other astrological mantras and mantra formulas used in Vedic and yogic practices. There are ways of correlating the Sanskrit alphabet with the planets, Nakshatras and signs of the zodiac. These are found in books on Vedic astrology and are too complex to bring in here.

Chapter 18:

Vastu and Directional Mantras

Mantra is not only connected to movement in time but also to location in space. The different directions of space convey various influences from nature, from other people, from technology, and from the greater universe that can be either helpful or harmful to us. We can use mantras to improve these "directional influences" in our lives that we otherwise have little protection against. There are universal directional influences, as well as those relative to the nature of the topography in which we live, and the orientation of our buildings, houses and rooms.

Most of us do not know how to create a sacred space around us. We may build a house to protect our bodies, but we don't know how to build a house to protect our minds. Nor do we know how to make our house not just a physical refuge, but a refuge for our inner being, a temple as it were. Our minds are vulnerable to directional influences, which carry negative thoughts, negative electrical energies or disturbances in our psychic environment. Many cultures speak of the danger of the "evil eye" or the jealousy of others. This is but one example of how negative forces can come to us like invisible arrows.

At all moments, there are influences coming to us through our environment as well as the thoughts that people are projecting towards us which, given human nature, are often negative in their orientation. We need to close our doors and windows to these negative influences, as it were, both outwardly and inwardly. Directional mantras help us to do that. Otherwise, we are making ourselves unnecessarily vulnerable to negative influences which, like bacteria and viruses, are there for everyone. It is like going outside without the necessary clothing to withstand the elements. Directional mantras can protect not only our dwellings but ourselves and our bodies, wherever we may be. They also serve to bring in positive energies from the Divine and cosmic powers.

Traditional cultures have special methods of honoring the directions, recognizing the type of forces that each direction brings to us. The cosmic quality of each direction can symbolically be regarded as a deity, a special power of consciousness and natural intelligence. The Vedic system presents one of the most comprehensive directional sciences available, and one that is closely linked with the power of mantra. Direction and sound are connected, as sound is the quality that relates to space as an element in yogic thought. Through mantra we can change the energy of our space and through that change the quality of our lives.

Vastu Mantras

Vastu is the Vedic science of architecture and directional influences. It has its own special "Vastu mantras", which are an important method for improving the directional influences in our dwellings. Vastu mantras can help promote positive energies and remove negative energies in the locations we live in, travel through or perform our work. Mantras are applied in Vastu to purify and energize the dwelling in which one is residing. They create a mind and a soul for the structure that we reside in. They are particularly important for sacred spaces, meditation rooms, temples and clinics.

Mantras are an important remedial measure in Vastu. They help clear the psychic and pranic energy in our dwellings and counter any negative effects brought about by improper orientation or "bad Vastu": inappropriate placement of buildings or of rooms within it. It is important to do mantras around the house, just as it is important to clean the floor or open the windows! Even mantras we otherwise may be doing can be performed in the eight directions to protect our Vastu.

Mantras for the directions are important not only in Vastu but also in Yoga. It is essential to have good directional energies relative to your meditation seat or the room where you perform your rituals. Generally, one sits for meditation facing the auspicious east or northeast directions. Mantras to directional deities are an integral part of traditional Yoga practices. Many spiritual traditions consider such directional influences and have mantras, prayers and offerings for them. Astrology and Vastu also correlate, with planetary influences corresponding to specific directions.

Directional influences primarily reflect the influences of the atmosphere or sphere of Vayu (Vayu mandala), which mainly affect Vata dosha, the biological air humor, through the forces of the wind and the weather. Our houses are built to protect us from the negative influences of the air and the seasons.

Directional Deities and Cosmic Principles

NW Vāyu Air	N Soma Mind	NE Īśāna Ether
W Varuṇa Water	C	E Indra Earth
SW Nirṛiti Intelligence	S Yama Ego	SE Agni Fire

Each direction has a "Directional Deity" (Dig Devata), which protects us from the negative energies and promotes the positive energies through their respective directions. The central direction is not counted in the sequence as it represents the place that we are seeking to protect.

Directional deities grant control of both the external and the internal elements and aspects of the psyche that they relate to: the five elements of earth, water, fire, air and ether, mind (manas), ego (ahamkara), and intelligence (buddhi).[111] These relate to the causal body or the prime energies governing our existence, which impact us through the directions. The directions are usually counted off starting in the east.

1) East – *Indra*, the deity of light and the Sun, who relates to the earth as an element and cosmic principle. His seed mantra *Laṁ* stands for the earth element, which he controls. His weapon is the thunderbolt or *Vajra*, which is the Divine light that protects us from the eastern direction. Its bija mantra is *Vaṁ*, which reflects its first syllable.

2) Southeast – *Agni*, the deity of fire and relates to fire as an element and cosmic principle. His mantra *Raṁ* is the seed sound for the Fire element. His weapon is the spear or *Śakti*, which is the Divine fiery energy that protects us from the Southeast.

Its bija mantra is *Śaṁ*, which reflects its first syllable.

3) South– *Yama*, the deity of restraint and death, who relates to ego as a cosmic principle. His seed sound *Māṁ* is that of the ego and grants control over it. His weapon is the *Daṇḍa* or rod, which grants restraint and counters evil influences from the South. Its bija mantra is *Daṁ*, which represents its first syllable and also gives self-control.

4) Southwest – *Nirṛiti*, the deity of dissolution, similar to Kali in qualities, who relates to intelligence (buddhi) as a cosmic principle. Her seed sound is *Kṣaṁ* which gives protection and support and also gives power to the intelligence. Her weapon is the *Khaṅga* or sword, which grants us protection and discrimination from the Southwest. Its bija mantra is *Khaṁ*, which reflects its first syllable.

5) West – *Varuṇa*, the deity of the ocean and the rains, relates to the water element as a cosmic principle, including both earthly and heavenly waters. His mantra *Vaṁ* is the seed sound of water. His weapon is the *Pāśa* or noose, which grants us protection from the West. Its bija mantra is *Paṁ*, which reflects its first syllable.

6) Northwest – *Vāyu* or the wind God relates to the air element as a cosmic principle. His mantra *Yaṁ* is the seed sound of the air element. His weapon is the *Aṅkuśa*, the prod or goad, which grants us protection from the Northwest. Its bija mantra is *Aṁ*, which reflects its first syllable.

7) North – *Soma*, the deity of the Moon, who relates to the mind as a cosmic principle. His mantra *Sauṁ* grants blessings, lunar energy and contentment to the mind, of which it is also the seed mantra. His weapon is the Gada or mace, which grants us protection from the North. Its bija mantra is *Gaṁ*, which reflects its first syllable. Sometimes Kubera, the deity of wealth and abundance, is placed here instead of Soma.

8) Northeast – *Īśāna* or the supreme Lord, who relates to the element of ether or space as a cosmic principle. His mantra *Haṁ* is also the seed sound of the Ether element. His weapon is the *Triśūla*, the trident of Lord Shiva, which protects us from the sacred Northeast direction. Its bija mantra is *Trīṁ*, which reflects its first syllable.

Two other important directional influences are also recognized:

9) Upward direction or above. This corresponds on a horizontal plane with ENE, the intermediate point between East and North East. It is the place of *Brahmā* or the Divine Creator, who represents the ruling spiritual energy coming from above. His mantra *Āṁ* grants expansion to one's being. His weapon or instrument is the Padma or lotus, which showers down blessings on us from above. Its bija mantra is *Paṁ*, which reflects its first syllable.

10) Downward direction or below. This corresponds on a horizontal plane with WSW, the intermediate point between W and SW. It is the place of Ananta, the serpent that upholds the worlds, who represents the support energy coming from below. His mantra *Hrīṁ* gives light and strength at the foundation of the world. His weapon in the Cakra or discus of Lord Vishnu, which protects us from below. Its bija mantra is *Caṁ*, which reflects its first syllable.

Mantras for Directional Deities

We can sanctify each direction through the mantras of its respective deity and its bija. Then we can protect each direction through the weapon of the deity, which has its bija mantra as well.

Directional Deity Name Mantras

Above - Oṁ Āṁ Brahmaṇe Namaḥ		
NW Oṁ Yaṁ Vāyave Namaḥ	N Oṁ Sauṁ Somāya Namaḥ	NE Oṁ Haṁ Īśānāya Namaḥ
W Oṁ Vaṁ Varuṇāya Namaḥ	C	E Oṁ Laṁ Indrāya Namaḥ
SW Oṁ Kṣaṁ Nirṛtaye Namaḥ	S Oṁ Māṁ Yamāya Namaḥ	SE Oṁ Raṁ Agnaye Namaḥ
Below - Oṁ Hrīṁ Anantāya Namaḥ		

Directional Weapon Mantras

Above - Oṁ Paṁ Padmāya Namaḥ		
NW Oṁ Aṁ Aṅkuśāya Namaḥ	N Oṁ Gaṁ Gadāya Namaḥ	NE Oṁ Trīṁ Triśūlāya, Namaḥ
W Oṁ Paṁ Pāśāya Namaḥ	C	E Oṁ Vaṁ Vajrāya Namaḥ
SW Oṁ Khaṁ Khaṅgāya Namaḥ	S Oṁ Daṁ Daṇḍāya Namaḥ	SE Oṁ Śaṁ Śaktaye Namaḥ
Below - Oṁ Caṁ Cakrāya Namaḥ		

Use of Directional Mantras

The simplest way to use these mantras is to recite the mantras of the directional deities in order, starting with Indra in the East, moving on to Agni in the Southeast and then clockwise through the remainder of the deities to Brahma above and Ananta below. This should be followed by their weapon mantras in the same sequence starting in the East. These mantras can be recited on a regular basis to sanctify the energy in your house; at least once a week is a good idea.

Relative to Yoga, one should recite these mantras before one does any serious ritual, practice or meditation. They can also be used to clear the energy from Yoga classrooms. One should face the appropriate direction while repeating the mantras for it. These mantras also protect us from the harmful effects of the elements that they rule over.

Bhuvaneshvari

The form of the Goddess governing space in general is *Bhuvaneshvari*, the Queen of the universe, whose mantra is *Hrīṁ*, the sound of the Divine light. This mantra can be used to consecrate all the directions of space along with honoring her as the deity.[112]

Planets and the Directions

NW - Moon	N - Mercury	NE - Jupiter
W - Saturn		E - Sun
SW - Rahu	S - Mars	SE - Venus

The planets correspond to the directions from which they cast their influences. These correspondences are a little different than those between the planets and the elements, reflecting more subtle qualities.

The Northeast direction has a positive or benefic Jupiterian energy and is good for spiritual and religious practices and influences. North has a positive Mercury energy and is good for learning, study and education. East is the direction of the Sun and is good for work, action, healing and spiritual practices. Southeast has a Venus energy and is a place of power, connection and expression. South has a Mars energy and inclines us to work, action, assertion and conflict. Southwest has a negative Rahu energy and is a place of rest and control. West has a Saturn energy and brings about decay and decline, but also maturity and detachment. Northwest has a lunar energy, but one that tends to be sensitive, vulnerable, changeable and unstable.

One can recite the planetary mantras relative to the directions around your dwelling to clear out any negative astrological energies, starting with *Oṁ Sūṁ Sūryāya Namaḥ*, the mantra for the Sun, in the eastern direction. People with planetary afflictions in their birth chart become vulnerable relative to the direction ruled by the planet. One can recite planetary mantras relative to the direction ruled by any negative planetary influences in one's birth chart for additional protection. Or if there is a very negative transit going on that may be affecting many people, one can chant the mantras of the planets involved with a directional orientation. This requires some knowledge of astrology or the help of an astrologer.

ॐ भूर्भुवः स्वः तत्सवितुर्वरेण्यं भर्गो देवस्य धीमहि धियो यो नः प्रचोदयात्
ॐ

Chapter 19:

Vedic and Vedantic Mantra Yoga

The *Vedas* present the oldest form of the Sanskrit language, the language of mantra. As such, they present us with the oldest form of Mantra Yoga. Mantra Yoga is the oldest and most central of all the Yogas. Classical Yoga evolved out of the language of mantra, which is the language of the spiritually awakened mind that reveals the underlying unity of all existence.

Some scholars argue that there is no Yoga in the *Vedas* because the term Yoga is rare in Vedic texts and no Yoga asanas are described. However, they miss the obvious point: the *Vedas* represent a path of Mantra Yoga, including the use of Divine Names. Mantra, more so than asana, is an indicator of higher Yoga practices and Yoga in general.

The *Vedas* provide a large number of names for the different Vedic deities. Some of these form special sequences, notably the twenty-one names of the Divine Mother. "The seers thought out the first name of the Cow and found the three times seven supreme powers of the Mother."[113] The *Vedas* recognize speech (Vak) as the Mother.

Her forms are different letters or different levels of communication. "The Devas generated the Word Goddess. Her animals of all forms speak."[114] Indeed the *Vedas* are always spoken of as the Mother or Mata Veda.

The *Rigveda*, the oldest and largest of the *Vedas*, speaks of seven levels of speech: 'seven Voices conceive a single child."[115] The voices are feminine and their child is Agni or fire, the Vedic deity ruling over speech. These seven levels of speech may refer to the role of mantra on all the seven planes or lokas of existence from the gross physical to the Supreme Absolute or formless Brahman and to the seven chakras.

The *Rigveda* projects a language of cosmic sound, reflecting the language of nature through the natural forces of light and energy. It consists of various rhythmic chants to the great powers of the conscious universe in order to draw their blessings into our lives. According to the *Vedas*, sound comes from the Sun, which has the nature of light. The Sun is continually chanting *Oṁ*.[116] There is a secret Sun hidden in our hearts. This is the origin of the unstruck sound or *Anahata* that gives rise to the inner sound current or nada.

Single syllable bija mantras are not as evident in the *Vedas* as in later texts. However, they do exist in the *Vedas*, particularly as hidden in the roots of words. Sanskrit words develop from root sounds. For example, the root "*Hu*", which we find in the fiery mantra *Huṁ*, also refers to fire as the invoker (Hota) and to fire offerings (Huti) and fire rituals (Havan, Homa). Sri Aurobindo notes that Vedic Sanskrit evolved from an earlier language of such root sounds, to which various inflections were gradually added.[117] These roots remain more alive and variable in Vedic than in classical Sanskrit.

This means that if one knows the prime roots of the Sanskrit language, one can understand most bija mantras, which are nothing but the language of the Sanskrit roots. Sanskrit etymology, called *Nirukta* in Sanskrit, is one of the *Vedangas* or "limbs of the Vedas" and an important aspect of Mantra Yoga. Such mantric roots are more alive in the Vedic language than they are in later Sanskrit. Vedic Sanskrit arose from these mantric roots at an early stage of human speech.

Vedic Suktas and Vedic Chanting

The *Vedas* consist of special poetic verses or Suktas, referred to as "hymns". Suktas are mantric verses to various deities, which represent forms and aspects of the Divine or Inner Self (Atman or Purusha). Hidden in these Vedic mantras is a complete inner Yoga of the chakras and realization of the higher Self, as well as the foundation for all the Vedic sciences. The *Rigveda* presents the greatest number of Vedic mantras in three tone chant. The *Samaveda* emphasizes a more musical type of chanting as its main form of practice. In fact, the *Vedas* honor the deity primarily as Svara or sound vibration, which is later equated with Shiva. "What is called Svara in the *Vedas* and what is established in the Vedanta, ...that is Maheshvara (Shiva)."[118]

Certain verses from different Vedic Suktas have become important mantras and prayers in their own right. A few of these Vedic verses remain popular in yogic circles. Most notable is the Gayatri Mantra to the Sun God Savita.[119] However, the Gayatri Mantra is one of ten thousand verses of the *Rigveda* and many of these verses have similar powers. The Mahamrityunjaya Mantra to Lord Shiva for warding off death also remains commonly used today.[120] Another very important Vedic verse is the *Haṁsaḥ* Mantra of Vamadeva.[121] Many significant Vedic verses are found in the famous Asya Vamasya Sukta of Dirghatamas.[122] Vedic Shanti mantras or peace mantras, Shanti Patha,[123] are another type of Vedic verse that continues to be widely employed. Many of these Vedic verses occur in the *Upanishads*.[124]

Vedic Suktas, particularly to Soma and Agni, are in my opinion the greatest works of Sanskrit literature, poetry and spirituality. These Vedic hymns have a density and power in the language probably unequalled even in later Sanskrit poetry or Kavya literature. Vedic mantras can be used according to certain methods of pranayama and meditation internally and according to special fire rituals externally, and remain very effective if so employed, even today.

Besides verses directly from the *Vedas*, there are special chants found in supplementary collections of Vedic verses. These include the Sri Sukta to Lakshmi, the Durga Sukta, Sarasvati Sukta, Narayana Sukta and Vishnu Sukta. Certain *Upanishads* are also commonly chanted today; notably the Taittiriya and Mahanarayana, the latter of which contains many older Vedic verses. Some Vedic chants derive from the *Yajurveda*, notably the Rudram, a long chant to Rudra-Shiva that remains the most popular of the longer Vedic chants.[125]

Many people today listen to tapes of Vedic chanting, such as are available from the TM (Transcendental Meditation) movement and other sources. There are several centers in the West that teach Vedic chanting, which is used in some Yoga traditions. The greater Vedic Mantra Yoga is less commonly taught or understood, but is gradually emerging once more.

Gayatri Mantra

The Gayatri Mantra is the most sacred prayer of the Hindus. It has been widely promoted by modern Hindu sects like the Arya Samaj and the Gayatri Pariwar, whose millions of followers recite it daily. Many western Yoga groups now chant the Gayatri as well, though they are not always aware of its sacred origins or intent.

The Gayatri is probably the oldest chant that has been continually recited in the history of the world, with an antiquity of at least five thousand years. It reflects the timelessness of the Vedic language. Below is the Sanskrit and a simple translation.

Oṁ Bhūr, Bhuvaḥ, Svaḥ, Tat Savitur vareṇyam bhargo devasya dhīmahi, dhiyo yo naḥ pracodayāt

Om Earth, Atmosphere, Heaven: We meditate upon the supreme effulgence of the Divine solar Creator, that he may direct our minds.

The *Yajurveda* reveals the sounds of the three worlds *Bhūḥ, Bhuvaḥ, Svaḥ* called *Vyāhṛtis* in Sanskrit, which are placed at the beginning of the Gayatri and other Vedic mantras and function as bija mantras. All three mantras are based on the root vowel-U, which projects a circular and expansive energy that can create and sustain the worlds. The consonant-Bha is the last of the series of the 25 Sanskrit consonants, except the M-sound, and is the most open and expansive of all the consonant sounds. It also relates to the sphere of light, *Bhā*.

Bhūḥ refers to being or existence in the realm of time and space as defined by the development of light. *Bhuvaḥ* refers to energy or becoming and relates to the Atmosphere or realm of intermediate space. Su refers to creation, expression, swelling, revolving and resonating. *Svaḥ*, also rendered as *Suvaḥ*, relates to light, sunlight and the realm of light or Heaven. The *Vyāhṛtis* are sometimes extended to seven with *Maha, Jana, Tapa* and *Satya* added for the four higher worlds of intelligence, bliss, consciousness and pure being.

Vedic Mantra Yoga and Bhakti Yoga

The *Vedas* consist of the human invocation of the Divine and cosmic powers, not only in the world around us but within our own psyche. They speak to the Divine as "Thou" as their main mode of address. Vedic mantras should be directed to the Divine with a sense of a personal and reverential connection in order to have their full efficacy.

In this regard, Vedic mantras promote Bhakti Yoga or the Yoga of devotion. They are directed to the Divine consciousness mirrored in the forces of nature like Fire, Wind and Sun, and in our own inner faculties of speech, mind and prana through various Devatas like Agni, Indra and Surya.

The *Vedas* promote various attitudes of devotion, looking at the Divine as father, mother, brother, sister, friend, master, and beloved. "Thou, O Indra, are our father and our mother, you who have unlimited power, as such we implore your grace."[126] There is no important aspect of devotion that does not occur among the Vedic chants, honoring the Divine as One, as many, as All and as beyond all manifestation, yet woven into a unitary pattern of sound and vibration.

Īṁ, the Supreme Bija Mantra of the *Rigveda*

The *Rigveda* speaks of the primal cosmic word called *Akṣara*, meaning what is imperishable. "All the Divine powers dwell in the syllable of the chant in the supreme ether; those who do not know that, what can they do with the *Veda*?"[127] The mantra *Oṁ* does not appear with any significance in the *Rigveda*, though it is well known in the Yajurveda, but other mantric sounds do occur. Most common in the *Rigveda*, is the mantra *Īṁ*, which is a common interjection in many hymns. The *Yajurveda* speaks with reverence of this word, "Reverence to the sound *Īṁ*."[128]

The great modern Yogi, Kavyakantha Ganapati Muni, the chief disciple of Ramana Maharshi, explains in detail the importance of *Īṁ* as the great mantra from the *Rigveda*, its form of Pranava, equivalent to *Oṁ*, as representing the Cosmic Word.[129] Ganapati Muni's disciple Brahmarshi Daivarata does so as well.[130] It was from Daivarata that Maharishi Mahesh Yogi received much of his Vedic knowledge. He brought Daivarata to the West and spent time with him in India.

Generally, *Īṁ* represents the power of Divine light and seeing, while *Oṁ* projects the power of Divine prana and hearing, though the two are closely linked together. *Īṁ* is the mantra of Indra, the supreme deity of the chant in early Vedic thought. *Oṁ* is the mantra of Shiva, the supreme deity of the chant in later Hindu thought. They are essentially two forms of the same mantra and of the same deity. Through the power of mantra *Īṁ*, the secret of all Vedic mantras can be revealed.

The mantra *Īṁ* is the foundation of most of the Shakti mantras discussed earlier in the book. It projects an energy and power of perception, the electrical force of seeing. It is the mantric sound of the eyes in the Mantra Purusha. The mantra *Īṁ* allows for the awakening of the Shakti of any mantra, and also provides the vision behind the mantra, its knowledge component.

The related Vedic mantra *Sīṁ* refers to the highest, the summit, the power of pure existence, while *Hīṁ* refers to the power of the Vajra or the lightning bolt of pure perception that Indra, the deity of cosmic prana, wields. Brahmarshi Daivarata revealed the great mantra *Īṁ Oṁ Śrīḥ*, which was followed by the Gayatri Mantra.[131] This he regarded as the mantric key to all creation and the basis of all the other Vedic mantras.

Orientation of Vedic Mantras

For all Vedic mantras, there are three primary factors. First is the deity or Devata to which the hymn is being addressed. Second is the meter (chandas), the rhythm or sound form the hymn takes, which is its means or vehicle of expression. The meters are regarded as feminine in nature and reflect the energy or Shakti of the hymn. Third is the rishi or seer who first cognized the hymn. The Vedic rishis have their own stories, energies and attributes which are relevant in understanding their hymns.

For a Vedic mantra to be fully effective, it is said that one should know and honor all three factors. One should chant the hymn according to an inner communion with the Devata, a feeling of the meter or energy power of the chant, and a regard for the rishi.

For example, the Gayatri Mantra is to Savita, who is one of the Adityas or solar Godheads. More specifically, Savita represents the Purusha or consciousness within the Sun as symbolic of the Divine light, especially the transformative power of light. Savita represents the power that changes night into day and day into night. This is why the Gayatri mantra is chanted at sunrise, noon and sunset, the transformational moments of the Sun's movement. In Vedic thought, the Sun is not simply a material globe but the source of prana, intelligence and Divine grace. The Sun is the primal guru. The Vedic mantras themselves reside in the rays of the Sun as powers of light and prana.

The Gayatri mantra was first cognized by the great Rishi Vishvamitra, the most martial and effort-oriented of all the Rishis. This means that the Gayatri is a mantra of effort and tapas, heat and transformation. Vishvamitra was known for his wrathful nature and was a manifestation of Agni or fire. Through the Gayatri mantra, he overcame his personal weaknesses and raised his energy into the highest light, charting a path for all humanity to follow after him and leave behind all their limitations.

The Gayatri mantra is named after the Gayatri meter in which it is cast. There are around two hundred and fifty Vedic hymns in the Gayatri meter, which consists of three verses of eight syllables or twenty four syllables each. The Gayatri meter is most connected to Agni or fire as a deity. It represents the power of the Goddess to move through all difficulties and causes her energy to arise within us.

The Gayatri mantra is a means of bringing solar energy of a spiritual nature into our deeper awareness. It should be chanted at the appropriate transformative moments along with reverence and humility. It can draw down a Divine solar power to energize our minds and prepare them for meditation, much like we use solar cells to electrify our houses. At the highest level, the Gayatri opens our minds and heart to the Supreme Light and grants the highest Self-realization, just like the great sayings and teachings of Vedanta.

Mantra Purusha and Vedic Mantras

The idea of the Mantra Purusha or body of mantra is one of the main Vedic concepts. It is based upon the same division of the types of sounds discussed relative to the Sanskrit alphabet.

The *Aitareya Aranyaka*, from which the *Upanishad* of the same name arises, states: "The consonants are the form of the Earth. The sibilants are the form of the Atmosphere. The vowels are the form of Heaven. The consonants are the form of Agni (light of Earth). The sibilants are the form of Vayu (light of the Atmosphere). The vowels are the form of the Sun (light of Heaven)".[132] This is the same concept as in Shaivite Yoga of the vowels as consciousness (light), the sibilants as Prana or Vayu, and the consonants as the material principle or Earth.

In another instance, the *Aitareya Aranyaka* states that there are 360 vowels, 360 consonants and 360 combinations of the two, referring to their variations and combinations, which relate to the 360 bones, 360 nerves and 360 bone-nerve connections in the body. This results in 540 sounds on the right side of the body and 540 sounds on the left side of the body.[133] These 1080 sounds in turn are said to correspond to the Sun and the 360 days, 360 nights and 360 day-night conjunctions of the year, so they are also part of a cosmic symbolism of light.

While I have not seen a presentation of the Mantra Purusha with the fifty sounds of the Sanskrit alphabet in the *Vedas*, we do find in these statements, a presentation of a Mantra Purusha with 1080 sounds, suggesting a yet more elaborate Mantra Purusha presentation that once probably existed.

Vedic Mantras, Ayurveda, Yoga and Tantra

The *Rigveda* is based on three primary deities Agni, Vayu and Soma, which outwardly correspond to the forces of Fire, Air and Water. Indra as the Supreme deity can be related to all three, but is generally placed in the sphere of Vayu. Surya or the Sun is the essence of all the three. We can find in these Vedic deities the basis of the three Ayurvedic doshas and their subtle essences with Agni, Tejas and Pitta dosha, Soma, Ojas and Kapha dosha, and Vayu, Prana and Vata dosha.

This means that we can repeat Vedic verses to Agni, Indra and Soma to develop the subtle essences of Tejas, Prana and Ojas within us, the spiritual essences of fire, air and water. These subtle essences are the master forms of the doshas that create positive health and help unfold our higher spiritual potential as well.

The hymns to Soma are particularly good to repeat for promoting meditation and samadhi. They aid in developing Tarpaka Kapha, which lubricates the brain and nervous system. The hymns to Agni grant us power of discrimination, speech and meditation. The hymns to Indra give higher powers of prana, will power and deeper perception. The hymns to the Sun or Surya give higher powers of intelligence, comprehension, prana and awareness.

Relative to Tantric principles, the Vedic Agni hymns help awaken the Kundalini Shakti or serpent fire in the root chakra, which is the Agni hidden in the earth of the root and in the recesses of our own psyche. The Soma hymns aid in the flow of Soma from the crown chakra or thousand petalled lotus and descent of Divine bliss and grace into us. Soma flows in a thousand streams covering all the petals of the crown chakra and all possible variations of sound and mantra. The hymns to Indra aid in the opening of the third eye and help us gain mastery over all external forces. The hymns to the Sun aid in the opening of the heart and contact with the omnipresent Divine light of truth.

Vedantic Mantras

The *Vedas* reach their culmination in the profound philosophy of Vedanta, the main principles of which are set forth in the *Upanishads* and *Bhagavad Gita*. The language shifts from cryptic symbolic mantras to profound philosophical utterances, in which the symbolism of light gradually merges into the supreme light of consciousness as Atman or Purusha, the higher Self.

Instead of rhythmical verses like the Gayatri, there are succinct statements of unity with the Supreme Reality, Brahman. These are called *Mahavakyas* or "Great Sayings". They teach and affirm the unity of the individual Self with the Supreme Self, which is the ultimate aim of Yoga. The special resonance of their sounds helps sustain the higher knowledge that they bestow to those who listen to them with an open mind and heart. There are a number of such statements in the *Upanishads*, of which perhaps six are the most important.

- *Aham Brahmāsmi*: I am Brahman or the Supreme Godhead.[134]
- *Ayam Ātmā Brahma*: This Self is Brahman or the Supreme Godhead.[135]
- *Sarvam Khalvidam Brahma*: Everything is Brahman or the Absolute.[136]
- *Tattvamasi*: Thou art That (the Supreme Brahman).[137]
- *So'ham Asmi*: I am He (the Supreme Self).[138]
- *Prajñānam Brahma*: Wisdom is the Supreme Brahman.[139]

All these great sayings are summarized in the single great mantra *Oṁ* that comes to dominate all mantras from the late Vedic era and also means "I am all". There are other important Vedantic mantras in yogic thought, for example, *Oṁ Tat Sat*. *Oṁ* is the Divine Word. *Tat* refers to the Infinite, from the root Ta meaning "to extend". Sat refers to pure existence, from the root As indicating being.

One repeats these mantras as the focus of one's meditation. In them, the meaning is most important, though the special nature of Vedic sound serves to support the meaning in a powerful manner. It is good to adopt one of these Mahavakyas as the great saying to guide one's life and promote one's deeper awareness, motivating us to Self-realization. They provide a higher intention or samkalpa to lead us beyond all lower inclinations.

Appendix 1.

Guidelines on the Chanting of Mantras

If you wish to use any of the mantras in the book, please make sure to keep the following factors in mind.

1. Chant the mantra with a sattvic or pure mind, which implies a peaceful intention and a calm frame of mind. Follow a sattvic or pure life-style while doing the mantra, including a vegetarian diet, refrain from negative emotions, take time in solitude and make your life into a form of service.

2. Honor the Divine power connected to the mantra before starting your practice, whether through mental acknowledgment, some form of ritual, or through a representative form like a statue or picture.

3. Seek further empowerment with the mantra from a guru, a holy site connected to its deity, or through the forces of nature like fire or water.

4. Make sure to pronounce the mantra properly. For this you may need to learn the basic rules of pronouncing the Sanskrit alphabet, starting with the Sanskrit pronunciation key in the book.

5. Initially chant the mantra out loud to gain a sense of its sound pattern. Then chant it softly on the breath to connect it to the prana. But most chanting will be mental while one is silent outwardly.

6. Chant the mantra in a regular manner at a certain time of day for a certain number of times. Generally, single syllable bija mantras like *Krīṁ* or *Hrīṁ* require at least 100,000 repetitions to energize, while longer syllable or extended mantras require at least 10,000, done in a series of regular sessions every day or week for a period of at least one month (often forty days is used). More repetition is generally better than less. Best is to repeat the mantra so often that the mantra starts to repeat itself continually and spontaneously in your deeper mind, even when you are not consciously trying to do so. That is a good sign you have really connected to the power of the mantra.

7. For counting mantras, it is best to use a mala or rosary of 108 beads. For single syllable bija mantras you can count 8, 16 or 32 repetitions of the mantra per bead to make it easier. 60 rounds are necessary for 100,000 repetitions at 16 per bead, 30 rounds at 32 per bead. For longer mantras, you can count one recitation of the mantra per bead. Chanting the mantra in a fast mode helps energize the prana. Chanting it slowly helps calm the mind.

8. Once the mantra has been energized, you can repeat it at will or follow its movement as it naturally arises within you. You need not continue to count it, though this can still be helpful.

9. It is best not to give to others mantras that you yourself have not already practiced or worked with for some period of time. Usually a year is a good minimum. It is better yet to only pass on mantras that you have been taught by a teacher or empowered by a tradition to teach.

Yantras and Colors

Mantras can be energized with yantras, which are geometrical designs. The mantra is the sound body of the deity; the yantra is its energy body. In this regard there are special yantras for all major Hindu deities, particularly the Goddess, and also for planetary deities. Yantra is an entire study in its own right. For higher Mantra sadhana, particularly Mantra Dharana or concentration on a mantra, the yantra is an important, if not indispensible tool. The chakras themselves are yantras or energy patterns that one can so meditate upon. The Shri Yantra, also called Shri Chakra, is the most important of the yantras and contains an extensive mantra sadhana of the Goddess.

Another way to energize mantras is through different colors. One visualizes the mantra in a certain color like golden for *Hrīṁ* or dark blue for *Huṁ*. One can use the colors of the elements in the case of mantras for the five elements,[140] or the colors of the planets for planetary mantras.[141]

Rituals

It is important to include some ritual or at least sacred attitude in the practice of Mantra Yoga. One can begin by offering the mantra to the deity with the folded hands of Namaste, or by offering a flower, candle, ghee lamp or incense to the guru, a sacred text or a sacred image before beginning the mantra practice. One can begin mantra practice with a simple fivefold offering. One can use the bija mantras to the elements for this purpose. These are:

1. A fragrant oil or sandalwood paste for the Earth element and the sensory quality of smell. *Oṁ Laṁ Namaḥ.*
2. Some sweet liquid food like milk for the Water element and the sensory quality of taste. *Oṁ Vaṁ Namaḥ.*
3. A ghee lamp for the Fire element and the sensory quality of sight. *Oṁ Raṁ Namaḥ.*
4. Some incense for the Air element and the sensory quality of touch. *Oṁ Yaṁ Namaḥ.*
5. A flower for the Ether element and the sensory quality of sound. *Oṁ Haṁ Namaḥ.*[142]

There are many traditional rituals or pujas that consist mainly of mantras and can be quite complex. These include gestures or mudras and a variety of offerings. Mudras are another important way to energize mantra and mantras are an important way to empower mudras, but also require a separate study.

Use of Different Kinds of Malas

Malas are important tools of both worship and healing. They relate to different deities and have their specific powers that can be used to hold the energies of mantras in different ways. When we use a mala with our mantra recitation, the power of the mantra enters into the beads of the mala, which become energized at a subtle level. The more often we use them, the greater their power becomes. The mala gathers and magnifies the power of the mantra forming a sphere of energy and protection around us.

Rudraksha is the most commonly used bead for malas. It is the seed of a special tropical tree. It comes in different forms, but overall it is heating and sacred to Lord Shiva, increasing Tejas and Agni. It also helps arouse the Kundalini. There are several types of Rudrakshas, with the smaller beads generally regarded as more powerful. However, the five-faced beads, though large, are also very powerful. They relate to the five faces of Lord Shiva. One faced beads relate to the Supreme Shiva and pure unity. Two face beads are Shiva-Shakti. Rudrakshas can be found with faces up to fourteen, which all have their special powers. Rudraksha, however, can be too hot for some people. One may need to combine it with sandalwood or crystal to make it suitable.

Sandalwood malas are cooling and soothing to the mind and heart. They are sacred to Vishnu. Those who find the Rudraksha to be heating can wear a sandalwood mala as well to help balance the energy of the Rudraksha.

Tulsi or holy basil malas are stimulating and help open the mind and heart and are often used relative to Vishnu, Krishna or Dhanvantari. They are made of the wood from the bush.

Crystal malas are cooling and clearing. They are often sacred to the Goddess, but can relate to Shiva as well. Combined crystal and Rudraksha malas are Shiva-Shakti.

Coral malas are warming and strengthening. They are often used to promote the Shiva energy as well. Astrologically, they relate to the planet Mars.

Malas can also be made of gems that reflect planetary energies. Garnet malas have a solar energy, pearl malas a lunar energy, coral malas relate to Mars, green gemstones like peridot to Mercury, citrine to Jupiter, clear crystal to Venus, amethyst to Saturn, hessonite garnet to Rahu and cat's eye to Ketu.

Malas can be stranded in gold, silver, copper or other types of threads. Gold is probably the most powerful. Wearing a mala, one should note, is not a matter for public display or a fashion statement. While one can wear a protective mala at all times, one usually keeps special sadhana malas away from public contact, viewing or touch. Remember the mala is a sacred implement that itself needs to be honored.

Mantra for purifying Rudraksha

Rūṁ Śrīṁ Hrīṁ Rūṁ Svāhā!

Repeat the mantra at least 108 times while first using the mala or whenever you feel a need to purify it (at least once a year).

Appendix 2.

Mantra Purusha and Marma Points

Mantra Purusha sounds relate to specific marma points and regions of the body. We can call these "Marma Mantras". It is not possible in this context to present a detailed account of the location or description of all the marmas mentioned. The reader is requested to refer to the book *Ayurveda and Marma Therapy* or other books on marmas for that particular information.[143]

The sixteen vowels for the head have important marma correlations. The short A-vowel that is the root of and prime tone behind all sounds, is only generally correlated to the head in most presentations of the Mantra Purusha. However, in the *Mantra Yoga Samhita*, it relates to the top of the head and would best correspond to Adhipati marma at the top center of the head. It connects to the crown chakra, our root prana and inner consciousness and helps balance our mental and energy fields.

The long Ā-vowel in most Mantra Purusha presentations relates generally to the face. However, in the *Mantra Yoga Samhita*, it relates specifically to the forehead, which makes more sense relative to marmas. I would relate it to the center of the forehead (Lalata marma) or to the third eye (middle of the brows), as governing the outer mind and senses, as opposed to Adhipati governing the inner mind beyond the senses. It may connect to the temples as well.

The I-vowels for the right and left eye probably best relate to the Apanga marmas at the outside corner of the eyes. However, they can be related to other marmas around the eyes. The U-sounds for the right and left ears probably best correspond to Vidhura marmas at the outside corner of the ears, though other ear marmas are relevant.

The vowel-Ṛ sounds relate to the Phana marmas at the outside corner of the nostrils. The vowel-Ḷ sounds seem best to relate to the Shringataka marmas on central cheek bones, which are the main marma in their region of the cheeks.

The E and Ai vowels relate to the points above and below the center of the lips. The O and Au-vowels relate to the points above and below the center of the front teeth. These are not classical marmas but are points that we can easily identify.

The Aṁ and Aḥ-vowels are often related to the short and long A-vowels in terms of their locations and indications. In the *Mantra Yoga Samhita*, they relate to the upper and lower region of the palate at the back of the mouth, which would make more sense in the sequence.

The twenty consonants for the arms and legs have clear marma correspondences, as they relate primarily to the joints. The mantras on the arms correspond to the joints of the arm, elbow and wrist. The shoulder mantras can be related to various shoulder marmas, mainly Kakshadhara, the main shoulder marma. The elbows and wrist have their own specific marmas, Kurpara and Manibandha.

The points at the root of the fingers correspond to the Kshipra marma, which though usually given for the joint between the thumb and index finger, has counterparts on the roots of the other fingers as well. The tip of the fingers can be corresponded to marma points on the inside of each fingernail, though these also are not among the main classical marmas.

The mantras on the legs correspond in the same way as those of the arms, first to the joints of the hip (Katikataruna mainly), knee (Janu) and ankle (Gulpha). The roots of the toes relate to the foot Kshipra marmas, and the tips of the toes to the points on the inside of the toenails, just as the points on the inside of the fingernails.

The five labial sounds cover the lower abdomen. Some relate to specific marmas like the navel (for *Bhaṁ*). For others, we can determine a location, though it may not be a classical marma. There are points on the middle abdomen to the right side of the navel that can correspond to the sound *Paṁ*, and points on the middle abdomen to the left side of the navel that can correspond to the sound *Phaṁ*. For *Baṁ*, which relates to the lower back, we could probably use the point of the spine opposite the navel, the point of the navel chakra. For the mantra *Maṁ*, the Basti (bladder) marma on the lower abdomen appears to be the best correlate.

The semivowels have three levels of relationships to our physiology. The first is relative to the tissues (dhatus). The second is relative the chakras. The third is relative the region of the chest around the heart. These can be related to different marma points.

For the chakras, we can use the respective chakra mantras for the points of the chakras along the spine: *Laṁ* for the base of the spine, *Vaṁ* for the region of the spine opposite the root of the reproductive organs, *Raṁ* for the region of the spine opposite the navel, *Yaṁ* for the region of the spine opposite the heart. We can also use these spinal points for the respective tissues that these sounds relate to (*Yaṁ* and plasma etc.).

Relative to the region around the heart in the front of the body, *Yaṁ* corresponds to the heart itself, *Raṁ* to the region to the right of the heart and the right nipple, and *Vaṁ* to the left of the heart and the left nipple. *Laṁ* may correspond to the region below the heart, perhaps to the base of the sternum, though it is usually connected to the energy flow from the heart to the top of the soft palate of the mouth.

The sibilants have several levels of correspondence. Like the semi-vowels, they correspond to the tissues and to the heart, but they relate more to energy flows or channels from the heart than to single locations. We can relate them to the marmas in the palms of the hand and soles of the feet where their respective energy flows end.

For *Śaṁ* from the heart to the right hand, we can use the right Talahridaya marma on the center of the right hand. For *Ṣaṁ* that relates to the heart to the left hand, we can use the left Talahridaya marma on the center of the left hand. For *Saṁ* that relates to the flow from the heart to the right foot, we can use the right Talahridaya marma on the center of the sole of the right foot. For *Haṁ* that relates to the flow from the heart to the left foot, we can use the left Talahridaya marma on the center of the soul of the left foot.

Some of the sibilants have additional correspondences to the chakras, *Haṁ* for the region of the spine opposite the neck, if not for the front base of the neck itself, and *Kṣaṁ* for the region of the spine opposite the third eye.

Relative to usage, one can chant the appropriate Mantra Purusha sound relative to the respective marma. This can be combined along with touching the point, directing one's prana there and holding one's attention there (dharana). The Marma Mantras serve to activate the mind or spirit of the marma and link prana, mind, marma and body. Their effects will reflect the general qualities and energetics of the particular marmas and mantras used.

For example, I-vowels for the right and left eye, can be used along with their marmas to strengthen vision and direct various healing energies to the eyes. On a yogic level, they can help open higher powers of vision and perception beyond the ordinary senses. All the indications provided relative the Mantra Purusha and how to use it can be brought in here.

Appendix 3.

Complete Mantra Purusha Nyasa

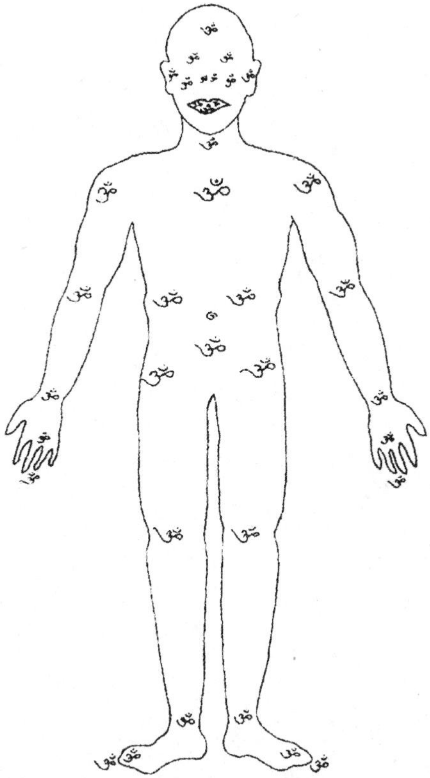

Below is the complete Sanskrit for the Mantra Purusha, which includes the bija mantras and the Sanskrit names of the bodily locations along with *Namaḥ*. This is for those who have interest in the complete Sanskrit renditions. The basic meaning is *Oṁ*, followed by the seed sound for the bodily location, *Namaḥ*, meaning reverence, to the name of the place. "*Oṁ Iṁ*, reverence to the right eye!" for example.

One can use these longer mantras in the same manner as indicated for the Mantra Purusha, including adding Shakti bijas and deity mantras to their recitation for additional effects. The goal of all such practices is to strengthen one's own Mantra Purusha or body of sound and use it to bring spiritual and sattvic qualities into the body and mind.

The Sixteen Vowels and the Head	
Oṁ Aṁ Namaḥ Śirasi	Head
Oṁ Āṁ Namaḥ Mukhe	Face
Oṁ Iṁ Namaḥ Dakṣiṇa Netre	Right eye
Oṁ Īṁ Namaḥ Vāma Netre	Left eye
Oṁ Uṁ Namaḥ Dakṣiṇa Karṇe	Right ear
Oṁ Ūṁ Namaḥ Vāma Karṇe	Left ear
Oṁ Ṛṁ Namaḥ Dakṣiṇa Nāsapuṭe	Right nostril
Oṁ Ṝṁ Namaḥ Vāma Nāsapuṭe	Left nostril
Oṁ Ḷṁ Namaḥ Dakṣiṇa Kapola	Right cheek
Oṁ Ḹṁ Namaḥ Vāma Kapola	Left cheek
Oṁ Eṁ Namaḥ Ūrdvoṣṭhe	Upper lip
Oṁ Aiṁ Namaḥ Adharoṣṭhe	Lower lip
Oṁ Oṁ Namaḥ Ūrdhva Dantapaṅktau	Upper row of teeth
Oṁ Auṁ Namaḥ Adho Dantapaṅktau	Lower row of teeth
Oṁ Aṁ Namaḥ Mūrdhani	Head
Oṁ Aḥ Namaḥ Mukhavṛtte	Face

The Ten Consonants and the Arms	
Oṁ Kaṁ Namaḥ Dakṣiṇa Bāhumūle	Right shoulder
Oṁ Khaṁ Namaḥ Dakṣiṇa Kūrpare	Right elbow
Oṁ Gaṁ Namaḥ Daksiṇa Maṇibandhe	Right wrist
Oṁ Ghaṁ Namaḥ Dakṣiṇa Hastāṅgulimūle	Right root of fingers
Oṁ Ṅaṁ Namaḥ Dakṣiṇa Hastāṅgulyagre	Right tip of fingers
Oṁ Caṁ Namaḥ Vāma Bāhumūle	Left shoulder
Oṁ Chaṁ Namaḥ Vāma Kūrpare	Left elbow
Oṁ Jaṁ Namaḥ Vāma Maṇibandhe	Left wrist
Oṁ Jhaṁ Namaḥ Vāma Hastāṅgulimūle	Left root of fingers
Oṁ Ñaṁ Namaḥ Vāma Hastāṅgulyagre	Left tip of fingers

The Ten Consonants and the Legs	
Oṁ Ṭaṁ Namaḥ Dakṣiṇa Pādamūle	Right leg
Oṁ Ṭhaṁ Namaḥ Dakṣiṇa Jānuni	Right knee
Oṁ Ḍaṁ Namaḥ Dakṣiṇa Gulphe	Right ankle
Oṁ Ḍhaṁ Namaḥ Dakṣiṇa Pādāṅgulimūle	Right root of toes
Oṁ Ṇaṁ Namaḥ Dakṣiṇa Pādāṅgulyagre	Right tip of toes
Oṁ Taṁ Namaḥ Vāma Pādamūle	Left leg
Oṁ Thaṁ Namaḥ Vāma Jānuni	Left knee
Oṁ Daṁ Namaḥ Vāma Gulphe	Left ankle
Oṁ Dhaṁ Namaḥ Vāma Pādāṅgulimūle	Left root of toes
Oṁ Naṁ Namaḥ Vāma Pādāṅgulyagre	Left tip of toes
The Five Consonants and the Abdominal Region	
Oṁ Paṁ Namaḥ Dakṣiṇa Parśve	Right side
Oṁ Phaṁ Namaḥ Vāma Parśve	Left side
Oṁ Baṁ Namaḥ Pṛṣṭhe	Back
Oṁ Bhaṁ Namaḥ Nābhau	Navel
Oṁ Maṁ Namaḥ Udare	Belly
The Ten Semi-Vowels and Sibilants and the Regions of the Chest, Tissues, Energy Flows and Essences	
Oṁ Yaṁ Rasātmane Namaḥ Hṛdi	The soul of the skin, the heart
Oṁ Raṁ Raktātmane Namaḥ Dakṣāṁse	The soul of the blood, the right side
Oṁ Laṁ Māṁsātmane Namaḥ Kakudi	The soul of the muscles, the palate
Oṁ Vaṁ Medātmane Namaḥ Vāmāṁse	The soul of the fat tissue, the left side
Oṁ Śaṁ Asthyātmane Namaḥ Hṛdayādi Dakṣahastāntam	The soul of the bones, the heart to the end of the right hand
Oṁ Ṣaṁ Majjātmane Namaḥ Hṛdayādi Vāmahastāntam	The soul of the nerve, the heart to the end of the left hand
Oṁ Saṁ Śukrātmane Namaḥ Hṛdayādi Dakṣa Pādāntam	The soul of the reproductive tissue, the heart to the end of the right foot
Oṁ Haṁ Ātmane Namaḥ Hṛdayādi Vāma Pādāntam	The soul, the heart to the end of the left foot
Oṁ Laṁ Paramātmane Namaḥ Jaṭhare	The supreme soul, the belly
Oṁ Kṣaṁ Prāṇātmane Namaḥ Mukhe	The soul of prana, the face

One can use these longer mantras in the same manner as indicated for the Mantra Purusha, including adding Shakti bijas and deity mantras to their recitation for additional effects. The goal of all such practices is to strengthen one's own Mantra Purusha or body of sound and use it to bring spiritual and sattvic qualities into the body and mind.

Appendix 4.

Sanskrit Pronunciation Key

These are some of the best English equivalent sounds possible, but note that they are only approximations and not a substitute for a deeper study of the Sanskrit alphabet.

1. Sixteen Vowels - Svara

अ - a, a as in *a*bout
आ - *ā*, a as in f*a*ther
इ - *i*, i as in *it*
ई - *ī* , as in s*ea*t
उ - *u*, u as in fl*u*te
ऊ - *ū*, as in m*oo*d
ऋ - *ṛ*, as in acr*e*
ॠ - *ṝ*, same as *ṛ* but longer
ऌ - *ḷ*, as in table
ॡ - *ḹ*, same as *ḷ* but longer
ए - *e*, as c*a*me
ऐ - *ai*, as in wh*y*
ओ - *o*, as in y*o*ke
औ - *au*, as in *ou*ch
अँ - *aṁ*, nasal mmm
अः - *aḥ*, soft ha sound

2. Four Semivowels and Five Sibilants or Nine Intermediate Sounds – Ushma/Antahstha

य - *ya*, y as in *y*oga
र - *ra*, r as in *r*ich (slight rolled r)
ल - *la*, l as in laugh
व - *va*, v as in vat
श - *śa*, as in *sh*ip
ष - *ṣa*, as in *sh*ut
स - *sa*, s as in sit
क्ष - *kṣa*, as in a*ct*ion
ह - *ha*, h as in hit

3. Twenty Five Consonants or Five Groups of Five

क- *ka*, *k* as in *k*it
ख - *kha*, as in block*h*ead
ग - *ga*, g as in *g*o
घ - *gha*, dog*h*ouse
ङ- *ṅa*, as in si*ng*

च - *ca*, as in *ch*urch
छ - *cha*, as in it*ch*
ज - *ja*, j as in *j*oke
झ - *jha*, as sled*ge*h*ammer
ञ - *ña*, as in ca*ny*on

ट - *ṭa*, t as in ar*t*
ठ - *ṭha*,as in ar*th*ouse
ड - *ḍa*, d as in har*d*
ढ - *ḍha*, as in har*dh*at
ण - *ṇa*, n as in hor*n*

त - *ta*, t as in stop
थ - *tha*, as in ho*th*ouse
द - *da*, d as in *d*ose
ध - *dha*, as in a*dh*oc
न - *na*, as in *n*ap

प - *pa*, p as in *p*it
फ -*pha*, as in to*ph*at
ब - *ba*, b as in *b*at
भ - *bha*, as in clu*bh*ouse
म -*ma*, m as in *m*an

Glossary of Terms

Advaita – Non-duality
Agni – cosmic fire principle
Aham – sense of I
Ahamkara – ego
Akshara – letter
Ananda – bliss
Anusvara – resonating final-m type sound
Apana – descending aspect of Prana
Artha – wealth and prosperity as goal of life
Astra – weapon
Atman – higher Self
Ayurveda – Vedic medicine

Bhakti – devotion
Bhairava – fierce form of Shiva
Bhairavi – Fire Goddess
Bija mantra – Seed mantra, single syllable
Bindu – point of awareness
Brahman – Absolute, Pure Being
Brahma – Creative aspect of Hindu Trinity
Buddhi – intelligence

Cerebral – sound made with the tongue placed at the roof of the mouth
Chakras – subtle energy centers along the spine
Chandi – fierce form of the Goddess
Chandra – Moon
Chhandas – meter
Chitta – mental field

Dakinis – Shaktis of the chakras
Dental – sound made with the tongue placed at the back of the teeth
Deva – Divine being or being of light
Devata – Divine or cosmic principle, deity, God or Goddess
Devi – Goddess
Dhanvantari – Vishnu as the deity of healing
Dharana – concentration as a limb of Yoga practice
Dharma – law of nature, vocation as goal of life
Dhatu – tissue of the body
Dhyana – meditation
Dosha - biological humor of Ayurveda
Drishti – gaze
Durga – fiery protective form of the Mother Goddess

Ganapati – another name for Ganesha
Ganesha – Deity of knowledge, teaching, speech and skill; portrayed with the head of an elephant

Gayatri – prime Vedic chant to the Sun as the Divine Light
Guna – quality of nature, especially three gunas of Sattva, Rajas and Tamas
Guttural – sound made in the base of the throat

Hamsa – swan or bird of the soul as power of breath
Hatha Yoga – Yoga of the Sun and the Moon, internal energy balancing
Havan – fire offering
Hridaya – spiritual heart

Indra – Vedic deity governing perception, also name of deity of the eastern direction
Ida Nadi – left nostril, lunar channel
Ishta Devata – chosen deity for worship
Ishvara – Cosmic Lord or God in theistic sense

Japa – repetition of a mantra
Jatharagni- digestive fire
Jiva – soul
Jnana – spiritual knowledge
Jyoti – Light
Jyotish – Vedic astrology

Kali – Goddess of transformation, dissolution, electrical energy
Kama – desire, happiness as goal of life
Kapha – biological water humor
Kavacha – shield mantra for providing protection
Ketu – south node of the Moon
Kilana – nailing mantra, to hold energy
Kirtan – chanting
Koshas – sheaths, bodies or fields around the soul
Krishna – bliss avatar of Lord Vishnu
Kriya – Yoga practice or action
Kundalini – inner power of Yoga, serpent energy of the chakras

Labial – sound made with the lips
Lakshmi – Goddess of preservation, support, nourishment
Laya – mergence, particularly into the sound current
Loka – plane of experience or world

Madhyama Vak – middle or pranic level of speech
Mahavakya – great knowledge affirmations of Vedanta
Maheshvara – Shiva as the great lord of the universe
Mala – rosary of beads for counting mantras
Manas – mind
Mantra Purusha – body or person composed of sound or mantra
Marmas – energy zones or points on the body
Moksha – liberation of soul from cycle of rebirth
Mudras – yogic hand gestures
Muhurta – timing science of Vedic astrology

Nada – vibration, generally sound
Nadi – pranic channel of the subtle body
Nakshatras – 27 lunar constellations
Namah – mantra of consecration or respect
Nirukta – Sanskrit etymology
Nyasa – consecration, usually through mantra of various parts of the body

Ojas – vital essence of Kapha dosha

Palatal – sound made at the soft palate
Panchanga – Hindu/Vedic astrology yearly almanac
Para Vak – transcendental level of speech
Pashyanti Vak – illumined or perceptive level of speech
Pingala nadi – right nostril, solar nadi
Pitta – biological fire humor
Prakasha – pure light
Prakriti – Nature
Prana – life-force and cosmic energy
Pranava- primal sound staring with Om
Prarthana – prayer
Pratyahara – yogic internalization of mind and senses
Puja – Ritual of offerings, mainly flowers
Purusha – Cosmic Person, higher Self

Rahu – north node of the Moon
Raja Yoga – Yoga of the eight limbs
Rajas – quality of energy and agitation
Rama – protective avatar of Vishnu
Rasa – essence
Rigveda – prime Vedic mantric text
Rishis – Vedic seers and yogis
Rudra – fierce or fiery form of Shiva
Rudraksha – Mala made of Rudraksha tree seeds

Sadhana – deeper Yoga practice
Samadhi – merged or deep meditation state of the mind
Samana – balancing aspect of Prana
Sarasvati – Goddess of Wisdom
Sattva – quality of harmony, balance and light
Shabda – sound vibration
Shakti – cosmic energy as form of the Divine feminine
Shankara – blessing or boon giving form of Shiva
Shanti mantra – peace chant or invocation
Shiva – cosmic masculine energy, Being of the Absolute
Skanda – fire God as son of Shiva and Parvati
So'ham – natural mantra of the breath
Soma – cosmic water and bliss principle, Moon
Sparsha – consonant

Stotra – classical Sanskrit hymns, chants and prayers
Sundari – Goddess of spiritual beauty and bliss, also called Tripura Sundari
Surya – solar Principle
Sukta – Vedic hymns, chants and prayers
Sushumna – central channel or spine of the subtle body and chakras
Svara – vowel, resonance, vibratory energy
Svaha – fire consecration mantra

Tamas – quality of darkness and inertia
Tantra – teaching or technical text of energetic Yoga practices
Tapas – power of self-discipline
Tara – Goddess of inner fire of knowledge
Tarpaka Kapha – Kapha governing the nervous system
Tejas – spiritual energy of fire

Udana – ascending aspect of Prana
Upaya – remedial measure in Vedic astrology
Ushma – sibilant

Vaikhari Vak – audible level of speech
Vak – Speech, Divine Word, Goddess
Varga – group of sounds
Vastu – Vedic architectural and directional science
Vata – biological air humor
Vayu – cosmic air principle
Vedanta – philosophical portion of Vedas, emphasizing Self-realization
Vidyut – electrical energy at a cosmic level, also produces sound
Visarga – aspirated final vowel repetition
Vishnu – Cosmic Pervader
Vyana – expansive aspect of Prana
Vyanjana – consonant

Yajna – fire ritual
Yantra – geometrical meditation designs
Yoginis – Goddesses as powers of Yoga

Bibliography

General

Ashley-Farrand, Thomas.
SHAKTI MANTRAS: TAPPING INTO THE GREAT GODDESS ENERGY WITHIN. New York City, NY: Ballantine Books, 2003.

Aurobindo, Sri.
SECRET OF THE VEDA. Twin Lakes, WI: Lotus Press, 1995.
www.lotuspress.com

Aurobindo, Sri.
SAVITRI: A LEGEND AND A SYMBOL. Twin Lakes, WI: Lotus Press, 1995.

Chopra, Shambhavi.
YOGIC SECRETS OF THE DARK GODDESS.
Delhi, India: Wisdom Tree Books, 2007.

Chopra, Shambhavi.
YOGINI: UNFOLDING THE GODDESS WITHIN
Delhi, India: Wisdom Tree Books, 2006.

Frawley, Ranade and Lele.
AYURVEDA AND MARMA THERAPY. Twin Lakes, WI: Lotus Press, 2003.

Frawley, David.
AYURVEDA AND THE MIND: THE HEALING OF CONSCIOUSNESS.
Twin Lakes, WI: Lotus Press, 1997.
www.lotuspress.com

Frawley, David.
AYURVEDIC ASTROLOGY: SELF-HEALING THROUGH THE STARS.
Twin Lakes, WI: Lotus Press, 2005.
www.lotuspress.com

Frawley, David.
AYURVEDIC HEALING: A COMPREHENSIVE GUIDE. Twin Lakes, WI: Lotus Press, 2001.
www.lotuspress.com

Frawley, David.
INNER TANTRIC YOGA: WORKING WITH THE UNIVERSAL SHAKTI.
Twin Lakes, WI: Lotus Press, 2008.
www.lotuspress.com

Frawley, David.
TANTRIC YOGA AND THE WISDOM GODDESSES.
Twin Lakes, WI: Lotus Press, 2003.
www.lotuspress.com

Frawley, David.
WISDOM OF THE ANCIENT SEERS:
SELECTED MANTRAS FROM THE RIG VEDA.
Twin Lakes, WI.: Lotus Press, 1999.
www.lotuspress.com

Frawley, David.
YOGA AND AYURVEDA: SELF-HEALING AND SELF-REALIZATION.
Twin Lakes, WI: Lotus Press, 1999.
www.lotuspress.com

Johari, Harish.
TOOLS FOR TANTRA. Rochester, VT: Inner Traditions International, 1986.

Raman. B.V.
MUHURTA OR ELECTIONAL ASTROLOGY.
Bangalore, India: IBH Prakashan, 1979.

Sivananda, Swami.
JAPA YOGA. Shivanandanagar, India: The Divine Life Society, 1992.

Swarup, Ram.
THE WORD AS REVELATION: Names of Gods.
Delhi, India: Voice of India, 2001.

Tigunait, Pandit Rajmani.
MANTRA AND INITIATION. Honesdale, PA.:
Yoga International Books, 1996.

Tyberg, Dr. Judith.
THE LANGUAGE OF THE GODS. Los Angeles, CA:
East West Cultural Center, 1976.

Vishnu-devananda, Swami.
MEDITATION AND MANTRAS. New York, NY: Om Lotus Publishing, 1995.

Woodroofe, Sir John/ Avalon, Arthur.
THE SERPENT POWER. Minneola, NY: Dover Books, 1974.

Woodroofe, Sir John/ Avalon, Arthur.
THE GARLAND OF LETTERS, NY: Dover Books, 1974.

Sanskrit Texts

Abhinavagupta. PARATRISIKA VIVARANA (Jaidev Singh translation).
Delhi, India: Motilal Banarsidass, 1988.

Abhinavagupta. TANTRASARA (Sanskrit only).
Delhi, India: Bani Prakashan, 1983.

AITAREYA ARANYAKA (with Sayana commentary, Sanskrit only).
Delhi, India: Ananda Ashram 1992.

AKASHA BHAIRAVA TANTRA (Sanskrit and Hindi). Nanak Chand Sharma, editor.
Delhi, India: Motilal Banarsidass, 1980.

Bhartrihari. VAKYAPADIYA (Sanskrit only).
Pune, India: University of Poona Sanskrit and Prakrit Series Vol. II., 1965.

Daivarata, Brahmarshi. VAK SUDHA (Sanskrit only).
Kolkatta, India: Madangopal Podar Charitable Trust, 1972.

Daivarata, Brahmarshi. CHANDO DARSHANA (Sanskrit and English).
Bombay, India: Bharatiya Vidya Bhavan, 1968.

Dikshit, Rajesh. THE DASA MAHAVIDYA (Sanskrit and Hindi).
Agra, India: Deep Publications, 2003.

Goswami, Lakshmi Narain. DURGA TANTRA SHASTRA (Sanskrit and Hindi).
Agra, India: Deep Publications, 2003.

MANTRA PUSHPAM (Sanskrit only).
Mumbai, India: Ramakrishna Math, 1994.

MANTRA YOGA SAMHITA (Sanskrit and English).
Varanasi, India: Chaukhambha Orientalia, 1976.

Patañjali, YOGA SUTRAS (Sanskrit only).
Varanasi, India: Bharatiya Vidya Prakashana, 1983,
with commentaries of Vachaspati Mishra and Vijnana Bhikshu.

Rao, S.K. Ramachandra. THE TANTRIK PRACTICES IN SRI VIDYA
(with Shri Sarada Chatussati, English and Sanskrit).
Bangalore, India: Kalpatharu Research Academy, 1990.

RIGVEDA SAMHITA (Sanskrit, with some English).
Bangalore, India: Sir Aurobindo Kapali Sastry Institute
of Vedic Culture, 1998.

Shankaracharya. SAUNDARYA LAHARI (V.K. Subramanian trans.).
Delhi, India: Motilal Banarsidass, 1986.

UPANISHADS, ONE HUNDRED AND EIGHTY EIGHT (Sanskrit only).
Delhi, India: Motilal Banarsidass, 1980.

Vasistha Ganapati Muni. COLLECTED WORKS OF VASISTHA
KAVYAKANTHA GANAPATI MUNI (Sanskrit only), in eleven volumes,
edited by K. Natesan.
Tiruvannamalai, India: Sri Ramanasramam 2003-2007.

VASISTA SAMHITA (Sanskrit and Hindi).
Lonavala, India: Kaivalya Dham, 1984.

YOGINI HRIDAYA TANTRA (Sanskrit and Hindi),
Vrajavallabha Dvivedi commentary.
Delhi, India: Motilal Banarsidass, 1980.

Resources

The Author and His Institute

Dr. David Frawley (Pandit Vamadeva Shastri)

Dr. David Frawley is the author of more than thirty books and several distance learning courses written over the past thirty years. His books are available in fifteen languages and include important publications in the fields of Ayurvedic medicine, Vedic astrology, Raja Yoga, Veda, Vedanta and Tantra. His works are noted for their depth and specificity and often serve as textbooks in their respective fields.

Vamadeva is one of the most respected *Vedacharyas* or teachers of the ancient Vedic wisdom in recent decades, East and West. He is honored in traditional circles in India, where his writings are well known. He is also regarded as a teacher or acharya of Yoga, Ayurveda and Vedic astrology, reflecting his rare ability to link different Vedic disciplines and teach them in an integral manner.

Vamadeva has worked with such important teachers as Swami Veda Bharati, Swami Dayananda Sarasvati, Pramukh Swami, Sri Sivananda Murty, K. Natesan, M.P. Pandit, Ram Swarup, Chakrapani Ullal and B.V. Raman, and such organizations as the Sri Aurobindo Ashram, the Ramanashram, Hinduism Today, Sringeri Shankaracharya Math, Ramakrishna-Vedanta, Chinmaya Mission, Vivekananda Yoga Kendra, Swaminarayan (BAPS), Paramarth Niketan, Gayatri Pariwar, Sivananda Yoga-Vedanta, Kripalu, Yogaville, and Self-realization Fellowship (SRF), among many other groups and organizations.

American Institute of Vedic Studies, www.vedanet.com

The American Institute of Vedic Studies is an internationally recognized center for Vedic learning, with affiliated organizations in several countries. Directed by Dr. David Frawley (Pandit Vamadeva Shastri) and Yogini Shambhavi Chopra, the Vedic institute serves as a vehicle for their work, their books, CDs and activities. Located near Santa Fe, New Mexico, USA.

The institute offers in depth training, including distance learning programs, in Ayurvedic medicine (Ayurvedic Healing course), Yoga, mantra and meditation (Advanced Yoga and Ayurveda course), and Vedic astrology (Vedic Astrology and Ayurveda course). The institute also conducts regular tours and retreats in India as well as various international programs and events. The institute website features extensive on-line articles, on-line books and a full range of Vedic resources for the serious student, including a regular newsletter and on-going newsgroup.

All institute courses and programs address the topic of mantra, notably our Advanced Yoga and Ayurveda course, which explains mantra and meditation relative to the chakras and deities as its primary therapeutic tool. Our work with Vedic astrology discusses planetary mantras, which we also prescribe for our clients. Our work with Ayurvedic medicine recommends special healing mantras, particularly for diseases of the nervous system and the mind, as well as for constitutional balancing. Our retreats and tours focus on mantra sadhana, particularly relative to the Goddess or Mahashakti and Parashiva. Please contact us for further information and current schedules.

Additional Resources

The American Sanskrit Institute, www.americansanskrit.com

Directed by Vyaas Houston, one of the most renowned western Sanskrit teachers, an important center for Sanskrit studies in the West, offers learning Sanskrit by CD, including a complete guide to Sanskrit pronunciation and reading of its script, Sanskrit alphabet chakra bija mantra CDs, and CDs of Sanskrit chants.

Thomas Ashley-Farrand (Namadeva), www.sanskritmantra.com

The works of Namadeva Acharya, Thomas Ashley-Farrand, give unprecedented, detailed instruction in how to *empower yourself* using the mantra techniques of the ancient sages and rishis. After many years of intense and prolonged daily spiritual discipline, he has published the techniques of mantra sadhana in which he was initiated over the course of decades by Eastern masters. Additionally, persuaded by his wife, Satyabhama, he has shared some of the moving experiences that he has had with spiritually advanced beings, and the lessons that he learned from each encounter. Namadeva's works are offered in a spirit of service.

Hinduism Today, www.hindu.org

Probably the most notable magazine and set of resources on Hinduism or Sanatana Dharma. Provides a wealth of resources on Yoga, meditation, mantra and ritual. Note also the related writings of Sivaya Subramuniyaswami, which contain much profound wisdom on all these topics and more.

Samskrita Bharati, www.samskritabharati.org

Worldwide organization teaching conversational Sanskrit and emphasizing all aspects of Sanskrit learning, including mantra, very active in India.

Sanskrit Sounds, www.SanskritSounds.com

Sanskrit Sounds is devoted to the preservation and education of the sciences and philosophies originating in India and recorded in the Sanskrit language. Nicolai Bachman, founder and director, has authored several important Sanskrit book/CD learning tools, particularly relative to the Sanskrit alphabet and its pronunciation, special terminology CDs relative to Yoga, Ayurveda and Vedic Astrology, and a course on the *Yoga Sutras.*

Swami Veda Bharati, www.swamiveda.org

Swami Veda is a Raja Yogi, meditation master, Sanskrit scholar, Sanskrit poet and Vedic adept since a child. He has spontaneously created new mantras in the Vedic style and is also a master of classical Sanskrit, as well as a great scholar of the *Yoga Sutras.* He can provide extensive instruction for serious students in meditation, mantra and all higher Yoga practices.

Yogini Bhava CD
Yogini Shambhavi Chopra
ISBN: 978-0-9102-6193-7
$16.95

Yogini Bhava, a wonderful CD by Shambhavi Chopra, contains many of the mantras used in this book, particularly those mantras addressed to the deities. Mantras contained on the CD include those to Shiva, Durga, Kali, Sundari, Sarasvati, Lakshmi, Annapurna, Ganga Devi, Ganesha, Dattatreya, Saturn, and the Hamsa Mantra to the Sun. These include many important bija mantras, invocations and Gayatris.

Shambhavi is preparing additional chanting CDs, including on the Sanskrit bijas and mantras to the planets, as well as additional chants to Shiva and the Goddess. Shambhavi's CDs are available through Lotus Press and complement Dr. Frawley's writings.

Shambhavi Chopra is one of the foremost women teachers coming out of India today, and the author of several important books on the Goddess *(Yogini: Unfolding the Goddess Within and Yogic Secrets of the Dark Goddess),* noted for their experiential approach. She also offers consultations in mantra sadhana and in Vedic astrology (www.vedanet.com).

Available at bookstores and natural food stores nationwide, or order your copy directly by sending the appropriate amount for the binding of your choice plus $2.50 shipping/ handling ($.75 s/h for each additional copy ordered at the same time) to:

Lotus Press, P O Box 325, Twin Lakes, WI 53181 USA
toll free order line: 800 824 6396 • office phone: 262 889 8561
office fax: 262 889 2461
email: lotuspress@lotuspress.com • web site: www.lotuspress.com

Lotus Press is the publisher of a wide range of books and software in the field of alternative health, including Ayurveda, Chinese medicine, herbology, aromatherapy, Reiki and energetic healing modalities. Request our free book catalog.

Endnotes

1 *Sri Aurobindo, Savitri: A Legend and a Symbol.*

2 *Sri Aurobindo, the Future Poetry.*

3 *Sri Aurobindo, Secret of the Veda.*

4 *As in the author's Wisdom of the Ancient Seers: Selected Mantras from the Rigveda. Many others were published in articles in various Sri Aurobindo publications like World Union and Sri Aurobindo's Action, mainly in the 1980-1984 time period.*

5 *Sarvam khalvidam Brahma, Chandogya Upanishad III.14.1.*

6 *Kashmir Shaivism has many notable books of Abhinavagupta and those in his tradition. Bengali Tantra is best revealed by the works of Sir John Woodroofe/ Arthur Avalon. Advaitic Vedanta Tantra is found in the poems of Shankaracharya and those in his tradition and is commonly practiced at the Shankaracharya Maths in India. Lakulish Shaivism has similar teachings.*

7 *This is stated with some qualification because there is also a tendency to bring into western kirtan not a sacred but a mundane entertainment that can be out of harmony with the deeper urges of Yoga.*

8 *Brahmabindu Upanishad 17.*

9 *Mantra and mantra japa are commonly mentioned in many yogic texts as an integral part of Yoga. Many yogic texts like the Yogi Yajnavalkya and Vasistha Samhita contain explications of mantras, particularly the Gayatri mantra.*

10 *While Pranava, which means primal sound or vibration, usually refers to Oṁ, there are other Pranavas or prime mantras for different traditions like Huṁ for Shiva or Hrīṁ for Shakti.*

11 *Patanjali, Yoga Sutras, I.25-28.*

12 *As the famous Mandukya Upanishad which is based upon an explication of Oṁ.*

13 *Note the Garland of Letters of Sir John Woodroofe.*

14 *The most important figure in the Shabda Yoga tradition was the great poet and yogi, Bhartrihari, who lived more than 1500 years ago, and his important text on Sound Yoga, Vakyapadiya. He explained how learning the Sanskrit language itself could be a powerful form of Yoga practice.*

15 *"Abhautika shabda", Ganapati Muni refers to this type of sound that is inherent in pure consciousness beyond the sound produced in the element of space or ether.*

16 *A common statement in Hindu scriptures and by modern gurus like Ramana Maharshi is shuddha ahara, shuddha sattva meaning "pure diet, pure mind".*

17 *These may include ritualistic pujas, nyasas (consecrations), purification of the senses (bhuta shuddhi), honoring of deities and gurus, ritual baths and cleansings, and so on, not done once but on a daily or regular basis.*

18 *Important modern Hindu movements that have brought the Gayatri Mantra, once kept secret, to a public usage.*

19 *There are a number of such self-proclaimed gurus or enlightened masters particularly in the West, who often use traditional teachings for their own advantage without truly representing it or being trained in it.*

20 Chandogya Upanishad I.1.2.

21 Udana Vayu in Ayurvedic thought, which not only governs speech but also effort, expression, will power and the ability to ascend in consciousness, including awakening the Kundalini.

22 Such is the importance of mauna or the practice of silence (not speaking) in yogic teachings, which is often regarded as the most important form of tapas or self-discipline.

23 Collected works of Vasishta Ganapati Muni, Vol. VI., Vishvamimamsa V.4.6.

24 Repeating the Sanskrit alphabet is an important Vaikhari practice, particularly as aligned with deities like Sarasvati, Ganesha or Matangi. It links the Vaikhari state with the higher levels of speech.

25 Prana mantras like So'haṁ and Haṁsaḥ are often used at this level, though they have deeper applications as well. Pranic deities like Kali, Shiva or Hanuman help us here also.

26 Bija mantras that are connected to the inner light, like Hrīṁ, are important at this level. The Goddess Tara in Hindu thought relates to this level, as also Chhinnamasta, who grants higher perception.

27 The Mahavakyas that we discuss later in the book in the chapter on Vedic and Vedantic Mantra Yoga, like Tattvamasi, Thou art that. The deepest level of bija mantras like Oṁ and Hrīṁ also takes us to this level.

28 Bringing the sound current and breath down to the belly and base of the spine helps unite the two opposite currents of our vital energy, allowing the Prana down to unite with the Apana. It is an important therapy for treating Vata disorders, for strengthening Prana and for correcting the adverse downward movement of Apana. Vata type people tend to breathe and speak shallowly and quickly. Such deep sound therapy helps counter this tendency. They can begin by learning to chant Oṁ from the belly so that it resounds throughout the entire chakra and nervous system.

29 It is also part of a process of balancing our energies to the right and left and above and below such as we will discuss later in the book relative to mantra and pranayama.

30 Note the Garland of Letters of Sir John Woodroofe.

31 Note Judith Tyberg's, Language of the Gods.

32 Sometimes only two types of sounds are recognized in Sanskrit, the vowels and consonants, in which case semi-vowels and sibilants are also classified as consonants.

33 The Sanskrit vowels are 16 in number, which is the number four squared. The semivowels and sibilants are 9, which is the number three squared. The constants are 25, which is the number five squared. If we add up these numbers, we get the number 50, which contains the key laws of manifestation. These are a few of the many mathematical connections which the Sanskrit letters have.

34 As discussed in Chandogya Upanishad II.22.

35 The principle of death, Mrityu or limitation in the Upanishads and Vedas (Chandogya Upanishad II.22). However, in some Tantric traditions, vowels are made into the Shakti principle and consonants into the Shiva principle as the Shiva principle cannot express itself without Shakti and is inert without her.

36 Chandogya Upanishad II.22. The three divisions here are svara, ushma and sparsha for the three groups.

37 As in the fourteen Maheshvara Sutras of Panini's grammar.

38 This is Sanskrit etymology or Nirukta.

39 Parama Shiva, Prakasha.

40 Specifically his Paratrishika Vivarana and Tantra Sara.

41 Nandikesa Kasika, Bulletin of the Government Oriental Manuscripts Library, Madras, (Chennai), Vol. III. No. 2. 1950.

42 Paratrishika Vivarana of Abhinavagupta, Jaidev Singh edition available.

43 Yogini Hridaya Tantra, Pujasamketa 30-31.

44 Aitareya Aranyaka II.3.8.

45 A is Ananta, the infinite, endless or boundless, an-anta. It is akshara, the primal letter, the central point, the undecaying a-kshara. It is Agni, the primal fire, the indestructible, a-gni, the inner guide ag-ni.

46 The Sanskrit long vowel-Ā serves as a prefix to intensify or to reverse the meaning of the words it is added to. For example, nanda means joy, Ānanda means bliss. Gacchati means "he goes", āgacchati means "he comes."

47 Particularly what is called the Jivatman.

48 Note Abhinavagupta's Tantrasara, third chapter, where he refers to the Shambhava Upaya.

49 Two key Sanskrit words for the meaning of the vowel-Ṛ are Ṛtam, meaning truth, particularly harmony and order in the cosmic manifestation, and Ṛṣi or seer, one who has the knowledge and energy of that truth.

50 It represents the dimension of will (i or iccha) as further brought into existence. Note the progression: short-vowel-I or will, long-vowel-I as ruling power, diphthong ai as majesty.

51 For example, the mantra Sau, which can be either Sauṁ or Sauḥ. Sauḥ is most common and is used to project energy or Shakti as well as the power of Soma.

52 The origin or root of the reproductive urge resides in the earth or root chakra while its expression or manifestation occurs in the water or sex chakra.

53 The doshas are those of the respective elements ruling the chakras. However, diseases manifest through the weakness of the chakra mainly. So high Vata or air, for example, is usually reflected in disorders or weaknesses of the earth and water chakras.

54 Aitareya Aranyaka III.3.2.1.

55 In the Yogini Hridaya Tantra, Mantra Samketa II.29, saṁ rather than the usual vaṁ is the bija mantra for the water elements and the Svadhishthana chakra.

56 In theVedas and opening and closing chants for Upanishads.

57 Like the Nandikesha Kashika.

58 Shaivite texts correspond the letters of the Sanskrit alphabet to the prime principles or tattvas of existence. However, there is some variation in how these are presented and a good deal of complexity, so we will not take up the topic in this book. Notably, Kashmiri Shaivism and the Nandikesha Kashika (and Mantra Yoga Samhita) correlate them differently.

59 In some texts like the Yogini Hridaya Tantra, Mantra Samketa II.29, kaṁ is the bija mantra of the heart, not yaṁ.

60 Brihadaranayaka Upanishad V.1.

61 Oṁ in the Upanishads is called Ud-githa, the high chant or upward movement, as Sri

Aurobindo explains in his commentary on the Upanishads.

62 Dakini, Lakini, Rakini, Kakini, Shakini, Hakini and Yakini are usually the Dakinis of the chakras from the root chakra up. Sometimes they are counted in a different manner, starting with Dakini in the throat chakra down to Shakini in the root chakra and up to Hakini and Yakini in the third eye and crown chakras. They are also correlated with the seven tissues of the body.

63 Mantra Yoga Samhita.

64 Notably for Tripura Sundari and Matangi.

65 What is called Kilana in Sanskrit.

66 The Tantrik Practices in Sri Vidya, p. 85, Sri Sarada Cahtussati 3.59.

67 Discussed in detail in author's Inner Tantric Yoga.

68 It is closely connected to Sri Vidya and Dasha Mahavidya.

69 Manomaya kosha in Sanskrit.

70 Like the author's Ayurveda and Marma Therapy.

71 There are some variations on the attribution of these mantras in different texts, notably the Mantra Yoga Samhita.

72 This second L-sound is the cerebral L, pronounced like the cerebral letters with the tongue at the roof of the mouth, as opposed to the dental-L, pronounced with the tongue behind the teeth.

73 Note Hatha Yoga Pradipika for its discussion of pranayama, Kundalini and Samadhi.

74 Or Ah can be used on inhalation.

75 The Para Vak of the four stages of speech.

76 Samkhya Karika of Ishvara Krishna, verse 22, Matharvritti commentary identifies the Cosmic Ahamkara principle with the Sanskrit alphabet.

77 Note the Self-inquiry method of Ramana Maharshi, which emphasizes tracing the root of all thoughts back to the I-thought in the heart.

78 Note the idea of lunar inhalation and solar exhalation in the works of Abhinavagupta, the main teacher of Tantric Kashmiri Shaivism, Para Trisika Vivarana, pps 263-264.

79 There are various yogic kriyas involving pranayama and mantra for guiding the energies of Fire (Kundalini), Moon (Soma), Sun (Surya) and Lightning (Vidyut) up and down the spine or to different chakras, depending upon the stage of practice and the development of the Yogi. How inhalation and exhalation function depends upon which specific energies one may be drawing in or releasing out. Balancing solar and lunar energies, however, is fundamental to all of these yogic pranayamas.

80 Another method is to use the So mantra to draw the Apana up from the root chakra to the navel and the haṁ mantra to enkindle Agni or digestive fire in the navel. This is a simple method to help balance Apana and Prana as lunar and solar forces.

81 This amounts to one breath every four seconds, about average for most healthy people. This number is found in the Shatapatha Brahmana XII.3.2.8, an ancient Vedic text.

82 Dhyana Bindu Upanishad 61-63.

83 The three lower chakras are commonly said to be the region of Fire or Agni and are named the kanda or bulb in Tantric thought.

84 The three higher chakras are called the region of the Moon or Soma in Tantric thought.

85 *The two bandhas, uddiyana and jalandhara, aid in these practices, uddiyana for the fire in the navel, and jalandhara for the nectar or Soma in the head. The mula bandha is important for drawing the Apana Vayu to the navel to unite Prana and Apana.*

86 *The Serpent Power of Sir John Woodfroofe.*

87 *An important aid to arousing the Kundalini is to draw the descending prana (Apana Vayu) upward from the root chakra, where its energy tends to get dispersed, to the navel and, conversely, to draw the ascending Prana downward from the throat and head, where its energy tends to get dispersed, to the navel. Uniting the Prana and Apana in the navel electrifies the nervous system and energizes the subtle body and its chakra system. In this respect, the Apana provides the fuel or food for the increased fire that is stimulated through the Prana. This can also be described as uniting the Apana or the lunar current with the Prana or the solar current in the navel, thus enkindling the fire principle, Agni or Kundalini. Many Tantric Pranayama practices reflect this approach.*

88 *A similar practice occurs in many Tantric teachings using the five element mantras to purify the Papa Purusha or dark man of sin in the lower left abdomen and transform it into a ball of golden light. The practices given here are a bit more complex and consider the Agni and Soma energies in both their locations.*

89 *Vasistha Samhita II.16.*

90 *Sometimes instead of Hūṁ, the astra mantra - Huṁ Phaṭ Svāhā - is used instead. This is a more powerful practice, requiring yet greater caution.*

91 *Generally repeated in numbers like 11, 27, 54 and 108.*

92 *Note the famous Dahara vidya in the Chandogya Upanishad VIII.*

93 *These eight are the five elements, ahamkara, buddhi and Prakriti.*

94 *This is also the teaching of Ramana Maharshi.*

95 *Tantra speaks of the knots of the root, navel and third eye centers. These are all part of the knots of the spiritual heart (hridaya) that the Upanishads speak of.*

96 *There are variations on this mantra that can be used to develop its energies in more specific directions.*

97 *Many famous Stotras were composed by the great Advaitic guru Shankara, particularly those to the Goddess and to Lord Shiva. Among the most beautiful of all Stotras are the Stotras to Krishna.*

98 *There are many CDs of famous Stotras that one can get from India, sometimes for the United States and UK as well.*

99 *Patanjali, Yoga Sutras I.23.*

100 *The vision of the Ishta Devata is also said to be the fruit of Svadhyaya or self-study in classical Yoga, Yoga Sutras II.44.*

101 *The terms are Agneya and Saumya in Sanskrit, not only fiery and watery but also harsh and soft, fierce or gentle overall.*

102 *The main deities that we find the bija mantras and letters of the alphabet most commonly used with are Ganesha, Hanuman and several forms of the Goddess, particularly Matangi, Sundari, Bhairavi and Tara.*

103 *Mantras relative to treating certain diseases are discussed in the author's book Ayurvedic Healing.*

104 *Other good Ayurvedic herbs for speech include shankha pushpi, manduka parni, and shatavari.*

105 *These include the Navagraha Sukta and the Nakshatra Sukta, as well as special Vedic mantras for the deity, over deity and supreme deity of each planet, examined in author's book Ayurvedic Astrology.*

106 *It is best to do some mantras for Ganesha before starting any planetary mantras, as Ganesha is the great Lord of Karma.*

107 *Some variations on these mantras exist particularly for Saturn, Rahu and Ketu.*

108 *Planets often have several names. Here Guru, the teacher, is the name used for Jupiter, which is also called Brihaspati.*

109 *The same Shakti mantras can be used as relative to the mantra to the Supreme Light (Paramjyoti Mantra) combined with or used apart from the usual bija Hrim, depending upon circumstances.*

110 *For more information on planets and disease, examine the author's book Ayurvedic Astrology.*

111 *These are called the Ashta Prakriti or the eightfold nature in Vedic thought and relate to the causal body and first eight of the 24 tattvas of Samkhya philosophy.*

112 *There are also special Tantric directional deities. One group is a set of Shaktis or Goddesses. The other set is a set of great deities, forms Brahma, Vishnu and Shiva. These are also used in directional Nyasas.*

113 *Vamadeva, Rigveda IV.1.16.*

114 *Rigveda VIII.99.11.*

115 *Vishvamitra, Rigveda III.I.6.*

116 *Chandogya Upanishad I.5.*

117 *Sri Aurobindo, the Secret of the Veda, section on the Origins of Aryan Speech.*

118 *Mahanarayana Upanishad, Dahara Vidya 12, last verse. This Upanishad has the most important Vedic mantras for chanting purposes, including Gayatri, Durga Sukta, Narayana Sukta, Shiva Upasana mantras and more.*

119 *Rigveda III.62.10.*

120 *Vasistha, Rigveda VII.59.12.*

121 *Rigveda IV.40.5.*

122 *Rigveda I. 164.*

123 *A few important Shanti mantras include, Oṁ Śānti Śānti Śāntiḥ; Oṁ Sarve Bhavantu Sukhināḥ; Oṁ Sahanavavatu; Oṁ Bhadram Karnebhi Śrinuyāma Devā; Oṁ Śam no Mitra Śam Varunaḥ.*

124 *Notably the Mahanarayana Upanishad, which has many devotional mantras, and the Shvetashvatara Upanishad to Lord Shiva, which contains many Vedic verses, particularly in its description of Yoga.*

125 *Most of these Vedic and Upanishadic chants can be found in a wonderful Sanskrit collection called the Mantra Pushpam published by the Ramakrishna Math. It contains a number of important Stotras as well.*

126 *Rigveda VIII.77.11.*

127 *Rigveda I. 164.39.*

128 *Taittiriya Samhita VII.1.19.1.*

129 *Ganapati Muni Collected Works Vol. VI. Vishvamimamsa V.4.18.*

130 *Vak Sudha Chapter 6 of Brahmarshi Daivarata.*

131 *Vak Sudha of Brahmarshi Daivarata, opening page.*

132 *Aitareya Aranyaka III.2.5.*

133 *Aitareya Aranyaka III.2.1.*

134 *Brihadaranyaka Upanishad I.4.10.*

135 *Mandukya Upanishad 2.*

136 *Chandogya Upanishad III.14.1.*

137 *Chandogya Upanishad VI. 9-16.*

138 *Isha Upanishad 16.*

139 *Aitareya Upanishad III.1.*

140 Yellow color for earth mantras, white for water, red for fire, smoky grey for air and dark blue for ether.

141 Red for Sun and Mars, white for Venus and Moon, yellow for Jupiter, green for Mercury, dark blue for Saturn.

142 One can use more complete mantras, for example: Oṁ Laṁ pṛthivitattvātmane namaḥ, reverence to the soul of the Earth element.

143 For those seeking more information on marmas, note the author's Ayurveda and Marma Therapy

Index

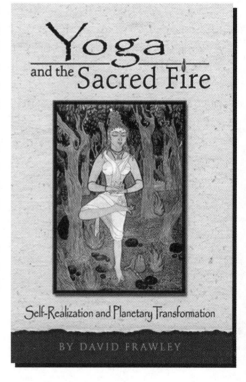

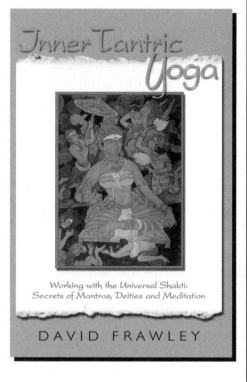